On Fire in Baltimore

On Fire in Baltimore
Black Mormon Women and Conversion in a Raging City

Laura Rutter Strickling

GREG KOFFORD BOOKS
SALT LAKE CITY, 2018

Copyright © 2018 Laura Rutter Strickling
Cover design copyright © 2018 Greg Kofford Books, Inc.
Cover design by Loyd Ericson

Published in the USA.

All rights reserved. No part of this volume may be reproduced in any form without written permission from the publisher, Greg Kofford Books. The views expressed herein are the responsibility of the author and interviewees and do not necessarily represent the positions or views of Greg Kofford Books.

Paperback ISBN: 978-1-58958-716-8
Hardcover ISBN: 978-1-58958-722-9
Also available in ebook.

Greg Kofford Books
P.O. Box 1362
Draper, UT 84020
www.gregkofford.com
facebook.com/gkbooks
twitter.com/gkbooks

Library of Congress Cataloging-in-Publication Data

Names: Strickling, Laura Rutter, 1956- author.
Title: On fire in Baltimore : black Mormon women and conversion in a raging city / Laura Rutter Strickling.
Description: Salt Lake City : Greg Kofford Books, 2018. | Includes bibliographical references and index.
Identifiers: LCCN 2018038731| ISBN 9781589587168 (pbk.) | ISBN 9781589587229 (hardcover)
Subjects: LCSH: African American Mormons--Maryland--Baltimore. | Mormon women--Maryland--Baltimore. | Mormon Church--Maryland--Baltimore--History. | Church of Jesus Christ of Latter-day Saints--Maryland--Baltimore--History.
Classification: LCC BX8643.A35 S77 2018 | DDC 289.3/752608996073--dc23
LC record available at https://lccn.loc.gov/2018038731

*Children, I beg you to love, for it alone will overcome hate . . . eventually. Misunderstanding abounds. It has no special resting place. Rich and poor, majority and minority, young and old, Black and White—all feel the sting of being misunderstood.
I am among those who fight misunderstanding.
The weapons I use are stories.*

Queen Mother Mary Carter Smith.
Baltimore's Griot

Contents

Acknowledgements	ix
Prologue	xi
Introduction: On Fire in a Raging City	xv
1. The Race Dilemma	1
2. Ain't Nobody Going to Drift Me	17
3. Salvation from the Dumpster	37
4. Delilah's Miracle	53
5. You Don't Have to Fake the Funk	65
6. I Could Never See Her Face	79
7. Having It Out With God	99
8. You Don't Serve God Then Drink With the Devil	115
9. Two Souls	125
10. The Healing Hand of Sister Clara Haynes	135
11. Pray for These Three Things	145
Epilogue: God Reclaims With Dandelions	161
Bibliography	165
Index	173

Acknowledgments

I am indebted to the Black church sisters who have made this book possible, and ask that they forgive the shortcomings of my work. Knowing them has changed the course of my life. I could not have written this book without the assistance and support of many people. My husband has been my most faithful supporter. He kept me focused through the years and has read more drafts than I can count. I am grateful to my son Benjamin who generously took time away from his family to read drafts and offer insights, and Alia who barricaded herself in the back room to read chapters while I watched her three children, then stayed up late with her husband Jeff to discuss edits. I would also like to thank my brother, Michael Rutter, my mother Josie Rutter, and friends Ruth Greaves and Margaret Hemming who were helpful at the early stages of the writing process. Finally, I would like to thank the editors at Greg Kofford Books, especially Loyd Isao Ericson for catching the vision of this book.

PROLOGUE

Mormons: The Farthest Thing Away from the Black Experience?

In the fall of 2009 I began recording the conversion stories of the Black Latter-day Saint (or Mormon) women from Baltimore who are featured in this book. It was also the semester that I took a graduate class on Africana race and ethnicity—three hours a week that left me painfully aware of how little I knew about the culture and politics of Black people. Professor Bryant, my African American instructor, deepened my anxiety on the first day when she announced that typically only Black students signed up for her courses, but this semester she had four who were White. She also informed the class that now she would have to start from an undergraduate level in order to get the White students caught up with the others because very few of them had a background in Africana Studies.

I am reluctant to admit that, in my case, Professor Bryant's assessment was true. I was a White student with little knowledge of Africana Studies whose interest in race had developed from graduate work in Intercultural Communication and Sociolinguistics. And while I had no reason to doubt the professor's expertise in her field, her pedagogical approach left me wary. I wondered if she really would revise her syllabus based on race. And if so, how would the other students take the dumbing-down of their coursework? The semester did not seem to be getting off to a good start. Already, the university had classified me as a "non-traditional" student because I was fifty-three years old returning to academia after decades of working in the trenches—raising four children and teaching high school Spanish. My fortitude waivered as I looked across the room at the savvy Black students.

Neeva was one of my African American classmates who entered the room with fiery confidence, colored scarves, and a head full of springy hair that augmented her self-assurance. She introduced herself as an entrepreneur whose expertise was Black politics and Hip Hop, and she came to class with questions and disputes that would spawn lively discussions. More often than not, she and Professor Bryant would start a conversation between themselves, and soon after, other Black students would chime in while we four White students sat clumped together on the left side of the room and watched. In fact, the more I learned about the layers of racism that existed in America, the more cautious I became of speaking, afraid that I would ignorantly say something that would reveal a Eurocentric view, which I surely must have.

"Can White people truly be Afrocentric?" Professor Bryant asked. "Do you think your race equips you for that?" She looked in our direction. I did not know. I wondered if I truly knew what Afrocentric meant.

So began an intimidating but thought-provoking semester when, for the first time, I read the works of James Baldwin, Marcus Garvey, Molefi Kete Asante, and Maulana Karenga, and when I was introduced to Pan-African film and began to understand Critical Race Theory. But more importantly, I began to examine my own White identity in relation to a Black perspective. I navigated through an evolution of emotions from feeling guilty for being born White and consequently with privilege, regret for belonging to a race who had enslaved another, inadequately prepared to resolve the racial discrimination I confronted, and acutely cognizant that my whiteness left me unable to understand blackness.

Yet, I felt at home with my Black church sisters and an affinity toward people of color in mixed social settings. I developed a keen interest in studying social contexts where African American English was spoken and decided to pursue this course of study in depth. When I mustered the courage to express these thoughts in class, Professor Bryant, instead of coming back with probing questions, paused the lecture and tilted her head to one side. I wondered if, for a brief moment, our racialized perspectives had found common ground.

After that semester, Neeva and I found ourselves working together as graduate interns investigating how White inner city teachers responded to students who spoke African American English. In addition to fieldwork, we talked about our families, complained about professors, and shared our academic goals. When I explained my interest in publishing the conversion stories of the Black Mormon women in my Baltimore congregation, Neeva asked, "You mean, there are Black Mormons?"

I assured her that there were.

"Then the thing I want to know . . ." she hesitated as if toying with the notion. "The thing I want to know is, why Mormon? How does a Black person get to be a Latter-day Saint? For me, the Mormon Church seems to be the farthest thing away from the Black experience—the Black Diaspora does not take *me* to Utah."

Neeva's question frames the purpose of this book. The conversion stories of these fifteen African American Mormon women will begin to explain how a Black person "gets to be a Latter-day Saint." With narrations of visions, healings, and miracles; life stories of violence, addiction, and Jim Crow racism, I tell how I come to love these church sisters and provide an intimate glimpse into how our Black and White racialized lives meet. As I traverse the crossroads of spirituality, culture, and race, I learn how these Black Mormon women reconcile their membership in a historically White church and begin to understand the depth of their faith that rises from a wellspring of experience so different from my own.

INTRODUCTION

On Fire in a Raging City

Baltimore is burning. Rioters are torching pharmacies, setting police cars ablaze, and throwing bricks at officers hours after thousands mourned the death of Freddie Gray. A weeklong curfew is in effect; the Governor has declared a state of emergency and called upon the National Guard to restore order in a raging city.

(*The Post-Standard*, April 27, 2015)

After the worst of the rioting in 2015, I called up Eunice to see how she was doing. Neighborhood stores had been destroyed in the rampage, reviving memories of the 1968 Martin Luther King riots, and older residents could not get out to buy food or fill their prescriptions. I wanted to see how Eunice, a seventy-two-year-old African American woman in my congregation, was getting along in the crisis.

"Oh, we're okay. We still have the Dollar Store—they didn't loot that."

"So you can get everything you need?"

"Yes, for now. I prayed for that. I prayed so they wouldn't loot the Dollar Store—so they wouldn't loot the Dollar Store *and* to put an end to this unnecessary nonsense."

After hanging up, I thought about Eunice's response. Baltimore, a city located on an estuary of the Chesapeake Bay, is home to more than six hundred thousand people. It is also home to multibillion dollar corporations like Under Armor and Legg Mason, as well as multiple international investment firms such as Morgan Stanley. The Baltimore Ravens, who play their football games in the seventy-one-thousand seat M&T Stadium, are valued just short of two billion dollars, and the Orioles baseball team at Camden Yards is valued at about half that.[1] The city's tourism industry offers dinners and harbor cruises with live music and "unmatched waterfront views,"[2] and the Marriott attracts a steady stream of vacationers and conference-goers. Yet Eunice, who was born and raised in Baltimore, lives a few blocks from the wealth of the Inner Harbor in a government-

---

1. Vasilis Lericos, "Forbes: The Baltimore Ravens Franchise is Worth $1.93 Billion."
2. "Spirit of Baltimore Dinner Cruises."

subsidized "mixed income community," previously known as The Projects. Even with government assistance she is not always able to spare the two-dollar copay to buy medications for her heart condition.

This disparity of life circumstance is not new; Baltimore has a history of discriminatory housing policies that have contributed toward the economic disadvantage of Black people. Apartheid-like practices became law in 1910 when the city enacted legislation that promoted the racial segregation of neighborhoods. It was called an "ordinance for preserving peace," one that would prevent "conflict and ill feeling between the white and colored races."[3] A multi-tiered real estate market was created where housing developments set up restrictive covenants delineated by racial lines.[4] In 1917 the ordinance was struck down by the Supreme Court, but not until Baltimore had become the national leader in residential segregation with other states following suit.[5]

Now, in the twenty-first century, if you are poor and Black in "Charm City,"[6] statistics show that your opportunity for a better life looks bleak. In the predominately Black Westside neighborhood where Freddie Gray had lived, half of the residents are unemployed; one-third of the homes are boarded up and vacant; sixty percent of people have less than a high school diploma; and the violent crime rate is among the highest in the city with sixty-six homicides in 2015.[7] Neighborhood violence like this has perpetuated Baltimore's nickname, "Murder City," breaking the city-wide record in 2017 with 345 homicides,[8] the highest rate per capita in the history of the city.[9]

That day, after Freddie Gray died in police custody with unexplained injuries to his neck and spine, rioting escalated in downtown Baltimore. More than thirty-six thousand Oriole fans were held at Camden Yards after a Red Sox game while they waited for law enforcement to push back protestors who had blocked a nearby intersection and were smashing win-

---

3. Baltimore, Maryland, "Ordinance No. 692," 337.
4. Erin Durham, "Mapping Inequality: Historical Context of Baltimore's Neighborhoods."
5. Matthew Yglesias, "How Baltimore Invented Neighborhood Segregation."
6. Baltimore was nicknamed "Charm City" in 1975 in order to promote the city and dispel its poor image. Gilbert Sandler, "How the city's nickname came to be."
7. Jamelle Bouie, "The Deep, Troubling Roots of Baltimore's Decline."
8. "2017 Baltimore City Homicides: List and Map."
9. Kevin Rector, "Baltimore Reaches Highest Per Capita Murder Rate on Record in 2017."

dows. The standoff lasted for several hours with the protestors throwing rocks and glass at police.[10] After peace had been restored, people blamed the underlying cause of the protests on general conditions in Baltimore: gang-related drugs, lack of employment among Blacks, and family instability.[11] Others traced the turmoil to Baltimore's segregated history and the despair born of decades of racial inequality, drawing on Martin Luther King's explanation, "a riot is the language of the unheard."[12]

Yet, when the protests were at their height, Eunice had not prayed for racial equality; she had not prayed for social justice. She had even rejected the backlash of Black rage that had resulted in violence and looting, calling it "unnecessary nonsense." Instead, she prayed to spare the Dollar Store. She prayed and, in Eunice's eyes, it had changed the course of events for the people in her neighborhood. I presume that the other sisters from my congregation had also been praying that day, and I wondered how their prayers had impacted their neighborhoods. I have known these faithful women for over twelve years and have learned to trust their praying.

My affection for these Black Mormon women began in 2006, when my husband and I moved to Baltimore and started attending church there. The first thing I noticed about our new congregation was the diversity of its female membership. We were accustomed to multicultural Mormons, since our family had attended meetings in Spain and regions throughout the United States, but this congregation of just about one hundred consisted of Latino, Nepalese, Nigerian, African American, Filipino, Korean, and White members. There were young mothers with newborn babies and ninety-six-year-old great-great-grandmothers. Some women came to the city to work on doctoral degrees, while others had dropped out of high school at age fifteen to take care of their aging mothers or young children. There were brand new converts, as well as members who had been raised in the faith with a heritage that traced back to Brigham Young and the Mormon pioneers.

On Sundays, conversations among the church sisters were often characterized by socioeconomic difference. In the foyer they talked about Food Stamps and Social Services, as well as cruises to Mexico and trips to Disney World. On the one hand, mothers were troubled about securing bail for a son in jail, and on the other, worried about sending a daughter to

---

10. Associated Press, "Fans at Orioles-Red Sox Asked to Stay in Camden Yards after Violent Protest."
11. "Crime and Despair in Baltimore."
12. Martin Luther King, Jr., "MLK: A Riot is the Language of the Unheard."

Europe. From an academic perspective, I was drawn to this linguistically-rich congregation and wondered in what ways these social and linguistic differences impacted our worship and influenced relationships.

What immediately caught my attention were the prayers offered by the African American women. For Mormons, prayer is one of the most frequent forms of shared worship. Members are called upon by church leaders to offer unrehearsed prayers at the beginning and end of most meetings, so on any given Sunday I could hear up to eight prayers. I noticed that many of the African American women in our congregation did not say prayers with the customary formal approach in which God was addressed with "thee" and "thou." Instead, they spoke with the informal "you." They talked to God about personal matters even though they were praying on behalf of the group, such as, "Father, I want to thank you for all you've done, for all our sisters and brothers, and thanks for the love that you've given to my dad who has cancer."

But what I really found intriguing were certain phrases that these church sisters said at the beginning of their prayers, such as "Thank you Heavenly Father for waking us up this morning in our right mind." I did not know then that they were opening their prayers in the tradition of Black preachers, praising God for another morning where "our sleeping couch is not our cooling board, and our cover is not our winding sheet."[13] In other words, the dearly assembled did not find themselves dead this morning, but rather, "clothed in their right mind." In addition, some of the African American women would approach the pulpit before bowing their head to pray with a version of "first giving honor to God who is the head of my life, and to Jesus Christ and the Holy Ghost, and to the Elders of the Church and the Bishop who is sitting behind me." I was not familiar with this kind of worship aesthetic and expression of faith in the Mormon community and wanted to find out more.

I began a study focused on recording the life and conversion of the African American women in my congregation—an endeavor that spanned over ten years and resulted in twenty-five recorded interviews and four hundred pages of transcription. But the interviews became more than data collection; they opened the door to sisterhood and sojourn into the Black community. Sitting side by side in their living room or sipping water at the kitchen table, these women would draw me into their narrative with Black vernacular, laughter, and tears. More than once I would find my-

---

13. John. R. Rickford and Russell. J. Rickford, *Spoken Soul: The Story of Black English*, 45.

self holding their hand as their eyes welled up from painful memories, or smiling at their sarcasm as they described a family member. And my association did not end with the interviews; the women would invite me to family celebrations and birthdays or ask for rides across town to pick up prescriptions. They would call me out of the blue because they "had a feeling," then tell me another story about their lives. These church sisters also let me know that they were interested in my work. "How are the stories coming?" some would ask as they passed me in the church halls. "We are praying for you," they would tell me as the unfinished book advanced from months to years.

But our time together was not always easy; sometimes there were tense moments that were difficult to navigate. My White rural upbringing did not lend itself to understanding the rationale behind the decisions these Black urban women made, and because of my ignorance I would find myself in a racialized snare that I could not resolve by intuition.

From an academic point of view, a feminist theoretical approach obligated me to be mindful of these emotions and enabled me to adopt a reflective process aimed at exposing my biases and questioning my responses. It provided me with the theoretical underpinning to acknowledge that, as a researcher, I would naturally affect the research I do, but also, in the process, I would be affected by it. Keeping this in mind, I documented the evolution of my thoughts as I interacted with these women and as I attempted to peel back the layers of my assumptions.

Feminist standpoint theory provided me with a rationale for addressing the longstanding and vexed topic of Whites writing about Blacks, a subject beset with accusations of neo-imperialism and "a certain kind of racism."[14] The contested issue is whether the line of propriety has been crossed when women research women unlike themselves—especially when researching women who, historically, have had little voice. This raises the question of who can speak on behalf of whom, and if such research would be better aimed at empowering women to speak for themselves. From the onset, my work was not intended to be a forum for giving voice to Black

---

14. Gabriele Griffin, "The Compromised Researcher: Issues in Feminist Research Methodologies," 333–47. Feminist Standpoint Theory assumes that men and women's lives differ systematically and structurally within unequal social locations; therefore, men and women cultivate distinct kinds of knowledge. Studying subordinate social locations not only provides insight into the lives of members of subordinate groups, but also casts light on dominant group practices. See Julia Wood, "Feminist Standpoint Theory."

Mormon women, but instead, it was a quest to gain insight from the distinct knowledge that only these women could have.

Similarly, I grappled with the question of whether, in the eyes of some research communities, my non-blackness would axiomatically invalidate my research on Black Mormon women or if my heightened reflectivity, due to the shifting relationship that comes with enacting an insider/outsider's role, would give me credibility. As a White person from rural Oregon I was an outsider to these Black urban women in my congregation who had lived in Baltimore for decades, yet as sisters in the gospel, I certainly shared conversion with them. I started by examining this intersection, the juncture at the spiritual crossroads of our Black and White identity.

But as the interviews continued and I began to know these women more intimately, I found that much of their conversion to Mormonism had risen from racially entangled events that produced a kind of despair that I had not experienced: of drug addiction and rape; of nights spent in jail and days looking for work; of single motherhood and grief for lost children; of relentless destitution born of scanty resources and the kind of desperation that comes from abandonment. Yet, their stories were filled with visitations from heavenly beings, dreams about deceased mothers, and protection from violence in the city. They talked about prayers, miraculous healings, and missionary messengers, and I came to feel that these Black sisters possessed a burning trust—an unquenchable spiritual fire—that I was not acquainted with. It was this fire, this spiritual strength, that I sought to understand.

Author's Note

While there is much debate on this topic, I have chosen to capitalize Black and White when referring to people of African and European descent respectively. Historically, the issue of capitalizing names when referring to the race or ethnicity of Black people has been fraught with racial politics and continues to be a rallying point today. My aim is to acknowledge that language matters and to recognize the campaigning efforts initiated by W. E. B. Du Bois in 1899: "I believe that eight million Americans are entitled to a capital letter."[15]

Every attempt was made to preserve the integrity and character of these Black Mormon women's speech. You will notice some African American English linguistic features in the transcribed dialogue, such as

---

15. W. E. B. Du Bois, *The Philadelphia Negro: A Social Study*, 1n1.

existential *it* which is generally equivalent to *there is* or *there are,* as in, "It was a lot of addictions in the city"; absence of *s* inflections as in, "I had to take my *mother* baby"; reduction of consonant clusters to a single sound, as in, "When I was sixteen, she *decide* for me to get married"; and stressed *been,* pronounced *bin,* which indicates a long time ago, as in, "My mother *been* join the Church way before I did."

I thought it best to regularize the spelling of most colloquial pronunciations for purposes of clarity and because the nature of written speech is inherently different than spoken. For example, it was not uncommon to hear "mother" pronounced as *muvah* or dog to be pronounced like *dug*—a distinctly Baltimorean pronunciation.[16]

Finally, the names and distinguishing features of the women featured in this book have been changed in order to protect their privacy.

---

16. See Inte'a DeShields, "Baldamor, Curry, and Dug': Language Variation, Culture, and Identity among African American Baltimoreans."

1

The Race Dilemma

Ruth's calm presence and quiet voice take the edge off my after-church hunger as we sit in an empty classroom. The room still smells faintly like the children who had occupied it just moments ago. There are crumpled papers with crayon drawings strewn on the table, so I scoop them up and lay them aside to make room for my recorder. On the wall behind us, a replica of Harry Anderson's "John the Baptist Baptizing Jesus" catches my eye. Other than the painting and two chalkboards, the burlap-covered church walls are unadorned and without windows. Ruth is sitting with a perfectly straight back in one of the hard, metal foldout chairs that are available in every room, but her hands are relaxed in her lap with her purse by her side.

I fill up my pre-interview preparations with talk about the weather getting colder and my kids in North Carolina. I also explain the need for permission to record her story. While Ruth signs the interview consent form, I study her face. Her olive skin is extraordinarily smooth for a woman in her fifties, and I wonder if it is the result of her placid countenance; I've never seen Ruth with a frown or her brow furrowed with annoyance. Her dark eyes, frosted with silver eye shadow, are serene, and her mouth, adorned with perfectly applied blush-colored lipstick, is relaxed into a smile. Shiny prism-like earrings catch the pale fluorescent light as her head moves ever-so-slightly in tandem with her hand signing her name.

"I love doing these interviews," I explain, taking a stab at getting the interview started, "because I feel like the sisters are with me every day when I listen to their recorded voices and transcribe their words." Ruth smiles at me and nods her head, and I'm feeling confident in the work I'm doing. But my satisfaction is short lived, and I am quickly reminded of how fragile the interview process can be. With my next comment, I fall from academic grace onto uncertain interview ground. I tell Ruth that I have run across colleagues who were surprised to learn that there were African American Mormon women in Baltimore, and that they were interested in hearing their conversion stories. Without a hint of accusation and with her customary mild voice, Ruth asks, "Are you only interviewing African American women? Because I'm not African American. My father was White and my mother was Native American."

I catch my breath for one speechless moment as a wave of panic washes over me. I had assumed Ruth's racial identity. After years of theoretical study regarding the hegemonic construction and social complexities of identity, culture, *and* race—how had I done that? In an attempt to cover my discomfort, I flutter out a bit of academic theory, saying, "ethnicity and race are social constructs..." but stop short, realizing that the Ivory Tower cannot rescue me now. Instead, hoping to regain my composure, I ask, "How do you identify yourself?" In good spirits Ruth replies, "Usually I say I'm biracial." Then she sets me back on track. "But can I *still* tell my story?"

I left the interview that day humbled and beset with questions. Why had I assumed that Ruth was African American? Clearly, I had misread cultural and linguistic cues somewhere along the line—but how? Had my perspective been biased because Baltimore is 63 percent Black?[1] Had I jumped to conclusions because of the non-standardized features in Ruth's speech? Was it her Facebook page that showcased photos and links of Black family and friends? What racial stereotypes had overshadowed my intercultural communication training where reflective practices are meant to replace the tendency to pigeonhole others? Ruth had identified as biracial, yet I wondered how often she still had been obliged to explain who she was. Did she traverse the Baltimorean borderlands of neither White nor Black nor Native American—finding herself cradled in one culture, sandwiched between two, and straddling all three?[2]

After wading through these thoughts, I resolved to take on the difficult task of unraveling assumptions that, for decades, had been intricately woven into the cognitive fabric of my world view. I began with an investigation of "the cluttered landscape of what is written about race,"[3] cluttered in part because, from a historical perspective, the concept of race is fluid, perpetually being redefined over time but always within a contested social terrain of struggle for control over one's destiny.[4]

---

1. "Race and Ethnicity in Baltimore, Maryland."
2. Gloria Anzaldúa, *Borderlands/La Frontera: The New Mestiza*, 78.
3. Ariela J. Gross, "Litigating Whiteness: Trials of Racial Determination in the Nineteenth-Century South," 114.
4. Ira Berlin, *Many Thousands Gone: The First Two Centuries of Slavery in North America*.

The Racialization of the Home of the Free

In North America, the institution of slavery created a society premised on race even though slavery was not immediately linked to blackness when the first Africans, seized by the Dutch from a Spanish slave ship, were brought to Jamestown in 1619. But by the time a generation had passed, European colonists had passed laws that differentiated White indentured servitude (a debt that could be paid off) from what became permanent Black indentured servitude. This then led to the legalization of slave labor. Whiteness grew to be synonymous with freedom, as well as a safeguard against slave status.[5] Justification for racial hierarchy was upheld by Whites seeking economic advantage and a biological essentialist ideology that characterized people of African descent as mentally and morally inferior.

By the late 1700s, the practice of enslavement had obscured the ideals upon which our new nation would soon be built. The contradiction between the human bondage that supported the economy and White men's "right to die freemen rather than live [as] slaves"[6] did not result in emancipation but the further dehumanizing of the enslaved. In the Constitutional compromise of 1787, Blacks were used as bargaining chips without voice, as Northern and Southern delegates vied for representation based on population. Southerners argued for enslaved Blacks to count as full non-voting persons, and Northerners resisted counting slaves at all, arguing that the South considered them "property, the same as cattle and horses in the North."[7] In the end, Black people were counted as three-fifths of a person.[8]

The compromise furthered a conceptual shift that had been progressing in the new nation. Black people were no longer viewed as enslaved men and women; instead they would be viewed as sub-human with inferior characteristics. Their social status as slaves had become an inherent embodiment of the traits that were the opposite of privilege, rights, and characteristics of the free.[9] Within this schema, "black" and "white" became antithetical absolutes, where social practice solidified legal pa-

---

5. Nadine Ehlers, *Racial Imperatives: Discipline, Performativity, and Struggles against Subjection*, 36.

6. John Dickinson and Thomas Jefferson, "A Declaration by the Representatives of the United Colonies of North-America, Now Met in Congress at Philadelphia, Setting Forth the Causes and Necessity of Their Taking Up Arms."

7. Mike Rappaport, "The Peculiarity of the Three-Fifths Rule."

8. U. S. Constitution, art. 1, § 2, cl. 3.

9. Ehlers, *Racial Imperatives*, 34.

rameters around blackness and whiteness, making the Black/White racial divide the deepest and most pervasive of all North American color lines.[10]

During the nineteenth century, free citizens throughout the country—but especially the South—became increasingly fearful that the mixing of "racial stock" would result in White degeneracy and cultural decline.[11] Because blood was believed to be the true essence of race, and "Black blood" was viewed as a pollutant that needed to be kept in check,[12] courts attempted to determine the exact fraction of blood that might constitute Black racial status.[13]

Racialized behaviors also became increasingly important to the differentiation of race. In court, witnesses could prove a man's whiteness by reporting on acts of citizenship such as voting, mustering for the militia, or sitting on a jury. Such legal proceedings further legitimized rights-holding as part of what characterized the nature of whiteness.[14] Also during this time, a variety of cases specified that certain offences were particular only to "Negroes." In inheritance disputes, for example, one claimant might allege that another was Black and could therefore not legally inherit property. In lawsuits for slander, a man who claimed White identity could sue for loss of status if another defamed him as a Negro.[15]

Following the ratification of the Civil War Amendments, racialization continued amidst the influx of immigrants to the United States, with the judicial system attempting to define who was White and what constituted citizenship. The Fifteenth Amendment had granted people of African descent to be naturalized but not other "non-White" groups, so courts drew upon the long-established 1790 Naturalization Act to set the precedence for subsequent acts. Whiteness became the key determinant of whether a group of people could be enfranchised. By the turn of the twentieth century, courts continued to rely on "common knowledge" and "you know it when you see it" observation as legal evidence and determined that such races as Chinese, Native Americans, and people who were half-White and half-Native American were "not White" and could not become citizens.

---

10. Werner Sollors, introduction to *Interracialism: Black-White Intermarriage in American History, Literature, and Law*, 3–16.

11. Edward B. Reuter, *Race Mixture: Studies in Intermarriage and Miscegenation*.

12. Gross, *Litigating Whiteness*, 113.

13. Nadine Ehlers, "Black Is and Black Ain't: Performative Revisions of Racial Crisis," 149–63.

14. Ian Hanley López, *White by Law: The Legal Construction of Race*.

15. Gross, *Litigating Whiteness*, 121.

The years that followed resulted in a confusing mélange of racial demarcation as states attempted to uphold discriminatory legislation regarding citizenship and civil rights. So it was, reiterated over time and grounded in practice, the discursive power of the courts and other institutional sites of White power continued to solidify the racial binary.[16]

By the middle of the twentieth century, the biologically oriented approach to explaining race had begun to lose coherence.[17] Scientific research had proven it impossible to arrive at a set of genetically quantifiable features where humans could be compartmentalized into pure races.[18] The concept of ethnicity emerged among academic and progressive circles, challenging previous ideologies and proposing that race is principally a social construct. Physical characteristics from common descent are but one aspect among diverse cultural and social factors such as language, customs, religion, and nationality—all of which impact the formation of human groups. Defining markers of ethnic groups are not inherited, but become imbued with meaning over time through early socialization, community interaction, and the reproduction of language. The ethnicity construct emphasized the complexity of individuals and the possibility of multicultural affiliations and biracial identities—a reality that Ruth had brought to light during our interview.

Notwithstanding the emerging evidence that race is a social construct, essentialist ideology continued to characterize Blacks as an inferior race. Opposition increased in the late 1950s as Black movements became increasingly radicalized and brought to light deep-seated racism. Ethnicity theory was critiqued as a Eurocentric perspective that had developed within the context of European immigration and focused on how groups modify cultural norms in order to assimilate into the dominant culture. This paradigm posited that Blacks could also become "successfully assimilated" into the melting pot of the American mainstream by adopting White group norms that could be brought to bear on their social circumstances. The theoretical underpinnings of ethnicity theory did not address the historically embedded White-biased legal system or our racialized social dynamic.

At this time, Black civil rights movements had formed in response to the racism that had persisted throughout the United States and especially

---

16. Ehlers, *Racial Imperatives*.
17. Michael Omi and Howard Winant, *Racial Formation in the United States: From the 1960s to the 1990s*, 15.
18. Wilbur Zelinsky, *The Enigma of Ethnicity: Another American Dilemma*, 8.

in the South, where poll tax and Jim Crow "separate but equal" laws had circumvented the Fourteenth Amendment and denied Blacks their civil rights. The movements' influential leaders called for Black solidarity as a means of amassing power, albeit often with differing conceptualizations of what solidarity entailed. Martin Luther King, Jr., for example, called for a partnership of "Negro unity with all people of good will,"[19] but other leaders espoused a more separatist stance. Black Nationalist Malcolm X advocated that "there can be no White-Black solidarity until there is first Black solidarity."[20] Consequently, he founded the Pan-African Organization of Afro-American Unity dedicated to the unification of all people of African descent, "so that the welfare and well-being of our people will be assured."[21]

Within two decades, Black movements had impacted the passing of the 1964 and 1968 Civil Rights Acts that prohibited racial and housing discrimination but also had put into action an ideological intervention that redefined the meaning of race. Black radicalism had exposed the political elements that were at the heart of racialization, and in doing so it expanded politics to include racial issues.[22]

Today, racial ideologies continue to diverge. The White supremacist narrative still lingers, as witnessed in the violent outcome at Charlottesville, Virginia, when a Unite the Right rally consisting of White nationalists, Klan members, and neo-Nazi protestors clashed with counter demonstrators.[23] Yet, a critical race perspective is also part of our twenty-first century dialogue. Critical race theory asserts that the formation of racialized behaviors and the classification of human bodies is a phenomenon that takes place within institutional power structures. This perspective maintains that a Black/White binary must be maintained in order for Whites to stay in power, and that White-over-color ascendency still exists in America today because it serves both a psychological as well as an economic purpose for those who identify with whiteness.[24] The acceptance of White ascen-

---

19. Martin Luther King Jr., "Statement on Poverty, Black Power, and Political Power, October 14, 1966."
20. Malcom X, *By Any Means Necessary*, 35.
21. Malcom X, 65.
22. Omi and Winant, *Racial Formation*, 99.
23. In Charlottesville, Virginia, August 12, 2017, a Unite the Right rally consisting of White nationalists, White supremacist, Klan members, and neo-Nazi protestors violently clashed with counter demonstrators. The skirmish resulted in thirty-four injuries and one death.
24. Richard Delgado and Jean Stefancic, *Critical Race Theory*.

dency—by both people of color as well as Whites—has served to maintain a kind of implicit racism that has become ingrained in the institutional structure and social fabric of American society.

During my interview with Ruth that Sunday, this racial binary, buried within the depths of my cognitive upbringing, had surfaced and overshadowed my theoretical knowledge of race. Instead of seeing the complexity of race and ethnicity, I had made an assumption through a dualistic lens. This perspective had been the cause of my "momentary crisis in racial meaning,"[25] when I had not been able to categorize Ruth as either Black or White. Even more troubling, I felt that labeling Ruth as Black had been a serious social transgression. In my subconscious, I had accepted that Black was the antithesis of White, and if White is desirable, then Black must not be. It surprised me how difficult it was to disentangle my racialized self in the heat of an encounter, how effortless it was to take whiteness for granted, and how easy to fall back on the racial instincts that my White American history had bequeathed me.

In addition to these complicated questions about race, I was wrestling with how to approach the race dilemma in my research. By dilemma I mean that, in terms of biology, race is a meaningless concept,[26] yet the social reality is such that race is *profoundly* meaningful. Race impacts educational outcomes, job prospects, housing, and everyday associations. Also, when Ruth had asked, "Can I still tell my story?" I was compelled to consider the racial criteria for the women I would interview. Do I exclude Ruth's conversion story because she does not identify as Black, or do I include her because she could provide a biracial perspective? How could I acknowledge and analyze the importance of race in these Mormon women's lives—and in mine—without re-endowing the concept itself with essentialist meaning? How could I examine the experience of these women—and my own—as racialized beings without espousing concepts produced by racist ideologies?[27] I doubted that I had the wherewithal to free up the language as novelist Toni Morrison had from its "sometime sinister, frequently lazy, almost always predictable employment of racially informed determined chains."[28]

---

25. Omi and Winant, *Racial Formation*, 59.
26. Duana Fullwiley, "Race in a Genetic World."
27. Bridget Byrne, *Troubling race. Using Judith Butler's Work to Think about Racialised Bodies and Selves*.
28. Toni Morrison, *Playing in the Dark: Whiteness and Literary Imagination*, ix.

During the time I was pondering these questions, I had an experience that provided me with clarity of purpose on the one hand, and the task of grappling with yet another layer of complexity on the other. However, such events are welcomed in feminist qualitative research where personal experience is accepted as an asset and where one expects methodological fluidity to be the natural companion to a heuristic research design. This refocusing process happened while driving south through Virginia on Interstate 95.

Black Stains on a White Shirt

My husband and I were on our way to North Carolina to visit our children who lived in the Research Triangle. During the six-hour drive, I planned to browse through books that might help me analyze transcribed interviews, particularly having to do with Mormons and race. I had recently run across Jesse Embry's *Black Saints in a White Church* online and thought that it might shed light on the subject.[29] So, riding down the freeway, I tested out the voice function on my new phone and Google-searched the book. Instead of *Black Saints in a White Church*, up popped, "Black stains on a white shirt." At first I laughed, but then the truth of the imagery persisted: Had not the purity of Latter-day Saint church history been stained with racist and misguided practices regarding members of Black African descent? Had not the first Black members, who had been ordained to the priesthood at the hand of Joseph Smith, become a "troublesome smudge" for subsequent church leaders that resulted in messy and contradicting justifications?

Joseph Smith was the first prophet and founder of the Latter-day Saint religious movement. In 1820, at the age of fourteen and amidst the religious fervor of the Second Great Awakening, Smith began a search for the right church, "So great were the confusion and strife among the different denominations, that it was impossible for a person young as I . . . to come to any certain conclusion." Seeking guidance, he turned to the Bible and read, "If any of you lack wisdom, let him ask of God . . . and it shall be given him." Taking this admonition literally, Smith went alone to a nearby woods to pray and received a divine visitation, "I saw a pillar of

---

29. Jessie Embry, *Black Saints in a White Church: Contemporary African American Mormons*.

light exactly over my head . . . and when the light rested upon me I saw two personages [Jesus and the Father] . . . calling me by name."[30]

Over the next two decades, Smith would divinely translate ancient scripture from the Americas and publish it as the *Book of Mormon,* organize the Church of Christ (later called the Church of Jesus Christ of Latter-day Saints) which was understood to be a restoration of the early Christian church, and dictate numerous revelations. Smith's followers gathered in Ohio and Missouri to build a communalistic American Zion, but after being violently ousted from Missouri, the community established a new settlement at Nauvoo, Illinois.

In 1844, Smith determined that none of the leading United States presidential candidates would support redress for the victimized Mormon Saints, so he ran for president on an independent platform. Amidst heightened racialization and division, he openly opposed slavery and questioned how a nation could "hold truths to be self-evident that all men are created equal, but at the same time hold some two or three million people . . . as slaves for life [just] because the spirit in them is covered with a darker skin than ours."[31] His platform called for Congress to buy freedom for the enslaved:

> Petition . . . ye goodly inhabitants of the slave states, your legislators to abolish slavery by the year 1850. . . . Pray Congress to pay every man a reasonable price for his slaves out of the surplus revenue arising from the sale of public lands, and from the deduction of pay from the members of Congress. Break off the shackles from the poor black man, and hire him to labor like other human beings.[32]

During Joseph Smith's ecclesiastical leadership there is no evidence of anyone being denied participation in Church ordinances based on race, and Smith endorsed the ordinations of Black men to the priesthood and their callings to leadership positions.[33] However, in 1852, Brigham Young, Smith's successor and then governor of Utah territory, publicly announced that Blacks were descendants of Cain and could no longer be ordained to the priesthood due to the curse God placed on Cain and his seed. The prohibition was not intended to be permanent, with Young prophesying that "[t]he time will come when they [Blacks] will have the privilege of all we have the

---

30. Joseph Smith et al., *History of the Church of Jesus Christ of Latterday Saints,* 1:3–5. The passage from the Bible was James 1:5 from the King James Version.
31. Joseph Smith, *General Smith's Views of the Powers and Policy of the Government of the United States,* 3.
32. Smith, 9.
33. "Race and the Priesthood."

privilege [of] and more." However, Young added that Blacks "should not receive the blessings of the Priesthood . . . until the last of the posterity of Abel had received the Priesthood, until the redemption of the earth."[34]

Following the death of Brigham Young, subsequent Church presidents continued to restrict Blacks from full access to church ordinances and advanced various theories to explain the restrictions. The curse of Cain was a common justification, not only among Latter-day Saints but also among other White Protestant denominations. But by the 1900s, another explanation had gained currency. Based on the Latter-day Saint doctrine of a premortal spiritual battle against Satan, Blacks were said to have been less valiant in the fight, and were thus restricted from certain priesthood blessings in mortality.

Confusing explanations persisted at all levels of church membership throughout most of the twentieth century. In 1907, Joseph Fielding Smith, then Church Historian but later prophet and president of the Church, commented that the "general belief among Mormons that the Negro race has been cursed for taking a neutral position in that great [pre-mortal] contest . . . is not the official position of the Church [and is] merely the opinion of men."[35] In contrast, in 1949, under the prophetic leadership of President George Albert Smith, the Church issued this official public statement: "The attitude of the church with reference to the Negroes remains as it has always stood. It is not a matter of the declaration of a policy but of direct commandment from the Lord on which is founded the doctrine of the Church from the days of its organization."[36]

By the 1960s, the "Negro dilemma" had intensified when Church headquarters became inundated with letters from many West African Christians requesting Church pamphlets and publications, as well as baptism into the Church. One of the requests had been spearheaded by a man named Anthony Obinna who, after receiving divine manifestations, had organized hundreds of Nigerians into an unofficial Latter-day Saint congregation. His conversion began with a dream that he did not understand at first:

> I was visited in a dream by a tall man carrying a walking stick in his right hand . . . He took me to a most beautiful building and showed me every-

---

34. "Speach by Gov. Young in Joint Session of the Legislature Feby 5th 1852 giving his views on slavery," reproduced in Russell W. Stevenson, *For the Cause of Righteousness: A Global History of Blacks and Mormonism, 1830–2013*, 26–63.

35. Joseph F. Smith, Jr., letter to Alfred M. Nelson, January 13, 1907.

36. "First Presidency Statement, August 17, 1949," reproduced in Stevenson, *For the Cause*, 310.

thing inside it . . . Then [years later] I picked up an old copy of the *Reader's Digest* and opened it to page thirty-four. I saw a picture of the [the Salt Lake Temple,] the same beautiful building I had been shown in my dream, and I immediately recognized it . . . From the time I finished reading the story, I had no rest of mind any longer.[37]

The Church responded to Obinna's request by sending the literature but because there were no White priesthood holders on location to provide baptismal ordinances, the Nigerians were told that "the time is not yet."[38] After years of letters sent to Salt Lake City, Obinna pleaded directly to the Quorum of the Twelve Apostles (the Church's second-highest leading body), writing, "There is no turning back until I achieve my objective. . . . Does our Lord not charge us to, 'Go ye into the world and preach the gospel?' Our claim is justified, therefore you must help us."[39]

It was not until 1978 that president Spencer Kimball and members of the Quorum of the Twelve Apostles received a revelation in the Salt Lake Temple approving their desire to end the restrictions: "He has heard our prayers, and by revelation has confirmed that the long-promised day has come."[40] The revelation rescinded the restriction on priesthood ordination for men of African descent and allowed temple ordinances to all faithful Latter-day Saint men and women regardless of race. When Obinna learned that the revelation had been received, he wrote to President Kimball personally, "We are happy for the many hours . . . you spent supplicating the Lord to bring us into the fold. We thank our Heavenly Father for hearing your prayers and ours."[41]

While the 1978 revelation ended the priesthood and temple restriction, it did not address the restriction's origin, leaving the speculative reasons largely in place in Mormon culture. However, in the twenty-first century the Church began an effort to examine its own history in a more scholarly and reflective manner, and in 2013 it released an essay entitled "Race and the Priesthood" that examined the restriction in the context of nineteenth century slavery and racism. While the essay did not provide a complete explanation for the ban, it explicitly disavowed the speculations that had been offered by members and leaders:

---

37. Anthony Uzidomma Obinna, "Story of a Nigerian Member: Obinna's letters."
38. Dale LeBaren, "African Converts without Baptism."
39. James B. Allen. "Would be saints: West Africa before 1978 Priesthood Revelation," 217.
40. "Official Declaration 2."
41. "Official Declaration 2."

Today, the Church disavows the theories advanced in the past that black skin is a sign of divine disfavor or curse, or that it reflects unrighteous actions in a premortal life; that mixed-race marriages are a sin; or that blacks or people of any other race or ethnicity are inferior in any way to anyone else. Church leaders today unequivocally condemn all racism, past and present, in any form.[42]

On the ride to North Carolina, the significance of Black Mormon women became increasingly clear. These women had converted to Mormonism in a racialized America, and while we all inherit the vestiges of our sociocultural racial history at birth, women of color have inherited the worst of racism over the decades. They might have been freed legally more than a century ago, "but the act of emancipation had no talismanic influence [for Black women] to reach to, to alter, or to transform [their] degraded social life."[43] In addition, Black *Mormon* women have had to reconcile their membership in a historically White church that, at one time, had denied them access to spiritually emancipitory temple ordinances. How did these women come to grips with their church legacy? What quality of faith did they possess that could attend to this reality? For surely, they possessed a spiritual trust that, as a White woman, I could not be acquainted with. "We who are dark can see America in a way that White Americans cannot," W. E. B. Du Bois had said,[44] but more fitting, *We, who are dark can see spiritual things in a way that White Mormons cannot*. Perhaps then, like nineteenth-century Black Nationalist Alexander Crummell suggests, I should look to these sisters' conversion stories as "windows into a different world, a [spiritual] universe that resembles my own but is based upon a strikingly different premise."[45]

Ruth

That Sunday, Ruth *did* tell me her story. Like Obinna, she had received a sacred dream; like Joseph Smith, a scripture and a heavenly visitation had changed the course of her life. As we sat in that small classroom, Ruth had folded her hands on the table, with eyes bright and mouth turned up into a gentle smile, and she began by taking me back to her childhood in the city.

"I grew up the only child, but with both a mother and a father in my home here in Baltimore. My parents, they believed in the Bible and were

---

42. "Race and the Priesthood."
43. Alexander Crummel, *Destiny and Race: Selected Writings, 1840–1898*, 214.
44. W. E. B. Du Bois, "Criteria of Negro Art," 290.
45. Crummel, *Destiny and Race*, ix.

faithful church-goers. They went to church every Sunday, except when they were sick. I was raised here and I went to school here. I've been in Baltimore all of my life."

"Where in Baltimore?" I ask, happy to get the interview rolling. I was still unsettled from my racial blunder, but Ruth appeared to be relaxed, having taken my error in stride.

"Definitely West. West Baltimore."

"So then, what's all this talk about East and West Baltimore?" I ask, having heard church members point out the difference.

"Well," Ruth smiles, "when I was a kid I heard some wild things about East Baltimore, like gang fights and division, you know like, my friends, when I was growing up, 'Don't you dare go to the East side! Don't cross the line!'"

"Isn't that funny," I smile, and Ruth laughs. "It was foolishness. I mean, I pretty much stayed in West Baltimore because that's where my parents lived."

Fact, folklore, and practicality surround allegiance to Baltimore's neighborhoods. Some of the women I interviewed had not ventured out of their side of town in decades. They had grown up, birthed children, and died all within a few blocks from where they were born. When asked which side of town was most dangerous, Eastsiders would tell me, "for sure the West." The Westsiders claimed that there was, by far, more criminal activity in the East. The FBI, however christens *all* of Baltimore a dangerous city—the fourth most dangerous in the United States with 833 violent crimes for every hundred thousand residents.[46] From a statistical point of view, in 2017 the Eastside was more dangerous with fifty-five homicides, and only forty-nine reported on the Westside. Yet, the previous year, the West claimed sixty lives while the East, considerably fewer, with forty-nine.[47]

"I had a pretty strict upbringing." Ruth continues. "My parents, they were very protective, expected me to follow the rules, like curfew and to take education seriously. My mom, she cleaned for Baltimore City Schools, and my dad worked for Sparrow's Point. Worked there his whole life then eventually retired."

During the time when Ruth's father was employed at Sparrow's Point, it was a three-thousand-acre facility owned by Bethlehem Steel. The site was originally inhabited by Native Americans who spoke Algonquian,

---

46. Megan Wells, "The FBI's Ten Most Dangerous Cities."
47. "Baltimore Homicides."

but around 1650 Thomas Sparrow, an English born planter, became the beneficiary to a land grant bestowed by the second Lord Baltimore. Later, Sparrow's son established residence on the peninsula and is said to have called it "Sparrow's Nest." The swampy terrain first became farmland, then by the late nineteenth century, home to Pennsylvania Steel. For three generations, local men and women worked shifts making steel for such structures as the Golden Gate Bridge and cables for the George Washington Bridge in New York. After changing hands several times over the years, steelmaking had come to an end and the plant was sold for scrap at auction in 2014. The site was then slated to become an industrial and transportation complex, and has been renamed Tradepoint Atlantic in order to attract business from Europe and Asia.[48]

"My father," Ruth continues, "he was different. He was quiet and pretty much to his self, you know like, he'd leave early in the morning for work and wouldn't come back until it was dark. So in the week I didn't see him much. He just had his own routine. He was quiet on weekends too."

"And your mother?"

"My mom, wow!" Ruth's face brightens. "She really made an impression on me! I remember, when I was younger, maybe eleven or twelve, I would walk past her bedroom and see her reading the Bible; she would be talking to Jesus." Ruth emphasizes, Jesus, not with a crescendo but by softening her voice. "She talked with the Savior as if she *knew*, he was, *right, there*." Ruth is whispering so softly now that I can hardly hear what she is saying. But what I find extraordinary is that her voice is full of intensity but quiet at the same time. I lean closer so I can hear what she is saying.

"What an impression it made on my mind! My mom felt the Savior's spirit and I believed he was right there too. I really did. She just kept her door open and I would never go in. But *what* an impression it left on me!" Ruth takes a small breath, and I sit back against my chair again. She is no longer whispering but has shifted back into her relaxed narration style as she begins to tell me about her conversion.

> I was a Methodist, pretty much living that religion because of my parents. So what happened was, my mother, she died first, before I turned eighteen. Then I stayed with my father until he died. I had two daughters by then and was raising them too. One day I was looking at the TV and I seen a commercial to advertise—it was for a free copy of the Book of Mormon and the Bible. I was curious you know, so out of

---

48. Jonathan Pitts, "Rebranding of Sparrows Point Bittersweet."

curiosity I called, and I requested a copy. But when I called they said, "We'd be glad to send you a copy, but could we have the missionaries bring it to your home?" So I was like, sure. Well, two missionaries came—they were young but so excited about the Book of Mormon. I was kind of taken with that a little bit. I was like, wow, what is all the excitement about?

So we met a couple of times and they started reading with me from the Book of Mormon and talked about getting baptized. I was really kind of reluctant because, even though I had this really good feeling each time we read, I've never known a church book outside the Bible. So I started feeling like, am I doing what's right here? I tell the missionaries I belong to the Methodist church and I'm really confused, and now you're talking baptism—I'm *really* getting scared.

But Ruth tells me that one of the missionaries instructed her, "Sister, we want you to pray to know for yourself if the Book of Mormon is true." Then he asked her to read a Book of Mormon scripture and Ruth recites it to me, "It says if you ask God with a sincere heart and pure intent, then the Holy Ghost will manifest the truth of it to you. I was like, wow, this scripture really spoke to me because I wanted to know if I should become a member of this church or not. I was at a point in my life where I wanted to know the truth. So I will never forget; I got down on my knees and I repeated the scripture to God." Ruth's eyes brighten at the irony of her reminding God of his own words, and she flickers an almost imperceptible smile.

I really, *really* wanted to know the truth. So it was the first time in my life I ever prayed like this, with all the faith I had. I prayed for two weeks. Then one night I went to sleep and received a vision of the Father and Jesus Christ. I mean, I actually seen them! They were standing there and their feet weren't touching the ground. When I looked upon them I could see the fire of eternity burning within them!

Ruth's voice is barely a whisper again because the more fervent her words, the quieter she becomes. It is not an airy whisper, not delicate or flimsy; it is firm with devotion and burning with confidence. And because of this incongruence between the tone of her voice and the meaning of her words, I begin to feel that there is substance in her quietness; that her calmness is the essence of her strength. I find that I cannot take my eyes off Ruth's face.

It is at emotionally-powerful moments like this when the role of interviewer becomes a burden. With unquestioning confidence, Ruth has revealed an intimate and hallowed event; she has handed me a sacred trust, asking me to cherish it too. My interviewer's role pales, then fades away as I feel the waxing of a friendship, a sisterhood. The life-changing significance of Ruth's story ties us together in silence, our spirits linked in an instant of time.

But just for an instant because I find that the ephemeral nature of the encounter does not sustain the intensity, and I am obliged to proceed. I resort to humor and break the spell, "So I guess you told the missionaries *yes* after that—that you'd be baptized?"

Ruth laughs, "Yes. Yes, I did." Then for a few seconds neither of us speaks. I check the recorder, as if the action will fill the pause. Ruth does not seem to mind the lapse of conversation between us; her face is contemplative. Then, she breaks the silence, "If I ever had any negative feelings about, you know, do I really want to be a part of this church, I just come to church anyway because now it's a part of me; it's definitely a part of me now."

I decide then, because I feel her good will, to ask Ruth about race. I ask her if friends and family had questioned her conversion; if they had called ours a White church.

"Yes," Ruth answers, "but you know, it didn't matter to me. It didn't matter to me what anyone said because I had a witness and nothing—nothing can *ever* change that." Ruth looks at me steadily, her hands anchored together in front of her.

> This is my foundation. This is the reason why I am a Mormon. I know that my Heavenly Father and his Son are alive because of what I saw. If it was possible to take all the faith I had, and pray to my Heavenly Father—that's what I did. And I believe that faith moves the hand of God. The Lord was teaching us the truth when he said, if you have the faith of a mustard seed you can move a mountain.

At this point, ordinary dialogue does not seem like it can match the power of Ruth's words, so instead, I thank her. Then, as we gather up coats and purses, Ruth turns to me and says, "I've prayed for you with this work, with the work you are doing with the sisters."

I immediately feel encircled about with Ruth's warmth and a rush of gratitude because at that moment I believe that her faith could call down miracles—not only for her, but for me also. Then, just as suddenly, I feel tired, drained of energy and the need to find a place where I can contemplate the significance of what I had just experienced. I hug Ruth, open the door, and we walk out into the foyer.

2

Ain't Nobody Going to Drift Me

"Opal, are you up there?" I knock on the door and yell at the same time. I had tried to call Opal the night before to remind her of our interview but kept getting the recording, "The person you are trying to reach is not accepting calls at this time." Having learned that this message can also mean that phone service has been cut, I take my chances and arrive on time.

Opal lives in West Baltimore in one of the forty-seven government-housing communities, more commonly known as The Projects. Her street had just missed the one hundred-block area slated for urban renewal. In 2010, the city of Baltimore had hired the Urban Land Institute to evaluate how the Westside could attract new residents and businesses, and the panel had determined that residential (rather than retail) development would lead to a "Westside Renaissance." The Renaissance would provide a "sense of place" for the new city dwellers.[1] The plan, however, did not acknowledge that, for the current residents, a sense of place had already been established through decades of family living and that they would have to be uprooted in order for the project to proceed.

"Who is it?" Opal yells from upstairs. I am surprised at the strength and confidence of her voice. At church, Opal is timid and speaks softly with a stutter.

"It's *Sister* Strickling," I yell, emphasizing my church name so my White voice will not be mistaken for a government worker. This is not an unfounded precaution. Over the years I have been mistaken for Housing Authority, Social Services, and Child Protection personnel when visiting The Projects. I hear Opal's brisk footsteps on the stairs.

"Did you remember our interview?" I smile.

"No," Opal laughs. "But come on up anyway." I follow her up a sharp incline of narrow stairs. When we reach the top, I am met with the heavy smell of musty walls and old cooking grease, and find that my sandals stick to the linoleum, producing a suction sound with each step. In the middle of the living room is a pleasant looking Black man—one that I immediately size up to be ten years older than Opal. He is sitting on a plastic folding chair.

---

1. "The Westside Baltimore: A Vision for the Westside Neighborhood," 9.

"How are you? My name is Laura." I reach out my hand.

"I'm Joe," he lets me know. His hand clasp is surprisingly meager given his muscular frame.

"We're doing an interview," Opal informs him.

"But you can stay, "I quickly add as the man gets up from his chair.

"That's okay. I gotta be doing some things," he tells us and smiles as Opal follows him to the stairs. Opal is a petite woman with delicate facial features that make her look younger than her near-sixty years. Her teeth are shaped in such a way that her mouth forms a perpetual pucker, and her small, wide-set eyes crinkle into a squint when she laughs. She has smooth terra-cotta skin and legs that are shapely and muscular. Today, Opal's hair is braided into cornrows, and she is wearing purple leggings and a long T-shirt that swaddles her figure as she talks to Joe.

Opal's apartment is small and dimly lit, and the walls, once painted in government-issue beige, are now a dingy gray. The living room, where I am sitting, connects to a small dining area and a kitchen with plywood cupboards and a white gas stove that is spattered brown from cooking oil. But what catches my eye is the coffee table next to me. It is covered with neatly arranged photographs of Opal's grandchildren next to a picture of the Washington, DC, Mormon Temple and another of Michael Jackson from the nineties. Among the photographs Opal has placed a figurine of the Virgin Mary and a Hindu princess, and next to that, a scene of The Last Supper with Black apostles at the table with Jesus.

On the wall, Opal's pictures are not hung around the room but arranged in one corner above the coffee table, like a memorial. On one side of the corner hangs three more photographs of Michael Jackson with the largest one saying, "R.I.P. Michael, we'll always love you." Facing these, Opal has placed two matching rectangular portraits of a Black child looking up to heaven with tears in her eyes; next to them a framed poster reads, "Where words fail, music speaks." I pause to consider the significance of this phrase for a woman whose speech is marked with a stammer. How often had Opal's words failed her? And when they did, what music spoke in her behalf?

I hear the downstairs door close, and Opal comes back up to sit next to me underneath the photographs. I start the interview with what I think to be a low risk question, one aimed at putting people at ease because it only requires a factual response. I ask Opal how long she has lived in her apartment. Her reply is not at all simple:

Well, I moved from here and moved in with my son. I was supposed to let my niece and them live here when I moved out 'cause they ain't have no place to live, and I still had my name on the lease. I let them move in, and it turns out they had moved here on a Sunday, and you're not allowed to move here on a Sunday because the office is not open yet. And so they went up my rent real high, so I had to take a bus down here and go to the office and talk to them, and they told me they raised my rent up because I was subletting. So I say, "What is subletting?" She says subletting is when you still have your name on the lease and you let somebody else live underneath your name. So then we had to get his niece—because first the kids' father supposed to be staying here—then the niece wanted to stay here and both them was here and everything. And I had to—eventually I had to move right back into my house.

"Whew! That sounds like a mess," I respond, still confused about the sequence of events.

"Yeah," Opal agrees. "But I'm here now."

"Have you always lived on the Westside?" I ask, wondering if Opal had spent her life on one side of town.

"Well, my mother done lived all over the place," Opal replies. "She lived in *Ma*—*r*yland Street, *Mo*—ser Street, Mc*Cu*—llah Street, oh and the *Pro*—jects, and *Broo*—klyn." Opal makes the list seem longer by drawing out the syllables of each location name. "It was kind of fun living out there in Brooklyn and stuff meeting friends and school and things."

"Did you like school?" I ask, wondering how a student who had moved so often would fare.

"Well, I think I was living—hmm, what Projects? On East Exeter Street. What's the name of those Projects? Well anyway I was living there and I used to go to school everyday. Back then I liked school because I used to work with clay making different things. I made a dog and they sent it away, got it shellacked and everything and when it came back it was nice and shiny black."

The Baltimore schools that Opal attended in the early Sixties were majority Black but not because of a segregated school system. Before the *Brown v. Board of Education* Supreme Court decision,[2] the city's educational ethos was, "where Negroes enjoy equal opportunities there are

---

2. In 1954, the *Brown v. Board of Education* case overturned *Plessy v. Ferguson* of 1896 and declared that "separate but equal" laws were unconstitutional.

no real differences in mental ability between the two groups [Black and White]."³ Even though the schools in the 1950s were still mostly segregated, the School Board had taken small steps toward racial integration. After *Brown* they opened up the city schools to all races voluntarily, but in order to comply with increased dependency on Federal funds, the city was compelled to further expedite school integration and impose mandatory redistricting. This hastened the process of White flight, which in turn, decreased the local tax base and triggered a dramatic demographic shift from a majority White student body to a majority Black one within a decade.⁴

"Coming up, I had three sisters, but only one was raised with me and my mother," Opal continues with her story.

"Did they live with your dad then?" I have not yet heard Opal talk about her father.

"No, because my father died of ulcers in his stomach."

"So you never grew up with him?" I ask, believing that my question would result in Opal confirming my question. Instead, I find that it spawns another extraordinary tale, but this one is about spirits and an after-death visitation.

> No, but I remember what he look like and everything. My sister, she been a baby when he died. And one day the strangest thing happened. Way back they used to have this place called the Domino Food Store, and you used to go there and get cheese and other kind of stuff, and they bag up your cheese and your milk and your cereal. Well, my mother left us in her boyfriend car while they go inside the place and get the cheese. And all of a sudden my sister said, "Opal," and I say, "What?" "I see a man." I say, "Girl, you see a man? I don't see no man." She said, "I see a man and he walking towards the car, and as he walk he going deeper and deeper into the ground." I said, "What he look like?" and she was describing him, like he had a hat on, how he was tall, skinny, and glasses on. And I say, "Girl that is our father!" And she say, "What?" I say, "Yeah! You just described our father. Girl, you

---

The court specifically ruled that separate educational facilities were "inherently unequal." This ruling paved the way for school integration.

3. Edward Berkowitz, "Baltimore's Public Schools in a Time of Transition," 413–32.

4. *Toward Equality: Baltimore's Progress Report*, 16. "There were over 58,000 Negroes in 117 biracial school organizations, whereas 41,000 remained in 54 all-Negro school organizations."

sure you seen a man going deep like that into the ground?" She say, "Opal I swear to God I'm not lying. I swear before God I saw him."

"This happened after your father died?" I ask, not sure what to make of the story.

"Yeah! Because like I said, my sister was a baby, so she never recognize what he look like. So I guess it was his spirit."

"Well, I guess sometimes children see important things that older people can't see," I offer, but wonder what the importance of her father's visitation might be for the two sisters. "What did your mother say about that after she came back from the store? Did she see it as religious or spiritual?"

"My mother say, 'Girl, you ain't seen no ghost! Like, that so real crazy!'" Opal laughs and crosses her legs, leaning back in her chair with her arms on the armrest. "I grew up Catholic. But there ain't no explanation there. They not friendly either. We just take the holy bread and everything, you know, being the body of Christ. And at the time everybody had to pay. They would have this long basket, and it come past every aisle, and we have to pay money for it—you know, put money in it."

"Then did you convert from Catholic to Mormon?" I ask, now seeing Opal's connection to the Virgin on the coffee table. "Tell me your conversion story."

"Well let me start from the beginning." Opal's voice brightens, and she appears to be enjoying the interview. "I happen to look out my window one day when I was talking to my mother on the phone, so I seen these two guys—two White men outside, it was. They had suits on and everything, suits and ties. They was talking to these children, and I say, 'Hey Ma, there's two White guys over here talking to the children. They have ties and everything.' Well, she said, 'Girl, those are the missionaries,' and laughed."

"Your mother knew about the Mormon missionaries?" I ask.

"Yes, my mother been join the Church way before I did, but I didn't know nothing about it," Opal explains.

Mormon missionaries are paired up into "companionships" and travel the city searching for people who will listen to their message about Christ. At one time, our Baltimore missionaries rode bikes, but they kept coming out of buildings only to find their locked bikes stolen, so now they get around on foot or hop public transit. I've been told by the missionaries that in some neighborhoods they are well known. People will say, "Oh they cool, they're the missionaries. Ain't no trouble with them." In other areas, with their white shirts and missionary badges, they are mistaken for police. One missionary told me:

> Once I was with Elder Wabash, and you know how he is, happy and oblivious to his surroundings. Well we were looking for this handicapped, homeless guy named Jeffrey, and we were walking down this alley. Elder Wabash walks up to these Black guys and says "Hey, do you know where Jeffrey is?" And they started coming at us, surrounding us—they were gang-type people. "Jeffery? What do you want with Jeffery? Why you asking about Jeffery?" And we started to back away. Then Jeffery actually rolled up the alley in his wheelchair and said, "Hey guys, get out of here," so we left in a hurry. Later, Jeffery said the gang thought we were cops.

Opal continues, "So I say to my mother, I said, 'Ma those missionary guys talking to these kids, and they not even scared,' because you know how some White people scared about being around Black people—at least a lot of Black people?"

Yes, I did know, but I did not know that Black people talked about it. But the question must have been rhetorical, because Opal moves on before I can answer. "The missionaries wasn't even scared, look so brave and everything, talking like they'd been in this area for a long time. So Mama said, 'I want to call the missionaries from my church Branch and have them come and visit you because you can join the Church with me.'"

Opal is speaking quickly and with ease, integrating her stammer into a narration of crescendos and laughter. She is also an active speaker, crossing and uncrossing her legs as her story changes, sitting upright in her chair, then sinking back down heavily with a thud. Sometimes she waves her long, thin hands for emphasis, making figure eights in the air. "So I said to my mom, 'What kind of church are they? What kind of rules of the religion do they have and stuff like that? Is this an all White church, all Black church or what?' And my mom, she says, 'Oh, it's all races. It's a mixed church, you know. They don't discriminate color and everything. We are all family, all a family of the church.' So I said, okay."

Distinct racial divides still exist in Baltimore even though the city, as a whole, is becoming more diverse.[5] Black residents live in a census tract that is sixty-three percent Black, and this demographic has hardly budged since the 1980s.[6] Neighborhood segregation today is a shadow of Baltimore's

---

5. Edward Ericson, "Mapping Baltimore."
6. Brian Resnick, "Zooming into Baltimore, a Segregated City."

past, where block-by-block segregation policies, created in 1910, stipulated that "no negro may take up his residence in a block within the city limits of Baltimore wherein more than half the residents are White."[7] After the Supreme Court struck down the policy, discriminatory housing practices still continued on through the decades.[8] Opal's experience attending church had been segregated until she joined the Mormons.

> So I was cleaning up and everything, and I got a knock on the door. The missionaries came in and talked to me about the Church. I asked them first if we had to pay, and they said, "We don't pass no basket around—but now we do have to pay tithings—it's like ten percent of your income." They said, "How would you like to visit our church and see how you like it? Then we can see about trying to get you into our church." So when I first came, the people shook my hand and said, "Hi, how you doing," like that. And when I went to the chapel everybody was saying "Hi" to me. Everybody was giving me a hug, saying "We all family here," and everything, "We love you." I say, "You don't even know me but you love me?" And a sister said, "Well, we all family no matter what, we still love you," like that. I said, "This is so friendly and nice."
>
> And I like the Mormons because you learn more than you do in the Catholic Church. They have classes in this church where you learn about different things—Joseph Smith and how the Book of Mormon came about. And it was interesting to me that they didn't say get rid of the Holy Bible and just use the Book of Mormon. I still could use the Bible; plus they combine together and use both of them. That's what really interested me. So we started talking about getting baptized. So they practiced baptizing, because I was scared I might drown. But on that day, I told the sister there, "I'm scared I might drown," and she said, "I'm going to help you through it. You're going to be alright," and she helped me through it. She walked me to the baptism water so I wouldn't be scared, then afterward, she showed me how to do my hair in the blow dryer, and the towels to dry yourself off and everything. So it was good.

"How about the rest of your family? What did they think about your baptism?" I ask.

---

7. "Baltimore, Maryland Ordinance 654," 377.

8. Garrett Power, "Apartheid Baltimore style: The Residential Segregation Ordinances of 1910–1913," 299.

Well my daughter said, "Why are you joining the Mormon Church? You know they have more than one wife." I say, "I never heard nothing like that—I mean, they don't have no all that many wives now. They was talking about like it was, like way back, you know? Then they changed everything." Then my daughter, she said, "It's all White church." And I say, "Girl, it's not all White church. We got Black, White, Hispanic, Chinese, Japanese, Pilipino, African—people come from all sorts of the world." That's what I told her.

Even though this multi-ethnic claim is true for our congregation, most of the missionaries who pass through the area come from White suburbia in the Intermountain West, "without much diversity," they told me. When asked what stood out as the biggest cultural difference in Baltimore, one missionary said, "Oh, it's definitely the language. We always say there are three languages in the city: English, Spanish, and slang. Black slang is hard to understand, and there's lots of swearing. One time, we lost our phone and called the number, and this Black guy had our phone. We couldn't understand what he was saying on the other end—not a single word."

A knock on the door downstairs interrupts Opal's story. "Who is it?" Opal yells, and a male voice calls up from below.

"Well, we ain't finished yet," Opal shouts back.

"But we're almost done," I join in on the yelling.

"I'm going to let Joe know," Opal tells me as she stands up then disappears into the stairwell. I hear Joe's husky voice punctuated by Opal's laughter down below.

"Well, anyone could have walked right in here," Opal tells me, laughing at the top of the stairs on her way back to her chair.

"Was the door unlocked?" I ask.

"Yeah!"

"Well, that's not good," I acknowledge, "not good at all."

"Girl, that's scary!" Opal confides. This is the first time Opal has called me "Girl," and even though I would not use this ethnic term of endearment in return, I feel that she has moved our conversation onto more intimate grounds.

"Now, where were we?" Opal asks.

"Well, I don't know. How about work? What were some of the jobs you've had?" I ask, and yet again I am caught off guard with Opal's response. My question spawns a story fraught with violence and sadness.

"Oh, I was way an adult when I started working."

"Oh, older?"

"Yeah, because I was pregnant at sixteen," Opal tells me freely. "And when I was pregnant, my mother never say, you know how some parents say, 'Get a job, I don't want you on welfare' and everything?" I nod my head even though I had no idea that this kind of conversation took place. "Well, I was pregnant, and the first thing that came out of my mother's mouth was, 'Opal, I need to take you down to Social Service so you can start receiving a check for your unborn child. You can get checks, and you need food stamps.'"

Opal is not critiquing her mother for taking her to Social Services; she is praising her. There was no tough-love approach to Opal's pregnancy, no yelling or accusing, no mandates to work or discussions of responsibility. Instead, Opal's mother was guiding her daughter through the bureaucratic red tape that would support her new motherhood. It was almost as if the trek to Social Services was a rite of passage for Opal, the proverbial door to adulthood and a ritual that would bond a mother to her daughter.

> So she took me down to Social Service, and they gave me a check for the unborn child and some food stamps. And my mother, she getting food stamps too. So you know how some kids, they have food stamps, but they don't want to share with their mother? They want to keep it all to theyself. Well we bought our food separate, but my mother, she said, "I don't want us to eat separate." If she wanted anything, what I have she can always go in and take it. And I could eat something of hers, you know. It doesn't matter what you eatin' long as you eatin'. So we did that together.

Opal is not the first Church sister I have interviewed who has been acquainted with free-wheeling and disengaged inner-city families. Sisters have described households where by age twelve they could come and go as they please, sometimes staying out for days at a time roaming around North Avenue, skipping school, and sleeping over with friends. Adults and kids alike wrangled food from kitchens, where food stamp purchases were guarded by the owner or when the voucher itself had been peddled on the street to satisfy a fix.

> We went shopping two different times. Like she went shopping first, you know at this one market and there weren't no sales, and she brought her food home. Then we turn around, after we put her food away, we go back to the store to get my stuff. And by the time we went back to the store to get my stuff, they had a good sale on. She'd

say, "Opal, they ain't had no good sale when I go, they must like you better than me." And we would laugh about that all the way home.

As Opal speaks, I see her as a young girl, clothed with buying power and the right to determine her own welfare check. She had become an invaluable contributor to the family, and her change in status had strengthened her self-esteem and put her, to some extent, on equal grounds with her mother. "So when I went to the hospital I was sixteen, but before I came home, I had a little birthday party in the hospital. They gave me a little cake with a candle on top of it. Yeah, I came home when I turned seventeen."

"And did you go back to school after your baby was born?" I ask.

"Well, at one point I was pregnant still going to school. I remember because the principal told me I had to leave school because I was pregnant." Opal brandishes a backhanded wave as if to dismiss the principal in one sweep.

And I said, "Why?" He said 'cause I'm a bad influence on the other kids. I said, "How's I a bad influence?" And he said, "Well we have a rule here that when somebody pregnant they have to leave the school." So I'm packing, getting my stuff out of my locker and everything. This girl comes up, said "Why you taking your stuff out the locker?" I said, "'Cause I got to leave because they said I'm a bad influence on you all because I'm pregnant." She said, "That's not right." I said, "I know but they telling me I got to get out the school and ain't no where else to go." So I stayed out of school and do the vitamins and the iron pills and go to the clinic and everything. And then my oldest daughter's born, and I stayed home and took care of her and everything.

"It was a girl, you had a baby girl?

"Yes. That was Daisy, the one—I think I told you about—that died."

"I don't think you told me."

"I didn't? Well, see, Daisy just graduated from high school and was going to college," Opal begins. "So, so what happened was she had got pregnant by this guy—" Opal pauses and for the first time, her stammer is becoming more pronounced. "And she told the guy she was pregnant, and the guy told her to get an abortion. But she was going to keep the baby, and they had been arguing back and forth and everything over the phone. Then he call her back, and he ended up telling her to come down to his room. He was a guard there."

"A guard? So he didn't go to school there?"

"No, he, he wasn't no student. He was one of those guards at the school," Opal repeats.

So Daisy was getting ready to go down there, and her, her buddies say, "Why you going down there? What can he say to you that he didn't say over the phone?" They said, "That doesn't seem right." And so Daisy's friend say, "Well how about we walk with you, because it don't sound right?" And they walked with her down there and everything. But the boyfriend was talking to her, and somehow he must have told Daisy to tell them to go away or something. Because all of a sudden Daisy told them that she was all right and go ahead to go back to the room. But they said, "Are you sure you all right? You sure? Because we don't want to leave if something happen." She said, "Girl, yeah, I'll be all right I'll be there later."

Then next thing you know he talked to her all nice and sweet, and he took her out for dinner. He said she had wine and dinner and everything. Then I don't know how they end up in the woods, but they end up in the woods and he, he had a shotgun in the back of the car. And when he went to pull the gun up, and Daisy ran through the woods. The guy took the gun and shot her in the back several times. And they said her back was so messed up that it was too much sight to see because her whole back was out. They say her whole back was out.

Opal is crying now, and even though she is gasping between wet breaths, she does not stop telling her story. I cannot keep tears from welling up in my eyes either, or questions from turning over in my mind. Why did Daisy's friends suspect that her boyfriend would take a violent turn? Had they witnessed his anger before? And how did this boyfriend, this guard who carried a gun, take the cognitive jump from arguing with his girlfriend about an abortion, to the premeditated murder of the mother of his unborn child?

They said they got this report that some man joggin' down the street, saw a car driving past him real fast. And the man was thinking that it was kind of strange zooming past him like that. So he, he went back and double check to see where the car come from. He said he seen um, the um, seen a body laying by the side of the road. And saw it was a girl laying on the side of the road. And took her and tried to give her CPR to bring her back. And he said at one point he did call her back, but she slipped right back away. So she was gone at that point and everything.

So I couldn't believe it when my sister called me on the phone, that something had happened to Daisy. I said, "Girl, you lie. Don't be lying like that. My daughter's in, is in college. Why you lying like that? Leave me alone." But my sister was crying too. Told me on the phone that she was gone, said, "I'm sorry," and told me to come over there because everyone was sitting around at her house and everything. But I asked, "I want to see the body because I still don't believe she was gone. So my sister found out she was downtown in a morgue. So I went down, but they say we couldn't see her. They used to let the people go back there, but they say they won't let people go back there no more because people used to try and take the body out the door and everything.

"What? Why would people do that?" This seems like an odd explanation from a funeral home.

"I don't know why," Opal answers, pausing for a moment to wipe her eyes with the back of her hand, then on her T-shirt. But clearly, this is not an important part of her story.

So they say the only thing he could do was go up there and take her picture and bring it down to us. Yeah so they took a picture and brought it down to us, and I saw her mouth laying wide open as if she was hollering, "Ahhh" like that or something. I told the man, "Yeah that's her, that's her," like that. "She's gone." So at the funeral, you know how you review the body? We had a viewing one day and the funeral another day. So I went to the viewing, and I was looking at her. And my sister was looking at Daisy and saw that she got somebody to polish up her nails for her and everything. She always liked her nails polished, so they put that on her nails and everything.

But it didn't really sit into me 'til I came home. Nobody don't know I was doing this because I came home after everything was over, and before we went to sleep I had got this feeling that Daisy was really, really gone. I guess she was telling me that she was really, really gone and that she's with God and she is okay. And I just bust, bust out crying and said, "She, she's really gone," like that.

Tears run down Opal's face. She apologizes as she sniffs back her runny nose, her face glistening below the shrine of pictures on the wall, and the crying-child-looking-into-heaven hangs like a Raphael cherub above her head next to Michael Jackson. Opal does not move to wipe away tears this time but leaves her arms limp, resting on the chair as if all her energy is required to speak. Her stammering seems to have become overwhelming, and I wonder if it were times such as this when music would speak for her. Was it Michael Jackson who would express her loss? "A star can never die. It just turns into a smile and melts back into the cosmic music, the dance of life."[9] But then Opal musters a breath.

> But my sister, she was thinking that since my daughter was living with her at the time that she feeling more strongly, that she was grieving more strongly than I was. Because Daisy was living there with her. But I was telling my sister that Daisy was *my* daughter, and *my* feelings—*my* mourn—is real, stronger than hers because my daughter came out of me. Although she was staying with you, she came out of me so it have to be stronger than what hers is, you know what I mean?

Yes, I knew about giving birth and motherhood, and had shamelessly flaunted it, at times, to gain status among beginning mothers. But Opal's claim to motherhood was more worthy. She needed to validate the authenticity of a mother's grief; she needed to feel that holding a newborn baby in her arms had not been in vain. But I was also wondering why Opal's daughter had not lived with her. And even though I sense that my question might open the door to more distressing events, I ask Opal to explain. I am about to find out that Opal was a pawn, as well as a player, in an even more troubling story, one that is shrouded in accusations, bewilderment, and denial.

"See, when Daisy first went to my sister's, she was a teenager. She lived with my sister throughout the growin' up years and everything."

"Why didn't she stay with you?" I ask.

"Well, she was living with me at first when she was a baby up to a certain age." Opal's face is tear-stained as she looks at me. Her hands are folded together, resting in her lap.

> See, because she was going to school and the school, had called me up, and they were saying that my other two kids' father, which wasn't *her* father, took her, and touched her in some kind of way. So they had the Social Service coming out. And they kept coming every so often to see how everything was going. Then, all of a sudden they brought these papers to me—pull these papers out of the bag and said they going to have to take my daughter today. I was crying, and they said, "We think we ought to take her now because we see that youse upset

---

9. Michael Jackson, *Dancing the Dream*, 15.

and afraid that you might hurt her." So I say, "Why would I hurt my own child? I love this child, this is my first child and everything." They said, "Well, you can always request to get her back if you want her back after a while, if we have her in this other place first." So they took her away.

"Do you think it was true?" I ask, because I cannot tell from Opal's narration what *she* believes. "Was it true that the father of your younger children was bothering—" I hesitate, carefully choosing my words so Opal will be free to explain in her own way.

"—that he was bothering Daisy?" Opal finishes the question for me.

"Was he like, abusing her?" I skirt around the accusation.

"No, rape." Opal replies bluntly.

"Yes, rape, sexual abuse—"

"—yeah, sexual abuse," Opal agrees and we have come to an understanding of terms. But I still did not know what Opal believed.

"And do you think it was true, or do you think it was—?" I start to ask but again, Opal answers before I finish.

"Well, to me it was true. At one point I *did* say that he might have done it, because, you see, they gave her a test, and they talked to her in court and everything, because see, right now he claim that he never touched her."

But something is amiss. I am not catching the significance of Opal's ambiguous response. She continues speaking but her tone becomes matter-of-fact and flat, as if like she were telling me a story she had seen on the news.

> But I know in my mind that he touched her one time when I went to the store. See, I kept asking my daughter did she want to come to the store but she said, "No, I'd rather stay here." I say, "Ain't going to be nobody here but you and him. Don't you want to go with me to the store so you won't be here alone. I don't like to leave you with just a man here you know—you here by yourself." She said, "Ma, I'll be okay." I said, "Girl, you look scared whyn't you come on with me?" But she kept telling me she wanted to stay there, so I let her stay there.
>
> Then when I came home she had showed me her bra torn in half. And said that he touched her, and he tore her bra off and everything. Well I'm in the bedroom talking to him about it. I said, "Why is her bra torn like that if you didn't do nothing?" So he kept at me, fussin' at me, and in my mind I was saying, "Damn, I got to leave this man, start all over again and find somebody else. That's going to be hard for me again," like that. "So I took it out on my daughter, saying to her,

> "You're lying, you're lying. Telling a lie. He didn't do nothing to you. Why you lying? You probably tore your own bra." But I always told Daisy if somebody do something to you and you tell somebody and if they don't believe you, you keep telling somebody until somebody out there believe you. And that's what she did. She told and they end up taking her out for therapy and everything.

There are inconsistencies in this story that I do not understand. Opal suspects her husband—or men in general—of sexual advances, so why does she leave her daughter vulnerable and alone with him? Is it that she does not see Daisy as a child, but as a woman who is "of age" who will allure her husband? Opal herself had gained woman status as a young teenager and perhaps she views Daisy in the same light. Opal also believes that she is faced with the choice to either continue with the stability her marriage offers her or side with her daughter. But does she also believe that if she sides with her husband, in the end, all will be well with Daisy because she will be "taken out for therapy"? And then, what is the significance of Opal calling her daughter a liar for blowing the whistle, yet praising her for the very same act? Are these the contradictions of a distressed mind, or is it that Opal's rationale is coming from a life paradigm I am not familiar with?

> They wanted Daisy to go to a camp, you know, her and my other daughter, so they took them to a camp for the summer. Then they supposed to be back for the winter. But they lied. Lied to me and put them on a plane by theyself without me being there. And I told Daisy, I told her, "Since I'm not with y'all, you the oldest one, and you got to act like youse me. You got to take care of your little sister make sure she all right. Don't let her run off. If she, like if she need something to eat, go get her something to eat," and everything like that. Then, at the camp they kept saying we couldn't talk to them over the phone, but her cousin used to call there all the time and he said they let him talk to the girls over the phone. So why they telling us a lie?

"What kind of camp was this?" I ask, hoping to piece together missing parts of the story.

"I don't even know. I think it was a therapy camp or something."

"And it was Social Services telling you this?"

"I don't know. I don't even know who was talking." Opal replies, sitting limp in her chair, like a ragdoll.

> So one day, all of a sudden the people called us and told us they were sending my youngest daughter back home on the plane by herself!

Now how she going to know where to get off and all that when she by herself? I mean they sending her by herself, and we had to meet her at the airport, say what? You know? They said they were going to instruct her and tell her where to go. They got people on the plane with her, let her know where to go and drop her off.

So we came and got her, and she was looking kind of funny like she was upset and everything. I was with my husband at the time, and my husband kept asking her questions. What happened down there, and why we couldn't talk to her over the phone? And she said that they kept questioning her different questions about her father and everything and she wouldn't tell them no information. Say, my father didn't do this and all that stuff, so they couldn't get no information out of her. Yeah, they sent her home. But they kept my other daughter because she was telling them all kind of things. How he tried to, you know, do something to her and everything.

In this labyrinth of affairs, it seems that Daisy is now at odds with the rest of the family who have united against Child Protective Services. She has become the "snitch," while the younger daughter is the loyal one who held her tongue.

"When did you see Daisy again?" I ask, wondering how this girl had coped with the swirling events that had suddenly engulfed her young life: first, court-appointed foster parents; then, a new school and friends; followed by an escorted plane ride; and finally, as I envision it, a summer camp with bunk beds, counseling sessions, group singing, and reflective journal writing. Was Daisy content with these new circumstances in which she seemingly had no choice; did she take solace in this new kind of adult care giving; or was she homesick, wanting the familiarity of her home and neighborhood?

"We saw Daisy when we went to court," Opal tells me, and her voice is pinched. "But I always find it strange that they were hugging her so tight, and I was saying, 'Hi, how you doing?' and as I was talking to her, the lady kept pulling on her arm, kept squeezing it real tight. I say, what? Why she hugging my daughter so tight and everything?" Opal is squeezing a fold in her shirt as she talks, wringing it out like a wet washrag.

So we testified and everything, and at one point they didn't let her come in and testify in the court, they had her a circuit TV and stuff. But they kept calling her a statue, and I couldn't understand why they kept calling her that. I'm saying she ain't no statue, she's a human being. I think that's their way of—I don't know. I don't know what they meant. But they said that the statue said that my husband put a pillow over her head so nobody can't hear her talk and was fondling her and everything. First they said that he did it, but then they changed they mind and say he didn't do anything because it never did penetrate. He put it near there, but he didn't put nothing in, they said. It didn't penetrate, he just attempt to do something.

Opal appears to be lost in a world that is swirling around her. She has been pulled into a vortex of laws and legal procedures where an unknown language is spoken. In this alien realm, "state statutes," a term meant to determine the meaning of rape and degree of offense, becomes dehumanizing terminology that has nothing to do with her daughter. Child Protective and Social Services are complex entities that give out checks and take away children, and the Courts are mechanisms that determine the fate of a family.

So after my husband been in jail for a long time, he come by here every so often. He showed me his papers, so now he trying to get it right, get on track because he say he can't get no house, he can't get no job, he don't have no rights at all because of what they said happen. So he trying to get all this straightened out and everything. And he wanted me to get some papers notarized and sign and everything, saying that it didn't happen. But now Daisy is dead and they still got paperwork and stuff left over on the computer. So you see, my daughter was long gone after the two missionaries came and I joined the Church.

Opal wraps up her story circling back around to the beginning. But I feel unsettled, and in a peculiar sort of way, abandoned, because I do not entirely understand Opal or the significance of the never-ending round of affliction in her life. A persistent critique of people who live in poverty is that they lack self-control, so instead of withholding short-term satisfaction for a future reward, they tend to make near-sighted choices that keep them in a vicious cycle of poverty.[10] For example, a Church sister who lived with extended family members on the same side of town as Opal received church and government welfare assistance. One day the family was bequeathed a gift of a few hundred dollars from an inheritance, but instead of putting the money aside for next week's gas and electric expenses, they decided to celebrate and spent the money in one fell swoop by feast-

---

10. Douglas Bernheim, et al., "Poverty and Self-control," 1877–1911.

ing on crab. This decision was frowned upon by the Church leadership who allocated welfare assistance—a disapproval based on assumptions of agency and character. But missing from the discussion was an inquiry into what a life of poverty might engender. Waiting for future compensation requires trust, and those who have lived with instability for generations have learned that the future does not pay off. Poverty necessitates people to think short-term and to live in the permanent here and now.[11]

Opal's decision to side with her husband and not her daughter perhaps was based on the reality of the present moment. Leaving her husband would mean immediate financial and emotional instability that would leave her vulnerable, like when she said, "Damn, I got to leave this man, start all over again and find somebody else." But it was this same frame of mind that became fertile ground for her faith. Opal did not need an explanation of why at one time the Church had practiced polygamy or had withheld priesthood ordinances from Black people, saying, "They was talking about like it was, like way back, you know? Then they changed everything." The Church, as it is in the present, satisfied Opal's spiritual needs.

Before packing up to leave, I ask Opal if I can take her picture, and she happily agrees but first asks me to wait while she changes clothes. In a few minutes, she comes back into the living room dressed in a sky-blue sundress and a shoulder-length wig with abundant brown curls. She stands in front of the photograph of Michael Jackson and poses, leaning to one side with her hand on her hip. Unflinchingly, she looks at the camera with confident eyes and smiles, then she waves, saying "Hi" to a faceless audience. I am surprised at Opal's enthusiasm and cheerful nature given the emotional story she has just finished telling me. I ask her if there is anything else she would like to say before I go.

"Yes," she says, "I love this church and knowing I am loved, if you happen to be upset about something going on, the Relief Society women will come to you and give you a hug and say what's wrong and try to figure out why youse upset and everything. They try to make you feel much better. Yeah, and they so lovely. And I never had no brothers and now I have a whole chapel full of brothers and that's making me happy." Opal's eyes are fixed on mine, "It's all making me happy," she says, and I wonder if this is Opal's message to me.

Then, what Opal says next strikes me as significant because it implies a shift in perspective, from one anchored in the here and now, to confidence

---

11. Elliot Berkman, "Poor People Don't Have Less Self-control: Poverty Forces Them to Think Short-term."

in the future. She envisions herself as the woman she will become—a strong, spiritual sister in the gospel, full of hope and perseverance—and trusts herself to get there.

"Yes, I really love this church," Opal says, "Ain't nobody going to drift me from it, because I'm really faithful and try to do all the rules and stuff like that. So, *this* is my church; *this* is the church I'm going to stay in always. I'm not going to leave it no matter what!"

3
Salvation From the Dumpster

It is a sultry, Sunday evening in August when Naomi, a Jewish friend of mine who had converted to Mormonism, pulls into the Westside Projects parking lot. When I open the car door, a merciless wave of heat hits my face even though it is seven o'clock and the sun is starting to settle in the West. I feel beads of sweat trickle down my neck and hope that Dee has air conditioning.

The neighborhood is deserted except for a tall Black man about our age wearing jeans and a T-shirt. He walks by and nods his head, acknowledging us. I smile back but feel his gaze linger too long and immediately become alert to my whiteness in a Black neighborhood. Then, not wanting to frame his attention in terms of race, I consider that maybe the man's glance has little to do with skin color; he could be looking at us because we are female, or perhaps because we are newcomers in a place where everyone knows each other. But upon further reflection, I decide that brushing aside a racial explanation entirely is not realistic, and I wonder if the tendency to do this is the result of an internalized perspective of whiteness. By this I mean: as a White person living where whiteness is linked to stature and is innately esteemed, I have acquired a kind of racial confidence and a blind eye that takes whiteness for granted. But at this moment, in the Westside Projects, I have become "raced," and not being accustomed to this kind of social disequilibrium, my inclination is to deny that race is the reason for his scrutiny. While I am carrying on this conversation with myself, Naomi, as usual, is oblivious to what is going on around her, chatting as she checks her purse to make sure she has not locked her keys in the car.

While waiting for Dee to open the door, I look across at the rows of duplicate apartments and notice that Dee is the only tenant who has a true yard. Her property is an oasis among the other dwellings that have dry clumps of dirt, scrubby grass, and stray pieces of trash for lawns. Around her front door she has fashioned a fence made of baby cribs salvaged from the dumpster, tied together with rope and twisted wire. The grass in her yard—which I would later learn she cuts on her hands and knees with a pair of sewing scissors—is green and thriving. Against the baby-crib fence grows roses, irises, and a tall berry-laden bush at the walkway. Dee has arranged a pile of rocks in the far corner of the yard next to two small tables that hold pots of wandering jew and colorful begonias. Against her house grows one hearty tomato plant, a patch of collards, and several yellow day lilies. This inner garden is enclosed by a border of cucumber vines that she has trained to grow on wire edging.

Dee has not yet answered the door so Naomi knocks again more vigorously. "I hope Dee is wearing her hearing aids," she tells me. Naomi lives only a few blocks away in Bolton Hill but in an entirely different community. Bolton Hill is now preserved as a National Historic District and was once settled by wealthy German Jews during the nineteenth century. The neighborhood later became home to such non-Jewish residents as F. Scott Fitzgerald and President Woodrow Wilson, but remained segregated from Black people except for servants who lived in alleyways or large homes with White families. Today, many of the ornate row homes have been converted into multi-family apartments.

Naomi had volunteered to come with me because I had just met Dee, and only in passing, whereas she and Dee had worked together as visiting teaching companions for several years.[1] A thin, personable woman in her fifties, Naomi would rather talk than eat. A conversation with her meant that you would need to understand Jewish conversation style—a kind of cooperative overlap that features simultaneous talking and quick turn-taking.[2] But today I am banking on Naomi listening to Dee's conversion story. Naomi had described Dee as "a spunky person and somebody who knows every street and back alley in Baltimore," then added, "and that's because she was a taxi driver at age seventy."

At ninety-four, Dee is the oldest member of our congregation, yet she is a convert of only six years. She walks to church, rain or shine, and sits in the middle row so that she can read the speakers' lips after losing the hearing aid she had been borrowing from a friend. Fascinated by any human who had lived almost a century, I was especially interested in hearing what Dee had to say about Baltimore's racial history and what had drawn her to join the Church at an age when most people were clinging to bygone memories and daily routines.

---

1. Visiting teaching is a system of care that was established church-wide among Mormon women, where a companionship of two visits several other women in their congregation. The companionship routes are organized by a female president, thereby creating a network of women who provide spiritual and temporal aid to each other.

2. J. Correspondent, "Interrupters: Linguist Says It's the Jewish Way."

At last Dee opens the door smiling and motioning for us to come in. Inside, the cool air is almost painful as it hits my face in stark contrast to the stifling heat outside. "I'm just eating a little salad from my garden," Dee explains as we take her cue and sit next to her around the kitchen table. Dee is a small, sinewy women with muscular legs and shoulders only slightly bent with age. She bustles about the room with arms in motion, stopping at moments to rest her hands on her swayed hips. She has smooth, vibrant, ochre skin and a sculpted face with a nicely-shaped nose that follows the lines of her high cheekbones. Her deep-set eyes take you in with the unspoken discernment that comes with age, yet entirely without suspicion. Her smile is wide, and when she speaks, her eyebrows move up into a questioning arch above her wire-rimmed glasses.

Suddenly, Dee pushes the bowl of cucumbers and tomatoes aside and says, "I'll tell you, after I came home from the hospital that time nobody in the Baptist church visited me so I didn't go back to that church anymore. That's when I prayed to find the right church." Dee had jumped right into her conversion story.

"Wait a minute," I stop her, "I don't have the recorder on yet." I fumble with the batteries. "But anyway, maybe you could start by talking about where you were born and how you grew up?"

Dee's apartment shows all the effects of having lived in one place for years. It is orderly, but jam-packed with household items. The kitchen counter is buried in newly-washed dishes drying on a rack. Plastic containers, cooking utensils, and pots of all sizes are stacked next to the rack, and loaves of bread, boxes of crackers, and cereal are arranged on top of a microwave that is wedged into the corner. The living room, which is an extension of the kitchen, is brimming with boxes of yarn and crocheted slippers, folded granny-squares, and a heap of stuffed animals stacked high on the back of the couch. There is a bookshelf directly across from the couch where, instead of books, Dee has arranged mismatched cups, medicine bottles, and a string of red and green plastic holly that appears to be a Christmas decoration. Even the steam heater serves as a shelf for artificial fruit, magazines, and a circular tin that once held butter cookies. The heavy curtains covering the windows are pulled shut to keep the room cool, but the darkness consumes what little bit of space remains.

"Okay. You got it on now?" Dee is asking. With the recorder ready to go, I soon discover the benefits of sitting next to Dee. When she talks, she touches whoever is close by with a series of gestures. She caresses your arm when she is giving you background information; when the narration picks up she pats you with her fingers, and at the climax of the story, she'll give you a little push while simultaneously exclaiming, "but I lived through it, yes indeedy—I sure did!" Dee speaks quickly with a flourish, arms always in motion, splashing out fragments of her life—often not in any particular sequence as they bubble up from the wellspring of her mind.

"I was born in 1914 on the Eastern shore in Pokomoke City. I was the oldest of eleven head of children." Dee is stroking my arm with her soft hand. "When I was five years old, I took care of my two little sisters while my mother went out to feed the chickens and hogs. I didn't want to be left alone, so I'd take my sisters and put them in the tub that you wash in, and drag them to my grandmother who lived in the woods. My grandmother used to fuss at my mother for leaving us alone too long."

Dee's mother and father raised their own livestock but also worked in nearby fields owned by White farmers. Outside of Pokomoke City during the early 1900s, most Black agricultural laborers worked fifteen hours a day and received about nine dollars a month.[3] With such a meager wage, families had to rely on gardening and hunting, as well as hiring out their children in order to get by.

"We had a coal lamp and one day it exploded," Dee continues, her eyes radiating vitality through the reflection of her glasses. "My mother was gone, and she had locked the door and we couldn't get out of the house, so I took my two sisters and wrapped them in a horse blanket and put them under the table. I told them not to get up. Then I sat on a stool where my mother used to do her hair because I thought the fire was only going to burn one room. But I got burnt up anyway—my hands and face—I was burnt up all over and was blind."

Dee emphasizes the word "blind" as she gives my hand a pat, punctuating the magnitude of her misfortune. "That's awful Sister Dee," I tell her.

"My father thought it was mama's fault I got all burnt up so he left us. He only came back to make more babies," Dee's laugh is childlike in spite of her age. After a few seconds she begins to stroke my arm again. "But I had a beautiful life, and don't you know, my sisters and brothers, they are all dead and gone now, but I'm still here."

"But Sister Dee," I object, afraid that she will forget to tell us the end of the story, "you haven't told us what happened after the fire."

"Well, my grandmother took goose poop and ground it up and mixed it with linseed oil."

---

3. "The State of Maryland: Not Much Work for Colored People on the Eastern Shore," 1.

"Goose poop?" Naomi responds before I can ask the same question.

"It was mixed with four things but I can't remember them all," Dee tells us. "My skin was so bad that she couldn't use her fingers to put on the ointment because when you touch the meat on my face it would come off. So she would get a goose feather and spread the poop on my skin. She told the doctor, 'Now you take care of Dee's eyes because I don't know what to do about that, and I'll take care of her face because I don't want her scarred up.'"

I scrutinize Dee's face while she speaks and don't see a single scar. No facial feature is disfigured, no blemish mars her skin. In fact, the smile lines around her mouth only highlight the smoothness of her cheeks. "Your skin looks so smooth!" I remark. "Can't you remember what your grandmother put in the ointment?"

"It was four things," Dee pauses. "But I can't remember the other two things."

"Well, maybe you'll remember later on," I encourage, hoping that she can recall how to make this miraculous concoction. "Can you tell us more about your childhood then?" I ask because not only am I interested in how Dee grew up at the beginning of the twentieth century, but I am imposing chronological sequence to Dee's narration. Otherwise, her stories would zigzag forward and back over the decades. I wondered if, after having lived so long, the tapestry of her life had become one interwoven design, a cohesive narrative where the materiality of time was no longer essential. Or perhaps the effects of old age had finally started to set in.

> Well when I was a little girl, maybe six or seven, where we lived was segregated—here and everywhere else. You didn't eat with 'em or go to a lunchroom with 'em nowhere. You couldn't go to a bathroom. You wash their toilets and their clothes, this and that, then you had to go out the back door. If you go down to buy a pair of shoes you had to put on the socks or something on your head for a hat. It was pitiful. But I learned to forget about it.

During the 1920s in Pokomoke City where Dee lived, segregation was highly formalized. For example, the Mar-Va theatre on Market Street featured movies for White kids on Friday and movies for Black kids on Saturday. Blacks were required to access the theater by a separate entrance with separate ticketing and seating, as well as "colored only" water fountains and bathrooms. City ordinances also imposed sundown curfew on Blacks, and during mixed race events, a strict code of social conduct applied. Blacks were expected to acknowledge their subservient status by their posture and manner of speaking.[4] But today, Dee, in a mode of retroactive defiance, does not even acknowledge the White people in power who had imposed these Jim Crow segregation practices; instead, she refers to the Whites only as *'em*.

> So when I was a little girl, and should'a had school, this lady wanted me to scrub her porch. And the whole family would get lice in their heads so I had to put this whatever-it-was on their heads to keep them from getting lousy. I'd go at eight o'clock and didn't get back until four, and she gave me a nickel. But grandmother told me, "I'm not going to let you work there any more because the lady calls you, *Girl*. That woman don't know how to talk to you, and you're too smart a girl for that, to listen to her that way." But I told my grandma, "Words don't hurt me none Grandma, I'm going to make that nickel."

Dee's grandmother had been born into slavery and had grown up at the end of Reconstruction when "separate but equal" laws were coming into full force. Surely she had borne the brunt of these laws, but young Dee, having lived within the relative protection of home life, might not yet have experienced the full magnitude of these discriminatory practices. She did, however, understand the impact of money for a family living in poverty.

> So after I growed up—I guess I was about seven or eight years or so—it was a school teacher, Miss Louise, and she lived in town, and she and her husband wanted my mother to let me come and stay with the children. My aunt already cooked and cleaned for them, so I went there to live and came home every other Sunday. One Sunday they took me to Snow Hill, which wasn't too far away, because they were going to have a family get-together up there. And when I got there Miss Louise's mother said, "Why would you bring Dee up here? You know I don't like colored people." But Miss Louise said back, "Mama, Dee's as sweet as she could be. Just put her on the sofa tonight, she'll be fine—just so no thunder and lightning come up 'cause then she'll end up in bed with you."

Dee laughs at how Miss Louise had used Dee's blackness to tease her mother. The intimacy of finding oneself sleeping in the same bed with a Black child must have been unimaginable to this woman who did not like "colored" people. Dee further explains the reason for Miss Louise's joke.

---

4. Thomas Ross, *Just Stories: How the Law Embodies Racism and Bias*, xi.

You see, at Miss Louise's I used to sleep in the room with the children so if they wake up I'd be there for them. And this one time a big storm come up. I run into Miss Louise bedroom. There wasn't much room but I ease in—kept easin' and easin' and easin' in. And Miss Louise husband said to her, "Louise move over. You push me out of the bed." But Miss Louise said, "Somebody's in here," and he turned the light on. It was me. He said, "Let her stay cause she's scared of the lightening."

Dee laughs, "It was fun then!" and gives my shoulder a little push.

Naomi smiles from across the table, "I love hearing your stories Sister Dee."

"Well, Miss Louise and her husband didn't send me to school like they was supposed to, because I was there with those babies," Dee continues. "I stayed at their house until I was thirteen, but Miss Louise taught me everything, and when I went back to school I could tell the teacher all what the other kids learned. Yeah that was good, yes indeedy." Dee holds my hand for a moment then unconsciously smoothes out the wrinkles on the back of my hand, as if she were flattening out a handkerchief.

"After that I went back to help my mother pick strawberries and lima beans in the field, and a whole lot of other stuff."

Dee does not mention a salary for her domestic work, but in the early twentieth century, the average wage for a Black woman in the South was about a dollar per week. A child's wage would have been less.[5] As a nanny, Dee also would have become intimately acquainted with the workings of a White family, and since her aunt was employed in the same household, she likely guided Dee's behavior to stay within the racial parameters of the day. But Miss Louise and her husband appeared to treat Dee with much of the same closeness as they would one of their own children—even allowing her to stay in bed with them when she was afraid. By age thirteen, Dee had lived with Miss Louise just as long as she had lived with her own mother, but Dee was an employee, and after years of service, she was no longer needed. This farewell must have been a heavyhearted moment for Dee and the children she had mothered at such a young age. The upside was that working seven years as a nanny would provide her with the valuable experience she would need for future employment. The downside was that her life back home was about to take an unfortunate turn.

---

5. David M. Katzman, *Seven Days a Week: Women and Domestic Service in Industrializing America*, 86.

When I went back home my mother married again, and my stepfather tried to get me. He say to me after Mama already gone, "You leave those dishes and get the children to go on to school, you can catch up with them later." I washed the dishes anyway and hurried up, but he was waiting there for me at the bridge. I had a coat on cause it was the coldest day of the year. But it didn't have a button so I stuck a safety pin on it. And he came out of the woods—right near the big woods you got to cross a bridge—and he grabbed me by the collar and was pulling me in the woods. Well, something said to me, "Pull the pin out." So I did, and it loosened my arms. He pulled on the coat, and I flew out of it and ran all that long way to school. And when I got there I was so cold icicles was on my arms and I was crying. They tried to warm up my hands, and I was just screaming murder.

My grandmother lived close, so after school that day I went to her house and I said, "Grandma, did you eat your dinner?" She had arthritis or something. And she said, "I haven't had a mouthful all day long; the children left out of here to work and didn't give me breakfast." And I said, "There's some of those greens in the garden you like. Can I fix them for you?" You see they had something called winter turnip greens and my grandma said, "Yes, but hurry up or it's going to be late and your mama'll kill you when you get home." And when I got the greens ready for her to eat she said, "Now go home 'cause the sun is going down and your mama be mad and beat you all up." But instead, I hid in her closet where they put fruit and clothes.

At nine o'clock my mama came with all the children in the buggy, and she say, "Have you seen Dee?" And grandma said, "She was here and feeds me the best little food, I hadn't eaten all day, but I sent her home." Well after my mama left, my grandmother come where I was, and I was peeking through her coat. She said come on out and tell me what happened, why you didn't go home. And I told her. Well she sent her sons up there, and they beat my step-father to pieces. Then when I found my father and told him, he went and beat him up again and said, "If you *ever* lay hands on Dee again I'll kill you."

But you know what? He did it again anyway—he got me. Well, my mother had a shotgun that I saw her shoot 'cause she used to kill rabbits and squirrels and stuff. I put it to my shoulder, and I shot at him. But he kicked it out of my hand and hit me hard and knocked me out. He coulda come back and kill me. I had a terrible time back then. It was terrible, but I lived through it 'cause here I am!

Dee gives me another little push signaling the end of that story then pats my arm as if to erase the shove.

"Well, I've never heard this story before," Naomi says. "What did you do after that?"

"After that I ran away from home from my stepfather, and I was out on the highway thumbing a ride like I saw all the people do."

"You were hitchhiking?" Naomi asks.

"Yes, and a man stopped—he was a mechanic—and he say, 'What in the world are you out here doing this for?'" Dee imitates the mechanic with a throaty voice.

> I say, "I don't know." He say, "Where you going?" And I said, "I don't know, I'm running away." He said, "Well come with me." He says, "My mother having a baby, and we are looking for somebody to help." See back then they stayed down a whole month after having a baby, the mothers did. So I went there and took care of seven or eight sisters and brothers. Cook and wash and iron, and they gave me two dollars a week. Well 'fore long the mechanic was liking me and the grandfather says, "He can't be liking her in my house like this. I'm gonna marry 'em." But he wasn't a real preacher, so he didn't turn in the paper. I lived with the mechanic for five years, and that's how we ended up coming to Baltimore. They were six generations of mechanics, and his uncle had a place for us where my husband could work as a mechanic so he sent for us. We came by car, and I've been in Baltimore ever since.

"Wow, you were so young!" Naomi remarks.

"Yes, that's how I came to Baltimore."

Then Dee tells us how, after five years of marriage, she left her husband because he was "acting like a muck" and was jealous all the time. He started slapping her in the face at church and accused her of enticing the deacons, saying, "They were looking at you." But Dee retorted, "Then why don't you go slap them? I don't see no man looking at me." One day, after Dee came home from work earlier than usual, she found her husband with another woman. "I couldn't see too good but I saw them through the hole in the door," Dee told us. "He was naked and so was she. So I went and found a whole pound of lard and melted it in a frying pan. Then I opened the door and throwed it on them. I done scald them, then I ran away to my uncle's house in East Baltimore to hide. I never went back. It was nice just to get away."

"I guess they got what they deserved," Naomi declares while I am contemplating Dee's creative method of retribution.

"I had three marriages but all of 'em are dead and gone. I wore them all up because I'm still here." Dee laughs and gives me a friendly tap, "Yes indeedy."

"That's why you're so happy," Naomi jokes across from Dee.

But then, out of the blue, Dee becomes indignant. "Somebody got my number and took money out of my bank account, and I don't know why. I gave myself to everybody all my life, helping people, and I don't think it's fair for somebody to go and take somebody else's money—with my little bit of money." It takes me a moment to realize that Dee is talking about the present.

"What do you mean, Dee?" Naomi asks.

"I don't get but six hundred fifty-nine dollars, and the rent is two hundred and something and if I get sick, I'm too old to work anymore."

"So they withdrew money from your account?" I ask, wondering how the scammer got Dee's information.

"See, this man, he call me and said, 'Are you Dee?' and I said, 'Yes, speaking. Who are you?' He said, 'I'm the man that got your money and if you want it back you better give me your new bank number.' See, I changed the bank number a month ago. But I said, 'You think I'm crazy?' And I started to tell him something that Jesus wouldn't like to hear, but the man got it—he got what I was saying."

"Did you get it straighten out?" I ask, smiling at Dee's fortitude.

"Well, I got the bank to send the money here, but guess what happened? The postman put my check in somebody else's box. Rent's supposed to be paid on the first and my insurance too. So Lord have mercy! Maybe they'll put me outdoors or something."

"I hope they don't," Naomi laughs, making light of the dilemma.

"You can hope all you want, but you've got to have faith for real," Dee tells us, but behind her lighthearted manner I sense her seriousness; that she understands, in a very real way, the quality of faith necessary for miracles. "The church people are coming and giving me money and bringing me food. I *am* happy about that."

"How about family, Sister Dee?" I ask. "Do you have any children or somebody who could help with this mess?" Dee must have someone who could step in and help her navigate the ins and outs of dealing with scammers and incompetent postal workers. But her response is entirely unexpected.

"Well see, I was raped when I was five years old by a cousin that was nineteen." Dee reveals this incident matter-of-factly, as if sexual abuse were yet another episode among many in the long list of trials she had endured throughout her life. "And I never had babies," she tells us. "They said I might get 'em but I never did—but it's okay because God sent me a baby and I adopted him. I'll tell you." Dee begins to stroke my arm again.

> One day my husband went to work and we didn't have any vegetables, so he gave me money to go to the store. Well, I couldn't find the money so I thought, I must have put it in the trash. I went out and sorted through the dumpster. And don't you know, when I was doing that, I heard a baby cry. I had to go get a step ladder to get into the dumpster. And I didn't know what to do when I got the baby out all wet and messed up. One of the ladies say, "Why don't you go to the police station and tell 'em." So I did. It was right on Pennsylvania Avenue by Dolphin Street there. So I carried him up there and the police said, "You know what? I'm going to send you downtown; say, if you found that baby and it ain't yours you need to adopt it." So I did.

"You saved a baby from the dumpster?" I ask, needing confirmation. These were stories that I had only heard on the news and even then, it was unimaginable that an innocent newborn could begin life so viciously. But I also questioned how easily the police had turned over the newborn to Dee. Was there no investigation into this attempted murder? No question as to the circumstances surrounding this act of child abandonment? Did the law just turn its head when dealing with family affairs in Baltimore's Black community or had Dee left out significant details of the story?

Instead of answering my question, Dee makes a declaration. "Let me tell you, everyone who has a baby is not a mother. Believe me when I say that."

I nod in agreement as Dee pats my arm, and I feel her nurturing touch validate her words. I look at her adept, shapely fingers, potent and full of life, and her silver bracelet dangling at her wrist. I see that Dee is not just giving us advice; she is telling us that mothering characterizes the essence of who she is. She was not able to give birth—tragically, that gift had been taken from her when she was only five years old—yet it was that very same age when her mothering began, and she had wrapped her sisters in a horse blanket to save them from the fire. Even Dee's yard, with its castoff babycribs that encircle thriving vegetables and healthy flowers, is a memorial to her maternal capacity and ability to nurture.

"I took care of lots of babies in my life," Dee adds, "a mother to lots of kids, yes indeedy!" Then, while I am still reeling from Dee's rape and adoption story, she jumps right into another episode of her life. "But I've got to tell you about my Jewish children too!" Her voice is full of energy as she waves her arms in the air and pats my back. "So I took care of children and worked for the Jewish people for years and years." Naomi nods and smiles because she has heard this story before.

I was taking care of the babies when their mother got sick. The mother got leukemia, and she calls me in and says, "I'm going to the hospital again but I don't think I'm coming back this time." She says, "you've been with these children, and they love you just like they do me. If anything happens to me will you stay here with them?" I told her, "I have a son remember? And Black children don't go to school with White people, so can my son stay here and can the children grow up together? Tell your husband that. And if he don't agree he can find somebody else." So I stayed and took care of four boys and two girls until they were teenagers. I taught them everything. I paid the bills, I went to the market, I cut their hair my ownself, and I even mowed the grass to save money. The kids, they'd be out playing but I'd make them come into the kitchen with me. I showed them how to set the table—one of them each day—and they would help me cook. And they'd go in the store to shop with me. Remember back then it was segregated, but they'd come right up to the counter with me and say, "Ma can I have this?" I wish you could a seen the clerk's face. "These your children?" he asked, and I said "Yes." Then when the kids were teenagers they went to boarding school. I didn't work there anymore because they didn't need me.

Suddenly, the phone rings and interrupts Dee's story. "Oh Lord," Dee exclaims looking at the recorder, "Can I answer the phone?"

"Sure, go ahead," I tell her and pause the recording. Dee jumps up and walks into the living room where her phone is plugged into the wall. Her voice takes on a quality of roughness that I have not yet heard. I wonder who could be on the other end of the line and why she appears to be irritated.

"It was Glenard," Dee informs us after hanging up the phone.

"Glenard! Tell Laura about him, Dee," Naomi insists, then tells me, "You'll like this story, Laura!" Dee appears to be happy to start a new account of her life drawing upon her unflagging energy and capacity for talking.

"Okay, see, years back this boy calls me at two o'clock in the morning and said, 'Are you Dee?' And I said, 'Yeah, who's speaking?' He said, 'My name is Glenard,' and I said, 'Are you my nephew from New Jersey?' I thought he might be my nephew." This time Dee lightly brushes my arm with her fingers at the end of each sentence. And while her touch might have been annoying to some, I welcomed her connection with me. Her need to touch was so involuntary that I doubted if Dee even knew she was doing it.

But Glenard said, "No, you don't know me." So I said, "Well how'd you get my number?" He said, "I closed my eyes and put my finger on the phone book. I wanted to talk to somebody that is not in the family. My father is leaving my mother, and I love the both of them, and I just want to know which one I should go live with." I said, "Glenard, does your mama own her own home—got a roof over her head?" and he said, "Yeah." You see, one of Glenard's uncles is a, you know, dead people, what you call them? A mortician. And he gave her a house, because the father didn't work so much. The mother was moving from place to place so the uncle gave her a house. So I told him, "Well, you go with your mama." Then he said, "Can I call you again? What's your number?" I said, "You called it once, find it again." He's been call me ever since. That was thirty-two years ago.

Thirty-two years ago? I was visualizing a child on the other end of the phone, or at the very least, an awkward and obnoxious preteen who had overstayed his welcome. But Dee's Glenard was a middle-aged man. I begin to be suspicious that Glenard might be some kind of free-loader or another scammer, but Dee enlightens us.

"I found out Glenard had something wrong with him," Dee says. "See, when he was a little baby his father and grandfather used to work all the time at the Royal Theatre playing music and singing." The Royal Theatre, first known as Douglas Theatre, opened in 1922 along west Baltimore's Pennsylvania Avenue. The Royal became the first theatre on the *Chitlin' Circuit*, a track of night clubs and theatres for Black performers that extended throughout the South, Chicago, and Texas. The biggest stars in Black entertainment such as Duke Ellington, Billie Holliday, Nat King Cole, and The Supremes performed at the theatre. Baltimore City's first talking motion picture, *Scar of Shame*, with an all Black cast, was also shown there. But unfortunately, during the Civil Rights riots in 1968, the theatre was damaged and from then on began to decline along with the entire Westside community. In 1971 the theatre was razed, and today, only a monument stands in its place.

"After playing the music they would go partying," Dee continues, "and one time, when Glenard's father was all drunk up, they had an accident and dropped him down the sewer hole. He never was right since then. Glenard is a mental case, but I took care of him and taught him to cook because they didn't teach him nothing and that's the truth."

Dee's cornucopia of life stories seem to abound with accounts of running away and saving others, of narrow escapes and rescues. But when I ask Dee to tell her conversion story, I find out that she did not escape the Mormon missionaries even though she tried.

"We're ready to hear your conversion story now, Sister Dee."

"Okay, well, when I had the mastecty the Baptists didn't come back to help."

"You belonged to the Baptist Church?"

"Yes, and when I go home from the hospital I got nobody—uh huh, and so I didn't go back to that church anymore. So I prayed. I said, 'I'm not going back to church Lord unless you send me somebody!'" Dee's eyes flash behind her wire rim glasses, and she puts her hand on her hip in defiance even though she is sitting.

> And he did, but it was years later. Yes, mm hmm. They knocked on the door, and at first I thought, "The Jehovey Witness are here." So I said I was going to put on clothes and go out the back so I wouldn't have to worry with them, but I didn't get dressed soon enough and the knock came on the door. So then I said I wasn't going to open it, but I went immediately anyway and two boy missionaries were there smiling. They showed me their badges and said they were from the Church of Jesus Christ of Latter-day Saints.
>
> I said, "I've never heard of you before, so come in and have a seat. I got two questions to ask you, and if you answer them correctly then you can talk. Well they didn't sit, they stood, and I ask, "Then where do people go when they die?" Because my grandfather preached everybody into heaven, and I couldn't understand how could they all go to heaven if they hadn't did right. Well they told me the answer and said, "What's the next question?" I said, "Do you celebrate Jesus' birthday?" Because the Jehovah's Witness didn't. They said, "Yes, Jesus is the name of their church." Then they said a prayer and read their favorite scripture in the Mormon book. Then they took my name and phone and was going to give it to the girl missionaries to come see me. When the lady missionaries called, I said "I'm sorry, I'm not ready yet. I got to pray on it." But before I hung the phone up I took their phone number. When I hung up something say to me, "How are you going to know what they're like if you don't listen?" So I called them

right back and told them I changed my mind. The day after they were there and I listened.

So the first time I came to church, I came too early, and I was sitting on these marble steps, and the White people was going by looking at me so funny. I felt so badly. But soon after that here comes Sister Kelly. I tell her I'm waiting for the missionaries but she said, "Oh, come on in here." You know how she's kind of bossy—she asked me my name and I told her. Then she says she introduce me to the members, "Now they reach their hand out so you reach out yours too. I'll show you, like this." And I'm so glad I did!

Dee rocks back and forth in her chair, unable to keep still. "And I got news for you—I'm so happy to be baptized! I don't know what to do I'm so happy. The Church is like family, yes indeed! This last time I been sick and the sisters would cook food and bring it! I couldn't use my hands because I had surgery and they *fed me*! Oh my goodness, I sucked it up too. I was enjoying it. It's just so nice to be loved."

The interview had ended that day with Dee showing us a windup monkey toy that someone had given her. "I wonder if he'll still do it," Dee had said as she put the toy by her feet. When she let go, the monkey clapped a pair of symbols together and scooted about on the floor.

"Oh my gosh, it works!" Naomi exclaimed, laughing at the performing vintage toy. A few minutes later after it came to a stop, I asked Dee about the big box of crocheted slippers she had next to the couch.

"I crocheted all these slippers," she replied, then suddenly, "Oh, wait! I didn't tell you this one last story about the slippers."

"Well, just a minute Sister Dee, let me turn the recorder back on," I told her, but she started her story anyway.

"When I was baptized Sister Kelly gave me a present. It was a book and you could put whatever in it. It was so nice because I never got too many presents. So I said, for whoever get baptized I'm going to give them a pair of slippers."

"Like the ones you made here?" I asked, picking up a double-crocheted pink slipper with red trim. "Yes, but I have to tell you, I was making granny squares and bedspreads all the time, but I wanted to make slippers. Now in my dreams I could make slippers, but I didn't know how to put them together in real life, and I worked on it for a whole month. It was like a puzzle and they wouldn't work right." Dee holds my arm as we stand in a circle around the monkey toy.

"Then I said, 'Well I think I'm going to say a prayer tonight and I'll ask the Lord.' I said, 'Lord, I done made all these things up here, and now I don't know how to make slippers. If it's your will, just tell me.' Then I dreamed these words, 'Try again.' That's all. That's all that come to me, 'Try again.' And guess what? I woke up and tried again and put them on the table and put the squares pointed and the two points together. It come to me and I made them! I made them and done been making them slippers ever since." Dee claps her hands together, then laughs.

After Naomi and I had hugged Dee and told her goodbye, we left with two gifts: a pair of crocheted slippers in our hands and Dee's stories etched upon our memory. As we climbed into Naomi's car and cranked up the air conditioning, I could still feel Dee's soft hand caressing my arm.

Baltimore saw record snowfall the winter Dee passed away. Right before Christmas, a blizzard shut down the city turning it into a silent, frosty dream world. Then in February, two more storms dropped waist-high snow and brought Baltimore to a halt again. Traffic lights dutifully continued to flash against the dark, gray sky even though no cars were waiting at intersections. There were no rowdy teenage boys walking home from Digital Harbor High in front of my window, no tourists that occupied sidewalks or puzzled over parking signs. The cars that lined the street were transformed into unblemished, white mounds and a blanket of unusual calmness settled over every neighborhood. Word got out that Dee had died and that regrettably, the funeral would have to be postponed for several weeks until the ground could be cleared of snow. For some reason this announcement filled me with warmth and made me smile. Strong and tenacious, full of vigor and playfulness, even in death Dee could not rest. It was then that I thought about something Dee had said in our interview, "All my life I wanted to learn how to do things; I wanted to try everything. I lived a long life and the only thing I haven't got to do yet is skydive. Yes indeedy!" Then she had laughed.

At the announcement of the delayed funeral, Naomi and some of the other sisters had joked that Dee was probably out playing in the snow. But if I were to place a wager, I would bet that Dee was out trying her hand at skydiving. She had waited on so many people in her life—babies in the nursery and children at church, young Jewish kids and older folk in rest homes—but now she would have one last fling while *we* waited on her and the final ceremony that would celebrate her life.

# 4

Delilah's Miracle

I called up Delilah to see how she was doing, because I had not seen her at church for several weeks. "Oh I'm feeling better. My tooth is much better."

"Your tooth?" I asked. Delilah did not always start a conversation from the beginning.

"Yes, I went to the emergency room on Thursday—was it Thursday?—no, I think it was Friday, because that was the day my son was supposed to come over." I had never met anyone who could glide so seamlessly from one topic to the next. Before I knew it I had spent forty-five minutes on the phone listening, and the story I was anticipating had just begun.

"I went to Emergency on Friday because on Thursday the dentist pulled my tooth and he must have cracked the one next to it," Delilah explained. "I could feel where the tooth was split and how the pain throbbed right up into my eye." The emergency room told Delilah they could not help her because they did not have a dentist on staff; instead they gave her Percocet. "Well, the Percocet didn't even touch the pain, so I prayed to God and he showed me what to do. I got some gauze, and I soaked it in Majors numbing liquid. I have pliers, and I sterilized them too. Then I put the gauze over the pliers."

"Delilah, you didn't!"

"It's okay," she replied calmly. "I took dental technician classes in high school."

But that was thirty years ago, I was thinking. And besides, high school classes?

"Well, I put the pliers on the tooth and jiggled it. I kept jiggling it slowly, then finally I just said, 'Here I go Heavenly Father,' and I yanked as hard as I could and pulled the tooth out. Then I held it up for Him to see."

Delilah had begun to pick up the pace because she knew she had me hooked. "It only bled about one-third cup. Then I stuffed the hole with gauze soaked in numbing medicine and left it there for a while. After that, I took a look at the tooth and could see the root so I knew I had it all out. And you know what? The pain was gone. This is a testimony of what God can do for you."

I was still trying to visualize the one-third cup of blood, but she continued on. "I was afraid of infection, so I went back to the emergency room for a prescription of antibiotics and faxed it to the pharmacy overnight so it would be ready for me in the morning."

"Really? You did all that?" I was impressed with Delilah's ability to keep a level head in the face of a crisis.

"Well, when I go back to the dentist next time I'm going to tell him about this tooth. I only go to the dentist about once every three years though because I hate needles."

"Delilah, you hate needles, but you can stick pliers in your mouth and yank out a tooth?" I could not help asking.

"Well, I used to see my dad take care of things that way," she said. "I've seen him pull out his teeth before."

When I first met Delilah she was using a wheel chair to get around. This was unexpected because, at first glance, you would take her for a woman who had barely reached forty. She wore a wig that was styled long and straight, with bangs across her forehead like a teenager. Her nails were fire-engine red, and she wore bright red lipstick to match. Delilah's wardrobe was reminiscent of the eighties—clothes she had bought forty years ago when she was working on Security Boulevard at the Social Security office: hot pink blazers with oversized shoulder pads, orange dresses, smelling slightly like mothballs and stamped with geometric designs, neon scarves, and black slouchy boots with pointed toes. Delilah's voice, like her boldly-colored clothes, was full of energy and purpose, but she would speak with vigor one moment then fall asleep in her chair the next. "It's my medicine," she would explain if you were sitting next to her in Relief Society[1] meeting, "it makes me drowsy." I told Delilah that I was recording the conversion stories of the African American women in our congregation and asked her if she wanted me to record her story. "Yes, definitely" she said, "I'll phone you when I'm ready."

Five weeks later, after I was sure Delilah had forgotten about the interview, she calls me. "I'm free this week if you want to come on over now."

"Great. I can come tomorrow," I let her know.

As I drive up to Delilah's house, I notice that her windows are decorated with purple crepe paper and a sign that says *Go Ravens*. Her efforts to cheer on Baltimore's football team seemed out of place next to boarded

---

1. The Relief Society was established in 1842 as the official organization for Mormon women.

up row houses and stairwells that had collected windblown trash. I get out of my car, step over the weeds that had made their way up through the cracks in the sidewalk, and begin to study the parking sign. I can't tell if parking is allowed there or not because of opposing arrows on the sign. I glance at the men milling around across the street. A few face each other coughing out hoarse puffs of laughter and cigarette smoke. Some are sitting on porch steps looking directly at me. While I figure they could likely explain the mystery of the sign, it would require girding up my emotional loins—the task of not only bolstering myself up against the vulnerable position of confronting a group of unknown men, but also a situation intensified by the gendered racial dynamic of White female approaching Black males. I decide to ask Delilah instead.

"Hi Delilah," I greet her as she opens the door, "so good to see you. How are you feeling?"

"Doing okay." Delilah smiles, and I can't help but notice the gap in her teeth where she had extracted the cracked tooth.

"Do you think it's okay to park there?" I ask, pointing to my car on the near-empty street.

"I only know that you can't park there on Tuesdays, because that's when the street cleaning truck comes by," Delilah explains as she peers out the door.

"Well, it's not Tuesday," I say, "but I still can't tell from the sign if it's okay."

"I think it's okay, but I'm not sure. How do you feel about it?" Delilah's response strikes me as unusual. How do I feel? Drawing upon one's sentiments does not seem like a good way to determine where to park in downtown Baltimore. After ten years in the city I knew, only too well, the erratic ticketing behavior of the city police. But I also knew that you could buy time in the run down parts of town where sightseers weren't scrambling for a parking space. I decide to chance it.

Delilah gestures for me to step all the way into the kitchen, then turns to lock two deadbolts and a chain latch. Entering her house is like a refuge. The kitchen is clean and spacious, furnished with new appliances, faux-granite counter tops, and off-white linoleum floors. Down the hall I see a mustard-colored velveteen couch draped with a crocheted afghan and lace doilies. A gilded flower arrangement sits next to that on a glass end table.

"Do you need something to drink?" Delilah offers, pointing to the refrigerator.

"No thanks, I'm fine right now."

On Delilah's refrigerator door, next to a *Go Ravens* magnet in the shape of a football, another large magnet catches my eye. It states, "God giveth but the government taketh away." I pause to consider this statement that would be more at home in my conservative brother-in-law's kitchen back in Idaho rather than urban Baltimore, where seventy-one percent of those receiving government assistance reside.[2]

As I turn to sit down in one of the two folding chairs Delilah has in her kitchen, I hear a dog's muffled barking upstairs. "Is that your dog, Delilah?"

"Yes, I locked Muffin up in my bedroom so he wouldn't bother you," she explains. "He's very protective." Muffin, a miniature Dachshund, is Delilah's official comfort pet, and the dog wears a badge to prove it. In church, Muffin sits in a basket attached to the front of Delilah's electric wheelchair, suspiciously eyeing Sunday worshipers as they walk past to greet each other. But sometimes, unexpectedly, Muffin will let out a series of sharp barks if a deacon steps too close with a sacrament tray, or when an unsuspecting child skips by. Usually Delilah can soothe Muffin with human conversation and a pat on the head. "It's okay, it's okay. They came too close, didn't they?"

"Muffin should quiet down soon," Delilah lets me know as she pushes aside a plate of half-eaten toast and a stack of newspapers to make way for my recorder on the table.

I take a few minutes to test my batteries while Delilah talks about the gas stove in the kitchen. Her voice is strong, almost boisterous. She will talk louder in the middle of a sentence, pick up the pace, pause dramatically, slide into filler phrases such as, "so therefore" and "you know," then crown the end with an inflected "okay?"—but without enough pause for me to answer. I make a mental note that Delilah likely prefers an overlapping discourse style. In other words, I will have to interrupt her in order to ask a question. The recorder is ready to go, but Delilah is talking about poor repair service, perhaps still in reference to her stove, so I jump in: "Okay, I think we're ready to start." I ask her to begin by talking about her childhood.

"Well I was born on the army base at Fort Meade and lived in the housing there. I remember that base distinctly because I had a really traumatic experience there—I contracted pneumonia as a young child."

"You were in the hospital?"

"Yeah. And I remember the doctors kept trying to come in, but I would scream and holler when I saw those white coats," Delilah laughs.

---

2. Donald F. Norris, "Addressing Baltimore's Population Meltdown."

"That's funny—the things that go on in a child's head," I say, then add, "We lived at Fort Meade too back in the eighties when our fourth child was born."

We had lived in military housing at a time when the medical facilities had been downgraded and were not equipped for surgery or childbirth. Camp Meade Hospital was first constructed in 1917, and at that time consisted of one temporary wood building and a smattering of tents. The Camp was expanded significantly with the outbreak of World War II to become a cantonment hospital with 545 beds. Later, called Kimbrough Army Hospital, the site continued to develop over the decades until the Cold War began to taper off. By the 1980s, Kimbrough had been downsized to a barebones outpatient facility and was jokingly called "*Kills*brough" by the military residents. Because of this downsize, our baby was scheduled for delivery forty miles away at Bethesda Naval Hospital. But the quick-paced nature of my labors increased our anxiety, because the last birth clocked in at fifty-five minutes, and all our previous babies had decided to come into the world at four o'clock in the afternoon—right at the peak of rush hour traffic.

When I tell Delilah about my lucky midnight labor that helped us dodge a Washington Beltway delivery, it spawns an exchange of birth stories. Delilah tells me that she was eighteen when she had her first baby, "and nineteen with my next because I didn't want to be an old mother." Her teenage labor and delivery soon became a family affair. "See, my first cousin came over to see if we had a baby yet, and I told him it was a false run. So he said, 'Oh, I'll make that baby come all right!' And he went to the kitchen and made some collard greens and mashed potatoes, and he cooked me a steak. I sure did enjoy that."

"And all that food was supposed to put you into labor?" I ask.

"Well, I'll tell you," Delilah replies. Her voice is strong and full of energy as she beckons me with her hands, inviting me into her story. "When my cousin was getting ready to leave, he comes upstairs and he says, 'Look at you! Look at you!' pointing at me. And that aggravated me and sent me into labor. I had to go into the bathroom because my water broke," Delilah laughs, and her enthusiasm fills the room. Muffin, whose yapping had started to taper off, begins barking again in earnest.

"When we went to the hospital in my dad's Ford, I was calm because I had prayed to have a boy. I wanted a boy, and I knew God would give me one. But I could tell it was going to be a hard labor, and I kept telling the nurse, 'I want to walk. I want to walk. It feels better that way.' But she said, 'You can walk after you take a shower.'" Delilah pushes her bangs to one side with her long fingernails and shakes her head. "But after that they took me to a maternity room and there was young girls there yelling, and screaming, Oh! Aw! Ow! It was scaring me, so I told them 'Will you *shut up*! I bet you wasn't screaming like that when you was making a baby, did you?'"

We both laugh at Delilah's audacious joke that had exposed her youthfulness and her attempt to manage her escalating pain. There had been no Lamaze class to tutor her breathing through the increasingly difficult stages of labor, no midwife's assurance, no doula to speak in her behalf. Even her mother, experienced at childbirth, had been sent out of the room by nursing staff for the time being.

Delilah was giving birth at one of East Baltimore City Hospitals, originally called Alms House in 1773, then Bay View Asylum in 1866, "a new institution for the paupers and the insane of the city."[3] Through the years, the hospital acquired an ominous reputation and became a name that Baltimore mothers would evoke to keep their children in line, saying, "If you don't behave, you're going to wind up at Bay View!"[4] By the 1970s, when Delilah was admitted, the hospital was on the brink of financial disaster. Nevertheless, it was during this decade when Maryland initiated a unique rate-setting system aimed at holding down medical costs—an initiative designed especially for low-income patients. Delilah, as a teen mother, was a beneficiary of this new system.

"Then, when they could see the crown of the baby's head," Delilah continues, "I asked the nurse again, 'Please, can I walk?' I felt like I *had* to walk, but she said, no. So when she was getting the stuff ready, I sneaked off the bed. And I almost got out of the room when the nurse turned around and said, 'Ah, ah, ah! Back up there. I'm going to have to watch you.'" I smile as I envision Delilah, an opinionated and impulsive teenager, ready to jump up and give birth in the hospital hall. But I also see that she was driven by maternal instincts that would make for an easier delivery—instincts that were not in keeping with the hospital's institutionally-managed childbirth protocol.

"So then, the baby's father shows up, and he says, 'How ya doing?'" Delilah's voice takes on a disparaging tone as she imitates him. "Well, I said, 'How you think I'm doing? This is painful.'" She rolls her eyes and shakes her head as she dramatizes her conversation with the baby's father.

---

3. John F. Weishampel, *The Stranger in Baltimore: A New Hand Book, Containing Sketches of the Early History and Present Condition of Baltimore, With a Description of its Notable Localities, and Other Information*.

4. Anne Bennett Swingle and Neil Grauer, "A Dream of a Deal."

"When my baby was born I didn't have a receiver to cover him up. I had an outfit, but it didn't fit him. But back then, they gave you so much, you know, that take-home packet. Like, if you didn't have a bassinet to put your baby in, they gave you a very heavily constructed cardboard bed with a little mattress in it." Delilah holds her fingers out in front of her to show me the size of the mattress. "And I was telling the father of my baby to be careful with the soft spot on the top of the baby's head, if anything happened to that, he's going to have problems with his brain."

I can't help but note that Delilah does not call her baby's father by name. She does not refer to him as "my partner," "my boyfriend," "my fiancé," or "my husband," but instead, a detached, "the father of my baby."

"So I went home to my parents, and the baby's father went back to his, because I had to plan everything," she continues.

"You lived separately?"

"See I had to pay for the baby, a little bit on it each month for the treatment and stuff. Because I said, I don't want no bill, you know what I mean? Six months later I moved out to an apartment."

"With the father?" I ask, but Delilah does not answer my question. Instead, she says, "It was such a joy being with those babies when they were growing up. And my daddy would say to me, 'You know, you've really got to let those children grow up without you sometime. Let me take them for a ride in the station wagon.' And my mother said, 'Now look. These are our grandchildren, you can leave them with us sometimes so we can babysit.' Finally I said, okay. I'm going to trust them." Delilah laughs at her new-mother jitters now that she is a grandmother of three.

"Well, we've all been through that," I confide, thinking back to the anxiety I felt mothering our first baby and the ease of grandmothering now.

"And my mother," Delilah continues, "was very close to me because I was the firstborn. She was not an *out woman*—never wore makeup, never wore revealing clothes. She was close to God and always used to take us to church. But my mom never finished high school, so when she got mail she would ask me to read it for her. The family depended on me greatly."

Woven throughout Delilah's childhood stories are accounts of the women who had raised her. She describes her grandmother as "a God-fearing women" whose last words were, "Delilah, see that light bulb? Well, keep your eyes on the light, child, keep your eyes on the light." Delilah said, "And I did. I prayed all the time. I prayed to pass school, I prayed for God to show me the way, for God to protect me."

Delilah describes her aunt Filia as "almost a White woman who wore bright red lipstick." It was this aunt who taught Delilah about "being a lady," and how ladies were not supposed to let men see them unkempt. "'Always wear nightgowns when you go to bed,' my aunt told me. And because I was so close to my aunt Filia, I was able to foresee her death. Let me tell you about that," Delilah tells me, beckoning me again with her hands.

I knew when my aunt Filia was going to die. I knew it would happen because there was this strange thing—it's not made up. So there was a pepper shaker, but somebody had poured the pepper out, and it formed a shape on the table. I looked at that shape as being bad because it was black, and it just made me think that aunt Filia had died. I didn't even know that she was sick or anything, or even that she had heart problems. So I pick up the phone and call my mother. I said, "Momma," I said, "listen to me." And she said, "What is it? What's wrong?" I said, "Aunt Filia is dead. You should call down to Virginia. She just died." And she *did* die just then. She died shopping. She just dropped dead in the store.

Delilah continues to tell me stories of her childhood as we sit together in her kitchen, one after the other, and as far as I could tell, in no particular order: Stories about stealing cans of mustard sardines and sharing the prize with her brothers, about how her mother had taught her to turn the knobs on the gas stove and use the heat to dry clothes, because it was her responsibility to do the laundry. Then out of the blue, Delilah says, "When I was seven, I experienced racism for the first time. Do you want to hear that story?"

"Yes, I do." I wonder what had prompted Delilah to want to share this story with me.

"Okay, well, we were one of the first Black people to move up in the Woodlawn area to have a house there. But the neighborhood respected my father because he kept the property clean. He would never throw his cigarette butts on the street or on the floor. And he trained us how to make beds and clean the way the military trained him." Delilah is slipping into story telling mode and begins to pick up the pace with increased volume. Even so, I do not hear Muffin upstairs and suppose that, exhausted, he has barked himself to sleep.

"Now my father, he didn't go to church with us, but I never held that against him. I think he had lost faith in God because when he was ten, his mom left the family. She was an alcoholic, but he loved her anyway even though she used to beat him with boards."

"With boards?" I ask.

"Yes, because that's how they disciplined back then. But my dad was good to us. He used to tell me, 'Now, I want you to learn. I want you to be understanding and get an education.' He would tell us kids to read a newspaper article every night, and when World Book Encyclopedias came out, he made sure that there was a set for our family."

"But first tell me the story about racism," I insist, afraid that Delilah is straying away from the story I want to hear. I can't help but make this request even though I am aware that I am imposing my topic-centered narration style on her. Delilah tends to favor non-linear storytelling, one that ties together loosely related events instead of introducing a topic and supporting it with details. Topic centered narration is often favored by Euro-Americans, while Black traditional storytelling takes the listener on "episodic journeys over tributary rhetorical routes but eventually leads back to its source."[5]

"Oh yeah!" Delilah acknowledges agreeably. "Okay, well, we went to make a trip down to Virginia, okay? And my dad, he wanted to take the long road down on Highway 301. See, he didn't want the state troopers to pull him over, because we had to get down there fast to my grandmother's funeral." Without stopping her narration, Delilah picks up some folded newspapers, arranges them in a stack, and puts them back exactly where they were before.

> What happened was, he went to stop at a gas station, and the car he had at that time, it was a older model before we got the station wagon. It was big, and I felt like I was riding in the huge car. Me and my mom was sitting in the back seat, and my mother said, "I don't think we should stop here Leon, see that sign? It says, *Whites Only*. Well, daddy, he got mad, and he say, excuse my expression, "I don't give a D what they say! We need some gas or we're not going to make it!" I remember the car encompassing me like it was a seat that was too big. See, it was an older model, and it was yellow. I don't remember the brand, he had so many cars.

I feel myself becoming impatient again. Why is Delilah spending so much time describing her family cars? Why is it important for her to tell about how she *feels* about the car? But then it comes to me—when we narrate our childhood we look back with the vision of an adult but with

---

5. Geneva Smitherman, *Talkin and Testifyin*, 148. "This meandering away from the point . . . though highly applauded by Blacks . . . is exasperating to Whites who wish you'd be direct and hurry up and get to the point."

memories experienced through the eyes of a child. Family cars had always been an important part of her childhood whereas adult race relations had not. Throughout the interview, Delilah's childhood stories had been punctuated with descriptions of family cars old and new, family seating protocol in the car, and rules for taking care of the family car. Her feelings about the car are the backdrop that ties her narration together.

> So, what happened was, mom said, "Let's, try to find another station." But dad said, "No, we need this gas, and I'm going to get it!" So the man came outside, and he said this, he said, "Cain't you read, boy?" I saw my father turn red, and he said, "I can read. All I want is some gas. Now you better give me what I want." And dad wasn't very polite with him either. So my mom, she said, "Leon calm down. Let's go! Calm down." But he said, "I'm going to get this gas Mandy!" So the man, he looked at dad and said, "You get that gas, and I want your butt gone!" But he didn't say it like that, he said the A-word. So my father got the hose, and the man looked at dad like, "Where did he get the money for this?" You know? I could feel it. I was young, but I could feel it.

Delilah finishes her story by telling me that her father and mother were not prejudice people, "We have White people in our family, you know, and as children we were not taught racism, but to love unconditionally." I wonder if these last sentences were for my benefit and if so, why? In what ways did *our* racialized upbringing shape the dynamic of this interview? Were there parts of the story that Delilah had sanitized for my sake? Had she selected words and changed register for me? In what ways had I done the same for her?

I glance at the recorder and realize that we have been talking for almost two hours, so I ask Delilah to tell me about her conversion. She shifts immediately to the new topic with cheerful energy even though she is describing what she calls, "the worst time in my life." Delilah had found herself alone, destitute, and depressed.

> See, I had left my husband because he was physically abusive. And he was a whoremonger—that's what the Bible states—a whoremonger. He lied to me, told me the transmission was wrong on the car but it wasn't, so I loaned him the money. He promised to pay me back, but he used the money to take women out. So he was a whoremonger, and that's when it went downhill. One day he got mad at me and pushed me down to the floor. Then he pointed a gun to my head. It was horrid. And he beat me up. After that, my brothers came and beat *him* up

because he had been so abusive to me. I couldn't take it any more after eleven and a half years, so I left. And I just didn't know what to do. I didn't tell my parents, because I didn't want to be a burden on them, but I had to raise my two boys, and there was nothing in the house. We didn't have food, no electricity, no heat, no nothing.

Sitting across from Delilah looking into her face, I do not see a victim. Even when she describes her homicidal husband, her penetrating brown eyes are bright. She speaks with natural confidence, and in those moments when she is not talking, the edges of her mouth rest into a natural upturned smile. It is as if the violence and betrayal she had endured are just another tale of her life, nothing more than an account of yesterday's doctor appointment—that is, until Delilah starts to tell me about how a different man, a man of God, betrays her. Then the intensity of her voice fills the kitchen, her eyes flash and her face glistens with beads of sweat.

Well, there I was sitting in the Baptist church, fed up. They were into all this luxurious attire, and they had started preaching worldly sermons—beyond the Bible. And that day the preacher says, "Okay, we need another hundred dollars for the building fund. Come on, he yells, you can do it! Give it to God and you'll be blessed. I promise, *you will be blessed!*" Well I had twenty dollars in my pocket book, and I believed him. I put it in when they passed the plate. Then after that he was like, "Okay we've reached our goal today, but you all still got a lot more to give tomorrow."

When I got home I suddenly realized that I had gave him the last of my money—all I had left! I didn't have money to go and buy soap powder or food for my kids. I was so upset, and I said, "I've had it!" I said, "This is it! I'm mad God!" I just screamed it out at him. I said, "God if you got somebody else to get me back into church you better send them to me, because this church is the wrong church! I have no money left! I gave it all away, and I can't do this anymore!" Then I threw my coat and my pocketbook on the ground.

Well, a few days later it was a knock on the door, so I said to myself, "I'm not expecting anybody, I wonder who it is?" I went to the door, and there was these two young White men there, and they said, "Hi, can we have a moment of your time?" I say okay, but I'm thinking, "Why are these White boys in this part of town?" Well they answer, "We're the missionaries from the Church of Jesus Christ of Latter-day Saints." Then they quoted me a scripture that I had just got done reading earlier that day so I knew they were for real. I said, "Come on in," and even though I did not know them, I said, "I've been waiting for you all."

I told them what happened to me with the Baptist church, and they said, "Well, would you like to learn about the plan that God has for you?" and I said, "I certainly would." They left me these three little books and said they would come back. But before they left they said, "You can come to church and find out what it's all about. We're hoping that you will accept this call from God." And I said, "I will, I will!" I was so excited. All of a sudden my world was changing. I'd found a church that preached truth—I could feel it in my heart. It seemed like my life was finally coming together and I felt whole.

"And your family?" I ask. "You are close to your parents—what did they have to say about you joining the Mormons?"

"Well I told my mother and father about the Church, and they had no judgment, they could see the light in my eyes. Mama was just proud that I'd reached out to God. She said, 'As long as you in church it's no problem.' But this church is nothing like any other church I've ever been to. Not at all."

Delilah's long fingernails click against the table as she reaches for the Bible in front of her. Apparently this is involuntary because she sets the Bible back down with another click. Before turning off the recorder, I ask Delilah if she has any final thoughts. "Yes. Yes I do," she tells me as she leans toward the microphone.

God performed a miracle on my life that day because the reality is, I could have turned out to be anybody. I knew what it was like to be hungry, to be without electricity, without money. I could have turned out to be a robber. I could have turned out to be on drugs. I could have turned out to be an abuser because I was abused. I could have run around fornicating. But I didn't elect to do any of those things. I trusted God. And the day the missionaries came, I was so happy because God had answered my prayer.

I reach to turn off the recorder, but at that moment Delilah inhales abruptly and I look up. She tilts her head to the side with a smile and adds, "Oh, but you know, I really shouldn't have yelled at God like that!"

5

You Don't Have to Fake the Funk[1]

I liked Pearl the moment I met her—gold tooth reflecting from behind her easy smile, graying dreadlocks bunched up into a pony tail high on her head, and the relaxed way she spoke to me. I had just moved to Baltimore, and we had been assigned to be visiting teaching companions. I was on my way to pick her up so we could visit Martha McCurdy, a homebound sister who I had not yet met. Pearl had been living at Madison Avenue Apartments with her mother, Grace, who, because of leg amputations, needed around-the-clock care. I pulled into the parking lot and gave Pearl a call. She came down from the high rise apartments with a Book of Mormon in her hand and a jacket under her arm.

"This is my inspiration," Pearl tells me as she balances the Book of Mormon on her knee so she can buckle her seatbelt. "I love it! My day doesn't flow without it, know what I mean?" She pats her book that is now in her lap. "It's like the other day I was reading it at work and the driver that relieves me, he says, 'Hey what you reading?' 'The Book of Mormon,' I say. 'You a Mormon?' and I say, 'Yeah I'm a Mormon.' 'Well ain't that a White church?' he says, you know, yaddy-yaddy-yadda this. And I tell him, 'Yeah we get a lot of that.' Then I tell him how the yaddy-yadda was back in the past, how Blacks weren't allowed to be in the Church and well, that's the past I'm not living in the past. I tell him, 'I'm living today with my spirit, and this is where I believe I should be. You praise your Allah, but I not only praise my God and my Jesus, I *talk* to them. I *talk* to my Heavenly Father and my Brother every day and that gives me the strength to go on.'"

So while Pearl helped me navigate unfamiliar city streets that night, we talked about church and family and began to get to know each other in the car. I tell Pearl about growing up in Oregon, and she tells me about living in Baltimore.

"I spent my childhood on this side of town," she points out the window. "Born in 1956."

"Well we're the same age," I let Pearl know cheerfully as we tally off our similarities. "So how about you? Are you an in-between child, like me?"

---

1. Parts of this story were printed in Camille Hughes and Laura Strickling, "Camille," 27–28.

"Yeah! And I remember when I was young, my mother came home from the hospital with my little sister bundled up in this white baby blanket and she was *so* brown! She was so chocolaty, chocolaty, and she had the prettiest dimples." Pearl pauses and looks out the car window. "Take a right at the corner," she directs me. "But I think after my little sister turned five or six—then the nightmare begin!" Pearl laughs at what must have been a family joke.

Later that year, I would interview Pearl's mother, Grace, and she would tell me the same story, but from a mother's perspective. In Grace's living room on the ninth floor she would sit across from me in her wheelchair, dress hanging limp where her legs should have been, and would talk about growing up in Baltimore and having children during the Depression. "I'm the mother of eleven," Grace had said, "but I only raised seven babies because of the ones that died. Seems I was always four, five months pregnant and would have a miscarriage. All of them were boys, the ones that died. Got pregnant at sixteen, then had another baby at seventeen. Got married at eighteen and left home. Went to live in a one-room apartment."

"Did you work back then?" I asked, glancing out the patio window at the evening sun reflecting on eastside Key Bridge and the rippling harbor water.

"Well, off and on," Grace had said as she also looked out the window. "And I went back to school three times but never finished. I ended up taking care of my kids. See, I almost graduated but when I was in twelfth grade, my mother, she had my baby sister, but she fell and broke her leg. And by her being so heavy and all, it was hard for her leg to heal. So I stayed out of school for six months to help. She tried to get me to go back. I wished I had, but I didn't."

"And your husband?" I had asked, wondering how he fit into the picture.

"Yes. My *first* husband. He was a large man," was all Grace said.

In the car that night, Pearl also had talked about Grace's husband—Pearl's birth father—as we drove through east Baltimore navigating around a stalled bus at the corner of Ensor, then dodging a teenager with a cell phone in her hand as she dashed haphazardly across the street.

"I remember my father being the Jolly Green Giant," she begins, "because he was so tall, but he wasn't jolly. Every Friday he would come home, and he had this black Chevy convertible. He would come in and you could hear all these keys jingling and the door open." Pearl sits back in her seat and looks straight ahead, her eyes fixed on the car in front of us. "The kids—it was six of us then—they would all run towards him to the living room, and he would have these pockets full of nothing but change. And the kids would get together and he would throw the coins up in the air and they'd scramble all over to get it. But I'd always sit back and look because I was afraid of my father. He come in and I'd go run in the closet or hide under the bed."

"Really? Why were you afraid of him?" I ask, looking at Pearl's face for just a moment at the stoplight, the red light flashing in her dark eyes.

"Well for one, he was so tall." Pearl pauses, "but he swung me out the window."

"Out the window? What do you mean?" I ask, as we approach the Maryland Penitentiary, a massive structure that looks like a castle and one of the oldest prisons in the country.

"Keep going straight under 83," Pearl gives me directions. "Well, I was being a child, you know. I was about eight years old, you see, and I used to pee the bed. And this one particular day he just—I guess he wanted to frighten me out of what I was doing, so he slung me out of the third floor window. He slung me like a roller coaster. He'd go up and down like this." Pearl moves her arms in a figure eight. "Then he let go and I went around in midair. He caught me on the way down. And all I could see was my mother standing there and all these people down below looking and everything. I was petrified—petrified of him."

"That's awful," I reply softly.

"And I remember him and my mother fighting," Pearl speaks quietly. "And I just couldn't—being a child, I couldn't do anything about it. I remember my mother having to go to the hospital because of him, and when she came home she couldn't go no further than the sofa. I was the one who helped her get back on her feet, you know. After that they split up. Then three years later he died."

This time, I don't say anything. I wished I could soften Pearl's violent and fear-ridden childhood, but I could not find the words. The mood in the car had changed from cheerful to somber as I pass a car with flashing lights stopped in my lane.

"At the funeral we all got dressed up in our best outfits and stuff and my mother had us sit age accordingly on the front row," Pearl continues.

> So my oldest brother got up to the casket and he cried real hard, and my other brother got up and he cried real hard. And I was sitting there like, you know, in a little white dress, my braids were real long and I had a bow on the side. I was just sitting there looking at him and thinking of the things that he did to me—sitting there, sitting there, sitting there, and I'm watching all the kids crying, but I'm not crying. So, just before they got ready to close the coffin my mother smacked

me up the side of my head and says, "That's your dad laying up there." She really hit me hard, and it hurt so I started crying real loud. Well everybody thought I was crying because my dad was dead.

This time Pearl laughs, but not free and easy like before. Then we are both silent. I am watching for sudden stops and cars making lane changes; Pearl is looking out the side window.

Grace would also tell me about her husband's death and how difficult it was to raise her children on one income. She worked any job she could find back then: cleaning for White people, doing assembly-line work in food processing factories, working as a nurse's aide. But the kind of work Grace loved most was sewing. She told me that she made men's suits and sewed gowns for graduations and weddings. "I learned to sew from my dad," she had said, "because he was a tailor. See, my dad worked at home, and we lived in a little alley called, Tyson.[2] It was a long strip and there was an opera house on the other side on Park Avenue. Our friends, because we all were Black, had to come out the back way into the alley. But there were coffee houses there and that's where the rich went to play the piano."

"The rich African American or—"

"Black."

"All Black?" I asked.

"Right. No Whites."

"Then, you were living in a segregated area."

"Yes, Tyson Street was segregated. And after school and work the kids'd get together and play—skate, ride bicycles . . . and steal ice from the ice man." Grace had laughed at that.

I smile too, remembering my own father who never stopped calling refrigerators, *iceboxes*.

"Back then we had an icebox," Grace explains, "and we didn't have bathrooms; instead, we had outhouses in the yard. We cooked on gas stoves in the summer and wood stoves in the winter, and we used the coal stove for heat. There was ten of us kids in our house, and during that time my father wasn't making more than about fifty-eight a week."

"Could you get by on that?"

---

2. Tyson Street is an alley located in the Mount Vernon neighborhood. In the 1940s, the neighborhood went through its first gentrification with the aid of Jewish artist Edward Rosenfeld, who owned a house on the corner of Tyson Street. In the 1960s, Tyson Street became known as "Beat Street" due to its coffee shops and bars that attracted artists. Especially popular was the *Checkmate*, a coffee shop frequented by beatniks.

"Well, I remember our rent was twelve dollars. We had a telephone, and sometimes the phone bill was two or three dollars a month. You could buy a loaf of bread—we used to call it a Pullman loaf—and it was double so you could go in the store and rip it apart and buy half for about thirty-eight cent. See, we all went to work when we got to be eight or nine. I started scrubbing steps at White people's houses and you'd get twenty-five cents for doors and steps." Grace stopped talking for a moment in order to push her arms against the wheelchair. With considerable effort, she managed to shift her torso into a more comfortable position. "And you made five cent by going to the store for somebody" she continued. "Then you went home and gave it to your mother. She might give you one, maybe two cent, and you could go to the store and get what they call grab bags. For two cents you'll get a pound bag of broken cookies. For a nickel you'd have cookies enough to last all day."

In the car, Pearl and I had just driven past Baltimore's Washington Monument located only a few blocks away from the street where Grace had spent her childhood scrubbing steps and playing with friends. The Monument had been erected in the early nineteenth century to honor George Washington, but more recently it had become a rallying point for activist demonstrations. In 2014, during the annual Christmas lighting celebration, groups had gathered there to protest the death of Eric Garner, a Black man who had been put into a chokehold by Staten Island police officer Daniel Pantaleo. Garner had resisted Pantaleo's arrest, denying the accusation that he had been selling single cigarettes on the street. When word came that the grand jury did not indict Pantaleo, protestors paraded around the Monument with signs that stated, "I can't breathe," the words Garner repeated eleven times before losing consciousness and dying on the sidewalk. The monument lighting ceremony that night had been cut short because the demonstrators were "peaceful but loud."[3]

Dusk is settling in, and the street lamps near the monument have started to light up. Pearl continues her childhood story telling me what happened after her father died. "My mother married again, and we left Baltimore for maybe a year because of the riots."

"The MLK riots?"

"Yeah. See, we went to my stepfather's farm in the country where it was safe. We came back in 1969, so as a child, I didn't do too well in

---

3. Colin Campbell, "Demonstrators Interrupt Baltimore Monument Lighting Event."

school. I always considered myself a dummy. I mean, I'm mostly street smart, not book smart because I couldn't read."

"But Pearl, I've heard you read in church."

"Well, now I can read—the Book of Mormon that taught me how—but back then I tried hard to do schoolwork, but I had a mental block. I just couldn't comprehend. They pushed me right through school out of the twelfth grade—and I couldn't read. I wanted to be more," Pearl arranges her shirt that has bunched up underneath her seatbelt, "but I dealt with what I dealt with." She taps her knee with her fingers.

"Are we almost to Sister McCurdy's apartments?" I ask while Pearl is between stories.

"We're almost there, but it's a one-way street, so we have to go down Cathedral first then turn right on Franklin."

At the next stoplight, Pearl tells me how her brother died. "I remember getting ready for the prom, that's when my brother got killed. They called it a cabaret at the time."

"A dance?" I ask.

"Yes, a dance. It was a Friday night, and we was going to this cabaret. And my mom had made all our gowns. Mine was white, and it had a cape in the back and was trimmed in zig-zag black lace. It was so pretty." Pearl points to an imaginary bodice across her front where the zig-zag lace would have been. "And we was getting all showered up to go to the dance when I got this feeling. I said, 'Mommy, call New York. I have a feeling something's wrong.' At the time I had that feeling my brother was being murdered."

"Did your mom call?"

"No, she didn't. She didn't call. She just said, 'Oh girl, go ahead and get dressed!'" Pearl imitates her mother's voice mildly, without sarcasm.

> So I went to the party, but I wasn't really there. I was clicking my fingers to the rhythm and watching the door. Then my sister runs in screaming from the top of her head, but nobody could understand what she was saying. I looked at her, and I knew my brother was dead. The friend he was living with in New York killed him because my brother wouldn't sell him his car. My brother's girlfriend said his last words were, "Mommy, give me a cold rag to wipe my face." It was hard. It was real hard.

Grace had told me the same story as we sat facing each other in her living room. The sun had set leaving only a trace of pink clouds. Grace pulled herself up in her wheelchair and looked at me with hazy eyes. "My oldest son, he asked me could he go to New Jersey to work. Had a good job there working for a toilet paper company. He was eighteen when he left; got killed when he was twenty." Then Grace told me how her son had decided to trade in his car for a new one instead of selling it to his roommate. "The fella stabbed my son one time in the heart with an ice pick, and it killed him."

"That's sad, Grace," I said.

"Yes," Grace had replied, exhaling slowly with little gasps. Then we both turned to look out the window.

"I always was a die-hard Baptist," Grace said.

"You were a Baptist growing up?"

"I was a *diehard* Baptist," Grace emphasized, "until the church wouldn't loan me money to pay off some of my husband's debt. I didn't ask them to *give* it to me, just *loan* it to me. See, I'd been going to the Baptist Church faithfully every Sunday, paying everything—the building fund, all the pastor's salary, the light bill, all that. So they come back and told me they couldn't loan me the money. I turned around and said, 'okay' then stopped going to church." Grace lifts herself up and leans to one side of the wheelchair.

> So Pearl asked me to go to church with her. See, they had a pot luck there, and I had such a nice time. Later, I sat down and had a discussion with the missionaries and read the Book of Mormon. They kept asking me when I'd join the Church, and they finally just wore me down. So I said, well I don't have much pleasure at the Baptist Church, because nobody talk to you—it's just, *Hi* and *Goodbye*. But in the Mormon church, people call and talk to me. Then, when my leg started acting up, and they had to take it off, members just swarmed around me. They took me into their care and I joined the Church.

On the way to Sister McCurdy's house that night, I learned from Pearl that her mother would have two more amputations; and that after the danger of complications had passed, Pearl would nickname Grace "Shorty" for laughs. Later, Pearl moved into Grace's one-bedroom apartment where she slept on the couch or sometimes in the same bed to make sure Grace was breathing. Sitting next to Pearl in the car it was good to hear that she had survived a distressed childhood with such a tender spirit, and that she did not blame her mother for her suffering. When I dropped her off back at Madison Apartments that night, and she turned to wave, I decided I would always remember Pearl just like that—with her effortless smile and Book of Mormon in her hand. I did not know then, that she had been battling with depression or her daily struggle with addiction. I did not know how it had consumed her adult life.

Our conversation on the drive to Sister McCurdy's house would be the last time Pearl and I would have a heart-to-heart talk until I visited her in the hospital six months later. We were soon assigned to different visiting teaching companions, and Pearl's work and my school sent us on our separate ways. Then, in April, Pearl did not come to church for three weeks. Ivy, who had known Pearl for a long time, had explained that spring was a sad time for Pearl because her daughter had died then. She said Pearl probably needed time to visit her daughter's grave, to withdraw and mourn. But we learned that after visiting the gravesite, she had admitted herself to the psych ward at University Hospital. Without explaining the reason for Pearl's admission, Ivy asked if I would like to go with her to the hospital.

The nurses let us into the secured ward to meet Pearl after we had checked our purses and coats into the hospital lockers and had been searched for sharp objects. Ivy carried a sack of grapes—a gift that had passed inspection—because Pearl loved fruit. Upon our meeting, it was clear that Pearl had expected Ivy's visit, but my presence had surprised her. "You came?" she remarked, and I had smiled, unsure if Pearl's response was an accusation or a declaration.

In the common room, under the vigilant eye of the medical staff, the three of us had talked about what was happening at church, cracked some jokes about how ugly the hospital was, and said a prayer. After that, our allotted twenty minutes were up. As we stood to go, Pearl said to me, "I always thought you were, you know, kind of finicky."

"What? What do you mean?" I had asked, but Pearl was not diverted from what she wanted to say.

"But, but when we connect eye to eye, you know what I'm saying? It's such a joy. And you don't get that with White people you meet on the street. It's like, when we all talk," Pearl moved her arm in a circle to indicate the three of us, "there's no color here."

From then on, our friendship took a turn, and we began to talk more openly about being Black and being White, about the racism Pearl had experienced intermittently in the Church, and about fishing. Pearl loved to fish. And even though I did not enjoy this kind of activity much, I would listen to Pearl's long stories about her technique for catching Rockfish in the Chesapeake and how she fell in the river once. She came out of the icy water, crying, with broken fingers and a sprained ankle—but she was not crying because of pain; it was because now she would not be able to fish for a several weeks.

In addition to fishing stories, Pearl would hop a ride to the temple with us, and we'd invite her to dinner. Then we'd both get busy and not see each other for weeks. But one Sunday, instead of going to Sunday School class, Pearl pulled me aside to tell me about an incident in the church. "I like White people," she had begun, "used to go out with a White guy, but there are some people in the church who don't like Blacks." Then Pearl proceeded to tell me about *a certain sister* who had said *certain things* to her, and who had walked right past her looking the other way.

"But Pearl," I had resisted, "are you sure it was racism and not just that this sister was preoccupied?"

"Well, it's possible," Pearl had answered, "but I can tell. I can feel it."

"Or maybe you misread the way she greets people," I suggested, drawing on my knowledge of cultural differences in communication style.

"There were other things too, things she's said, but I don't want to make this a big issue," Pearl explained. "I just think maybe we could have some kind of a lesson in Relief Society—not bringing up *my* thing, but maybe in a soft sort of way. In the right way."

"We could. But let's think about it—how to go about it," I said.

"Yes, it has to be right."

We both paused to think for a moment then I asked, "So what did you do? About the sister."

"Well, I took her aside and told her how I felt—don't know if it will change things," Pearl had answered. "Sometimes I talk to people about racist stuff; sometimes I ignore it and go sit on the other side of the chapel. In the end we all have to come face to face with Jesus Christ," she had resolved, "in the end."

Later in the summer, not long after that conversation, I met with Pearl in her apartment to record her conversion story. We had just finished a dinner of baked catfish and potatoes. Pearl had spent a good ten minutes explaining how she had caught and cleaned the fish, how she had soaked them in milk to sweeten the taste, then how to bake them so they are just right—nice and tender but not overdone. We were now settled in her living room on an overstuffed couch, blinds pulled tight so the room is dark and lamps on low.

"So, you want to know how I stumbled in on the Church?" Pearl had asked.

"Yes, I do." I answered as I took a sip of mint tea and Pearl held onto her glass of ice water.

"Okay," she smiled, "this is my story." Then Pearl took a long, slow drink and began.

Back in 1982, I was, let's see, a mother of one child at the time, and I worked as a nursing assistant. I was an alcoholic then, trying to put an end to it. One day I went to my aunt's house, and when I came in, I had a beer in my hand. I saw these men in black and white, and one asks me a question about Jesus Christ, but I told him, "Wait a minute, I got to go—I got to go and come back in." So I went out, put the beer down and came back. But this time, he had my full attention. I had never heard nobody speak like that—that way, you know. It was just like me talking to you but spiritually. I could feel something, and it was totally different. The missionary ask me would I be interested in taking the lessons and I'm thinking, "I got to read—read everything too, and I don't really know how. And I'm going to have to reevaluate things." But I said yes anyway; nobody forced me to do it. The missionary told me, "You can take some time and pray about it you know," and I did. I felt like it was my destiny, I mean, I toyed with it for a little while, but I knew it was my destiny.

So, I got it together, put the drinking aside, and the missionaries came to the house. I would fix dinner, and we had a nice little chat and everything. They were telling me about the fall of the church and how the Church of Jesus Christ of Latter-Day Saints was established and everything. Then they asked me would I be interested in joining the Church. So, I took the lessons and me, being an alcoholic, I kind of put alcohol aside. I stopped drinking, and I was baptized and that lasted a while—until my grandmother got sick and died. Then the devil got a hold of me again. Seemed like it just—a volcano erupted, you know, and from there I stumbled into this business, my restaurant business. And I couldn't establish being in a restaurant business and having a bar, with church. I couldn't put the two of those together. But I worked with it that way for nineteen years. And when the nineteenth year came around, I had been praying to God to get me out of this business. See, I was going to church at the time but I wasn't feeling it. I knew I had to put my business aside because it dealt with drinking and drugs and all of that stuff. So, I went to therapy for my drinking and smoking. And eventually it sunk in, and I quit doing the drugs. And I would come to church, and I would look at the women, and I would see how happy they were and how honest they were in this religion. So I pressed on. I stopped drinking.

Around that time my daughter told me she had cancer. And I knew that in order to serve God and be a good mother to her in her endeavor with this cancer, I had to become a real mother and set aside my lifestyle and live for her—for whatever years she had left. Well, one weekend, I had her child, my granddaughter, with me. And at the time I was like, on the verge of stopping my habits, my problems, my situation. But I was still playing with it. And this night I brought my granddaughter home, and I went out to buy some drugs and got locked up. Well, that night I had to call my daughter and tell her that her daughter was in the house by herself. I had gotten high and left a child at home. And it tore her apart as well as it tore me apart. So later, at home with my daughter, I cried. I did the little cry thing and told her I was sorry. And you know Laura, she was knitting that pink afghan over there. She was laying in that bed on that pillow right there. She was like this, knitting and never looked up at me. And when I had finished telling her what I said, she said, "Mommy," she said, "That's okay." She said, "We all fall down and we pick ourself back up, you know?" And then she said, with a distinguished, clear voice, she looked me in my eyes and said, "Don't do it again." That is the night that I *really* surrendered. I put my hands in the air and I said, "God, I surrender all." And I did, I surrendered. I put everything aside—except for the smoking, smoking cigarettes.

Then, one day I was at church and one of the sisters had been asking me, "Can I do anything for you," and I would always say no. But I went home and thought about it. I said the next time she asks me, I'll tell her, I'll tell her. So she came the next Sunday, and she asked me, she said, "Pearl, can I do anything for you?" And I said, "Yeah." I said, "I'm having a problem with my smoking, and maybe we could, um, get together and you know, work on it." And she was excited. She was really excited. And she came to my mom's house, and we sat down, and we talked. And that night, we read a scripture, and that scripture was, "He who lack wisdom let him ask." And the scripture kind of stayed in my mind. And she tells how she smoked and she drank and she did her little worldly thing so I didn't feel so bad. And this particular day she asked me did I, in my heart, really want to stop smoking? And I said yes. Now, I had just bought—I didn't buy a pack of cigarettes—I bought four single cigarettes on the street. I smoked one before she came then

I put one in the drawer—I used to hide them from myself, and I put one behind my daughter's picture. She hadn't passed away yet, but she was going through her crossing over at the time. And the sister said that if I really had faith in God I could stop. And my faith at the time was growing. And it grew so much it kind of amazed me.

So that night I gave her the two cigarettes that I had bought, there were three cigarettes in the house but I only gave her two. I forgot where I had put the other one at the time. So, she told me that night that I had to set a time limit. I told her if I could go five days, I got this thing licked. So, that was a Sunday; I gave it up on a Sunday. The next Sunday I went to church, and I told her, it's seven days. I made it to seven days! And you know, I was so happy and it didn't bother me not to smoke. In the past, I would always stop, I would give me five days, but I would always go back and smoke again later. But this time, I took five days and I stopped. And when I got to the ninth day I was cleaning my mother's apartment and I found the other cigarette. And oh man, it was, it was like a baby finding a piece of candy, you know? So I picked the cigarette up, and I was like, nobody's here, I could smoke this cigarette. And I'm standing in mommy's living room, and all I could see was the big sky. That's all I could see. And, in that sky, my thought was that my Father, Heavenly Father was looking at me. But then the devil was saying nobody's going to know if you smoke this cigarette. And in my mind I said, "God would." And I curled the cigarette up, and I put it in the trash can. And it's been a year, well, I guess it was two years, and I haven't had a cigarette. But it gave me strength to deal with my daughter crossing over.

After the passing of my daughter it was just like I was going through a tunnel, not knowing where this tunnel was leading. But seeing the things that I saw, the things I'm about to tell you now, Laura, made me a true believer. Because when we read about Joseph Smith going into the grove and then a pillar of light, seeing the Spirit, I mean, it was *really* like this for me. Because my spirit was broken you know. I was at that point where it says a contrite spirit was broken. And I stayed in it—broken. I would always go to work and read the twenty-third Psalm and then read on a couple pages more, then I'd take my lunch break and read The Book of Mormon too. But the day before my daughter died, that's when I saw an angel.

See, I was working at the hospital and I was visited, out of the blue, by two Relief Society sisters. They came up to where I was, and I was amazed. We sat during my lunch break, and we talked. And I was so lifted by the Spirit. All that day the Spirit was so alive, I could feel it. After they left, I was working up on the seventh floor, and I walked into a room. That's when I saw the Spirit. I actually saw it come out of me. I was standing there, and as I walked it came out of me. I was looking through this big glass window and I was seeing this happening, right? And I'm like, "This is not real," I was thinking this because I couldn't talk. And I turned around to see if it was just a mirror thing, and as I turn around, my eyes behold the Spirit. And I stood there for a good ten seconds. It was close, like you are to me. So I walk toward the window and say, "When I turn around it will just disappear, just a figment of my imagination." But when I turn, it was still there. It was a man, and he had on a pure white robe, and his feet didn't touch the ground. His hands looked like they were like a big man's hands. Then all of a sudden it glided and descended into the wall. I could actually see it descend into the wall.

When I got home that night, the movie, *Jesus of Nazareth* was on the television. I stumbled in—now Laura, this is amazing—I stumbled in on the part of the show where Christ says, "You saw me heal the sick. You saw me raise the dead, and all of this you've seen, but yet you don't believe." And I look upon that and upon what I saw, and I know it was real. And that day I could deal with the fact that my daughter was going to die. And from that day to this day, I've been clean. And I just, in order to keep where I'm at, I found the definition of diligence. And I use it to my advantage. I'm constantly reading the Book of Mormon, and I'm constantly praying, because, just like that Spirit I saw that was so real, the devil is *more* real, and he wants a part of that. But I can't, I can't let my religion go. You know what I'm saying?

"Yes, I think I do." I told Pearl.

"I know I had a fun life but the whole time I was in the world, I prayed to get *out* of the world. And here I am, I'm out of the world."

"You are."

"And this life here, it's a happy life. It's real. Because I don't have to fake the funk anymore. I can stand up and *really* testify in church. And I bring *me*, the real Pearl. When I step into that chapel the world doesn't even exist. I don't think about anything. All the bad goes away and I can concentrate on the energy of love. I can't explain it really, but that's how it is."

6

I Could Never See Her Face

After my mom died I would dream about her all the time, but I could never see her face. And every time I would dream, she was in a wheelchair or sick in bed. I would see her three times a week, and this was sad for me. I dreamed like that for two years, and I was grieving, oh, I was grieving! So Laura, when I finally got to go to the temple[1] to do the baptisms for her—now I guess people think I'm making this stuff up, but I tell you, this is the honest truth—after I did the temple work for my mother, I dreamed about her and she wasn't sick anymore. I could see her face, and she wasn't in a wheelchair. And me and her was being together, you know, just doing things together.

When Sheera told me this story, we were sitting in the church Primary room on small chairs made for children. The room was bright with sunlight and colorful posters of Jesus surrounded by happy children. On one side, a wall was covered with construction-paper cutouts of small hands, each tagged with a name and the pledge *I will choose the right.*

"My mom, she was a very strong woman," Sheera had said. "She wasn't a Mormon, but she was a devout pray-er and she had strong faith. Everybody say, 'Oh your mother so sweet. All she talk about is the Lord.' And that was the truth."

Sheera had requested that we have our interview at the church because "my house isn't together yet," she explained. Besides, on Saturdays she was already at the church working at the clothing exchange downstairs. Sheera's job was to sift through donated clothes and castoff shoes and stock the shelves for patrons.

"Before I joined the Church some strange things happened. I don't know if it was a vision or a dream, but I saw heaven," she tells me in the

---

1. Temples, for Mormons, are sacred buildings where members receive spiritual strength, make covenants, and participate in ordinances or rituals. They also learn how to prepare for life that continues after death. All temples contain baptisteries where members can perform proxy baptisms for people in their family and others who have died and have not yet participated in this ordinance. Temples also have sealing rooms where the ordinance of eternal marriage takes place and where children can be sealed to their parents.

Primary room. Sheera is a muscular woman with youthful mahogany skin that belies her age. She cuts her own hair using two mirrors, wears loose midi skirts reminiscent of the Seventies, and walks with a limp because of a bad back. Sheera speaks with quiet confidence and soft South Carolina vowels in the church halls, but in Relief Society she goes "kickin' up dust," taking on a preacher's voice that can be heard way to the back of the room and probably out in the foyer. "Sisters, I got to tell you all something—something I've been working on all week. Now there's a lot I don't know . . ." Sheera pauses while the sisters in the room stop chatting and smile. "But I *do* know we got some beautiful sisters in this *Ra*-lief-So-*ci*-ty." The women look around the room and nod. "And we gotta help each other, lift each other; we got to *pray* for each other! You know what I'm saying? Can ya'll hear me?" Then Sheera would "bring it down" dramatically, beseeching the captivated sisters. "But listen now," she modulates into a fervent whisper, "what I really need is your help. I'm not kiddin', I really need you to *pray* for me. I'm going through something right now and I'm in danger of fallin'. Every day I fall more, and I'm afraid. Can you pray for me to overcome? Can y'all pray for me to rise above my weakness and not fall into temptation?" The sisters, their eyes fixed on Sheera, nod their heads with one accord and some call out "yes!" One sister seals the pact and springs from her chair calling out, "We love you Sister Sheera!"

That's how we start our meetings when Sheera conducts the class.

"What was heaven like?" I ask Sheera to explain her dream.

"Well, let me tell you; let me tell you what I saw," Sheera shifts into a story-telling rhythm. "The street was like glass, and it looked like God was sitting on a throne. It was *so* beautiful, so beautiful to see! He had on red—well, I guess it was Jesus with the red—so he had on white and it was amazing! So, *so* amazing that I had a dream like that." Sheera pauses and moistens her lips, and I'm expecting her to tell me the significance of the dream; instead, she moves on. "So I've just had strange things happen to me before I joined the church. A lot of things I hear *now* in church are things I heard before. It was like, preparing me—even when I was a kid in South Carolina I was preparing, preparing for the Church."

Sheera's gold loop earrings flash in the sunlight. She takes a moment to adjust her Nike ball cap and pull down her men's polo shirt that is two sizes too big—her Saturday work clothes. "My childhood was really good," Sheera explains. "And I had very caring, loving parents. My father spoiled us rotten, and my mother was the disciplinarian, but, oh gosh, she was the best mother in the world! We lived in the country; we rented a house, and my father was a mechanic." Sheera pauses then adds, "He also was a bootlegger so we were pretty comfortable."

"A bootlegger?" This was a profession I did not hear about very often. The name became popular in the nineteenth century when temperance movements were gaining traction and the smuggling of illegal liquor in boot tops became common practice. By 1920, a national prohibition of alcohol was adopted with the ratification of the Eighteenth Amendment, but this legislation only increased black-market liquor production and sales.

"Were customers coming to your house all the time?" I ask.

"Yes, but my father, he had a room so we wasn't usually exposed to that."

"Did he have a still?"

"Out in the woods." Sheera smiles.

"Seriously? So did he ever get in trouble with the law?"

"Yeah. Internal Revenue. They always try to catch the bootleggers because there was a lot of them. Took my father out to court a time or two but almost everybody in South Carolina knew my dad so they usually didn't keep him long."

During Prohibition, access to good liquor was in high demand, so bootlegging became one of the few occupations where Blacks and Whites could be on equal business footing.[2] Since it was common for people in a community to know who the bootleggers were, if arrested, their activity was often considered a misdemeanor, and many were quickly released and back in business again.[3] By 1933, the Twenty-first Amendment had repealed Prohibition, but bootlegging still continued to thrive alongside "dry" counties that have prohibited liquor on into the twenty-first century.[4]

"My mother, she was a homemaker and we did farm work," Sheera continues. "We farmed out to people picking cotton—we did tobacca too."

"You picked cotton?" I ask, my curiosity piqued. I had not seen a cotton plant until I was an adult living in North Carolina where cotton stripper machines had done the work. I was intrigued by this plant that was not part of my western upbringing and the commodity that had been the rationale behind centuries of slave labor.

"I hated it! My goodness I hated it!"

"Well, tell me what you had to do."

"Okay, I'll tell you, Laura. I'll tell you how it's done," Sheera prepares me for her story.

---

2. Mark Schultz, *The Rural Face of White Supremacy: Beyond Jim Crow*, 63.
3. Thomas Fleming, "Reflections on Black History: The Great Experiment."
4. Phillip Smith, "As If Prohibition Never Ended."

They have this big, old field of cotton, and you get a sack and you put it on your shoulder. Some people stood up and picked, most people crawled. You got down on your knees and picked the cotton, put it in a sack, pick the cotton, put it in the sack, move on down the row. That's how you pick cotton—on your knees—that's really the only way you *could* pick. Man, I hated it! We would each have a row, and every one of us would pick the rows on up. But I would always be behind. My mother used to say, "Girl you better pick that cotton and get up here." We would pick all day long in the sun. Sunup to sundown. And when the sack got full you would take it to the end of the row. They had these sheets spread out there, and you would empty the sack on the sheet, go back and pick some more cotton and empty it on the sheet. But I was so lazy I would go down and empty my sheet, and my mom'd say, "Now you go down and empty, then you come right back in this field." I'd say, "Okay Ma," but then I'd go down and get some water and lay down in the shade—and get some cotton off other people's sheets 'cause they were all spread out, you know.

"You stole other people's cotton?" I wondered how Sheera could get away with that.

"I was a crook then," Sheera admits, smiling." And I probably made—okay, the most I ever made was sixty cent a day. My mom, she could pick about two hundred pounds so she made about three, four dollars a day. I probably picked about fifteen pounds!" Sheera laughs, amused at her immaturity.

"I guess that's not much for a day's work."

"No, not much. But now, tobacca—" Sheera's voice takes on new vitality. "Oh, I loved the tobacca! That's when we moved up here to Baltimore, but I would go back down south and stay with my brother."

"Is there a trick to picking tobacco?" I ask. I had seen tobacco on the North Carolina Eastern Shore, but I never saw anyone working in the fields.

"No, you don't *pick* tobacco, what you do is this—Laura, let me tell you how to do it," and Sheera begins to explain the process of tobacco harvesting. "They go in the field, and they *crop* tobacco, then they come back with a wagon full. You take it off the wagon, and you'd have to *horse*—something they call *horse*—you'd have a stick on there." Sheera twirls her hands to show me how the harvesters would string tobacco on both sides of a stick that was set in the notches of a looping horse. "You'd have people that would hand tobacco to you off that wagon, then you string it, chhh, chhh, chhh, chhh. String it up, get a stick full." Sheera demonstrates the looping technique with her fingers. "Then they had stick toters—children that tote the sticks. I was a stick toter until I learned how to strang. They had croppers, strangers, handers, and stick toters."

"Like an assembly line."

"Yeah, and when the people would get their whole stick filled up they'd yell, "stick," and the kid would get the stick and take the tobacco off and take it in the barn and hang it up in the ceiling. When I learned how to string, oh my goodness! Man I loved that! I was about eleven and they would let me string."

"And this was more fun than picking cotton?"

"Oh my gosh, yes!" Sheera twists her hands as if she were still stringing tobacco. "But we moved to Baltimore because my father got sick. I had an older brother and sister here, and they wanted my dad to go to Johns Hopkins." Sheera stops her imaginary tobacco stringing and rests her hands on the table. "But he never regained his health." She pauses and looks across the room. I follow her gaze and notice rays of sun reflecting against dust particles in the air.

"You were talking about all the strange things that happened to you before you joined the church," I remind Sheera.

"Oh yes! Okay, so I got married when I was nineteen."

"Up here in Baltimore?"

"Yeah, and what had happened was this, I dropped out of school." Sheera moistens her lips and settles into her chair.

> I was in tenth grade, and one day I was smoking cigarettes. We were in the bathroom, because children used to sneak in the bathroom to smoke. I went in there and came out and the principal saw smoke coming out of my mouth. So, I got suspended and never went back. I got married when I was nineteen, then I got pregnant. After I had my baby I went back and got the GED. But then, my father said he wasn't going to live long and my mother had a major stroke so I had to take care of my parents. After that, my college and whatever I wanted to do just went away. And you know, often to this day I regret that I wasn't able to go to college—but I'm thankful I was able to take care of my parents.

"Was this about the time you joined the Church?"

"No, I joined the Church later," Sheera replies. "See, I can never remember a time when I have *not* gone to a church. Oh gosh, there's never been a time! But I was going to the World Church—I call all the other churches the World Church—and I began to realize that something wasn't there; something just wasn't right. On Sundays, I would come out of church and go around the building smoking a cigarette then go back into church. Well, I got to thinking how it was so empty and why I did that. I felt like a hypocrite." Sheera laughs, but it is a meager laugh, without mirth. Then she looks at me intensely. "See, Laura, I was *so* into church. I would have people coming over to the house, and I'd be preaching to them. People always say, 'Oh gosh, here she go with that preaching again.'"

"Kind of like you do in Relief Society," I say, and Sheera smiles.

"So this one time, Laura, let me tell you about this one time." Sheera clears her throat and leans forward.

> I had a lot of my family over to my house, and I was reading the Bible to them and talking about the Lord. And something happened, my voice went and I couldn't speak. Everybody was standing around me, and I was trying to talk and nothing was coming out of my mouth. And they was calling me and I couldn't say anything. They just kept saying, "What's wrong with her?" They thought I had a stroke or something, but I couldn't open my mouth and talk. You know, this is similar to what happened to Joseph Smith, when he was overcome with the Devil. And I remember thinking in my mind, I need to call on the Lord's name. So I said, "Jesus," because you know, back then we said "Jesus" a lot, and when I did, my voice came back. So I started going to different churches because this was a sign. Well, my apostolic cousins had been trying to get me to join their church because I talked about the Lord so much; I would go to their church off and on. Then one day I finally told them I would join, but this was before I had seen this commercial on T.V. about the Mormon Church. On the commercial they said, "Call this number and get The Book of Mormon." So I started getting up to call, but I sat back down and said, "No this might be some kind of Devil work." I said, "No, I better not mess with it." So I sat down and thought about it—I did this three times. Finally that third time I got up and made the call. They said, "We will send you the Book of Mormon."
>
> So during this time, my cousins and I was going to be baptized in the Apostolic Church. But the strangest thing happened. They were trying to fill the font, and the water wouldn't come out. It just would *not* come out! So they said, "Okay, we'll baptize you on another date." Finally, it was a day or two before I was supposed to get baptized when there was a knock on the door. I went to the door and peeped out,

and I see these two White boys standing there and they said, "We are from the Church of Jesus Christ of Latter-day Saints." I say, "Who are these White boys?" And they said again, "We're from the Church of Jesus Christ of Latter-day Saints, and we come to bring you the Book of Mormon." Well I'm hesitating because I'm saying, "Wait a minute, I didn't know people come along with the book! I thought I was just going to get the book in the mail." I'm standing there hesitating saying, "Man, this might be some kind of cult or something. They're going to get me to Devil worship." I'm sitting there debating all this stuff, right? But finally, I got this feeling this was the right thing to do.

So, they come in and tell me about the Church. They told me what to read in the Book of Mormon and I was glad when they left because I took it and ran upstairs and opened the book. I started reading it right then and there, and it just seemed like I was being pulled. Something was saying to me, "This is serious. This is it." I was nervous because it was so powerful and I told myself, "This is it, Sheera. You've got to be really sincere." So Laura, the thing is, I started studying with the missionaries, but I still had to quit smoking so I could join the Mormon Church. I'd gotten myself down to two cigarettes a day for a whole year—see, I was preparing myself for those missionaries—but I still sucked on those two cigarettes; I couldn't get off. Finally, I only had one whole and a half a cigarette left. I went upstairs to the bathroom, and Laura, I was just standing there with my half cigarette. I'm standing up there and the Spirit said—I didn't realize it was the Spirit then—but it said, "What do you want? Do you want that fleeting minute of pleasure or do you want eternal life?" So I took that cigarette, that half butt, and threw it in the toilet. But I kept the whole cigarette and here's why. When the missionaries came back again I said, "I want you to write a scripture on this cigarette for me." So they took it and wrote a Book of Mormon verse from Ether.[5] I still have that cigarette today. That was fifteen years ago and I have never smoked a cigarette since.

Later, Sheera brought her scrapbook to church to show me the cigarette. On the page, right next to her certificate of baptism, was a flattened

---

5. "And if men come unto me I will show unto them their weakness. I give unto men weakness that they may be humble; and my grace is sufficient for all men that humble themselves before me; for if they humble themselves before me, and have faith in me, then will I make weak things become strong unto them." Ether 12:27. *Book of Mormon*, (1981), 510.

Newport in a ziplock bag with the words "Ether 12:27 page 510" written in ballpoint pen. Above that she had added "My last cigarette."

"What did your friends and family say when you joined the church?"

"Just that the church was a cult and that it was all White—you know, the White-church thing. But it wasn't something I really had to contend with. It wasn't a problem because you see, I'm stubborn and I'm bossy." Sheera flashes me a wide smile displaying rows of dental work. "And besides, I was busy preachin' at my daycare job," she adds. "I mean, when the kids would take their naps I would get out my Book of Mormon, and because I was the assistant director, I would make them all come back there and sit around the table and I would preach to them. Got my friend Harriet to join and my cousins Sarah and Rachel. They all worked in the daycare with me, and I told them Heavenly Father was saving them to join the Mormon Church." Then Sheera smiles and says, "And he was!"

Sheera's Friend, Harriet

When I interviewed Harriet she told me, "We worked at the daycare with Sheera and when she got converted she tried to get me. First she got her cousins, Sarah and Rachel, and I was the last one she got."

Harriet is a large, slow moving woman with a round face and hair pulled back in a tight bun, like a Buddha. She wears slippers and a blue or yellow Muumuu at home, and lipstick and a wig when out shopping. Her face is placid with flat, motionless eyebrows, and she speaks in a leisurely sort of way with comfortable pauses and mellow laughs. But from time to time, when she becomes animated, her voice will rise to a squeak. When I first met Harriet she was walking with a cane, but her condition had deteriorated, so now she moves about leaning on a "rolodex," a Baltimore nickname for a Rollator walker. When Harriet tells me her story, we are at Monument East apartments on the second floor. She is sitting high in her walker seat, looming over me because I am sitting down low on a couch with broken cushion springs and no legs.

> See, I was going to United Baptist, but I got tired of everybody hollerin' "yes" and "amen." I didn't understand one word the preacher was saying, so Sheera said, "Why don't you come to church with me?" Sheera told me they have classes for the womens, and Sunday School with teachers so you can learn more step by step. I said, "What?" and she said, "Yeah." So I said, "Now I have to see for myself." So I went and I enjoyed it. Said hey, I can understand what they're talking about.

I learned the Bible, read the Book of Mormon, and said, "Well this is just about the same, but the Book of Mormon got more in it than the Bible does." I said, "I'm learning more than I was learning in the Baptist Church." So I'd meet Sheera downstairs on Sundays for her to take me to church, 'cause we lived in the same house together. First, I was living at my house, but the house got condemned because of a tree growing out of the wall. The birds had bin dropped seeds and stuff down there in the bathroom window. They would sit on the ceiling, and the seeds had got down in there, and a tree started growing from the basement on up. Finally the walls started coming in. You could stand there and see the sky. We lived there for a long time, then the health department came and said, "No. Ya'll can't live here. You have to go."

"What? A tree was growing up out of your house?"

"Yeah, it was growing right out the wall."

"But it must have been growing for a long time," I say, but my statement is meant to be a question. I'm wondering why someone didn't dig up the tree when it was still a tender sapling in the basement.

"Yeah, it was a long time for a tree to get like that. Then finally the walls just started coming in," Harriet tells me, almost as if she had told a joke. But Harriet has an uncanny ability to insert a laugh into her narrative without smiling, so I find myself unsure if I have heard humor or not. "See, when I was young," she continues, "my mother and my sisters, we moved back to east Baltimore. My father was drinking and beating on my mother, so we left and moved in with my grandmother—it was my *grandmother's* house." I take Harriet's explanation to mean that the tree had already grown into the structure of the house by the time she and her family had moved in—long past the time for easy removal.

"We was raised right there with my grandmother," Harriet tells me as she shifts her weight precariously in her mobile chair and holds on to her cane for support. Harriet had been in the hospital last week because her toes were turning black from lack of circulation. The doctors had increased her Lasix prescription from twenty to eighty milligrams, and it had done the trick. Now she was back home, rolling the walker around.

My grandmother made us learn, wouldn't let us get out of it, taught us to cook—how to cook collard greens and season them. All kinds of vegetables. And then, a man in a wagon would come along selling peaches. She'd buy three baskets, then we'd have to can them. Take the skins off, cut them in half, put them in the jar. It would be so hot in the house—it got to a hundred and three degrees—and I hated it. But grandma said, "You're going to learn to love it 'cause then you'll have fruit when it's cold." My mother and grandmother both worked at Sinai Hospital; they assisted doctors in the operating room, but she was not a full-pledged nurse. Back then, womens went to school for nursing for about a year, then graduated. My mother worked up at Sinai cleaning too. Later on, I worked there.

A scuffle outside the door interrupts Harriet's story. I hear a stream of profanity, a high-pitched female voice, then a door slams shut; after that, more profanity from a male voice followed by footsteps pounding away down the hall. I look at Harriet but apparently she does not notice the disturbance.

"So, when I was older in seventh grade I went to live with my aunt because me and my father didn't get along," she continues.

"So your father came back?" I ask while still keeping an ear out for more turmoil in the hall.

"Yeah. He would come and visit my mother and bring her supporting money. Then he would come drinking and comin' on—talking about my mother going with this man and that man, and she wasn't. It was in his mind. One day me and him got into it. I took a frying pan and hit him with it. So my mother sent me to live with my aunt because she said, 'You're too young to have a juvenile record.'"

As Harriet speaks an odd mixture of pungent sweetness and burning garbage begins to seep under her door, and I realize that someone is smoking marijuana outside in the hall. Within a few minutes, however, the stench fades with quiet footsteps and the rustle of plastic bags in someone's hand. Harriet keeps on talking through the odor, telling me stories about growing up in the sixties, how she could get into bars even though she was only seventeen, and how she would listen to Marvin Gay and the Temptations while dancing and shooting pool.

"Do you remember the MLK riots in the sixties? I ask.

"Sure do. I was still living with my grandmother and working at the Sinai Hospital and everything. The National Guards was taking us to work and bringing us back home. And when I got home I couldn't sleep, because my mother had a house full of people sitting there."

"Talking about the riots?"

"Well, *and* because my sister was raidin' one of the stores across the street from the house. She got caught in the store with a lot of stuff, because they was only one door and it was narrow. Everybody trying to get out and couldn't, so the National Guard caught about six or seven of them. My mother had to go down to the jail and find my sister, but by her being a minor, all they had to do was sign for her and let her out."

"What kind of stores did the kids loot?" I ask, wondering if there was a rationale behind pillaging.

"Well, they went into Old Town Mall down the street, and when they got in there they tore that place up and everything. My sister said 'Aren't you coming on inside Harriet?' I looked at her and say, 'Do I look like a fool?' And they would shake their head and say, 'Well, you ain't getting nothing from us.' But I said, 'I don't want nothing if unless I can buy it.' Later my grandmother said, 'That's right.' She said, 'Everything we have in our house, we bought. I got the receipts to show it.'"

The remnants of Old Town Mall still exist across the street from Harriet's apartments. First constructed in the early 1800s, Old Town grew to accommodate the growing immigrant and working class population with more than sixty-four row home shops. By the twentieth century, Old Town was bustling with middle class commerce and featured Victorian and Art Deco storefronts. But Baltimore's urban renewal efforts after World War II (and again in the sixties) left what was now, Old Town Mall, surrounded by public and subsidized housing, so businesses began to cater to the Black population.[6] After the 1968 riots, the Mall never recovered its original vitality.[7] Today, patches of asphalt replace missing bricks in the pedestrian walkway, and weeds have overtaken the center where flower planters once were. A few businesses remain in operation: Cooper's Liquor, Upscale Fashion Wig, and Old Town Pawn Shop, but most are boarded up, left vacant with metal pull-down store fronts marked with gang graffiti.

"After that," Harriet continues, "the National Guard started going door to door to see who have people's furniture and stuff because people had broken into furniture stores and everything. When they tore up the stores down there in Old Town Mall, I said, 'Hmm that doesn't make no sense,' and I shook my head."

The rioting that followed the assassination of Martin Luther King, Jr., later dubbed the Holy Week Uprising, prompted Baltimore's mayor, Tommy D'Alesandro, to call for help. More than five thousand National Guardsmen were deployed, along with four hundred state troopers and a thousand city police to quell the looting on the East side of the city. Three days later, looting and violence had shifted to the west side, so Governor

---

6. Spence Lean, "Oldtown Mall: Youtube Worthy."
7. James Singewald, "Photographing Old Town, East Baltimore."

Spiro Agnew petitioned the White House for even more assistance. Five thousand army troops were eventually sent to contain the chaos. By the time the rioting had simmered down, the toll was six dead, more than seven hundred injured, over five thousand arrested, and one thousand businesses—owned mostly by Whites—had been looted, vandalized, or set on fire.[8] People who witnessed the outpouring of rage reported that the sky was April blue on one side of the city and blackened with the smoke of seventy-two fires on the other.[9] The National Guard remained for ten days after the worst of the rioting. With bayonets fixed to their rifles, they patrolled the streets in tight formation, enforced the city-wide curfew, and slept on the hoods of cars in Druid Hill Park until Baltimore sent them home.

"After the trouble was over and everything," Harriet tells me, "I wound up getting married to the National Guard who was taking me back and forth to work."

"Really? How did that happen?"

"We fell in love, him taking me back and forth," she says unceremoniously. "We got married at my mother's house—didn't have no big wedding or nothing, we just got married at the house." Then Harriet points to one of the photographs on the wall behind me. "After that, my first baby was born, but my husband got called back to active duty, and he went to Vietnam." I turn to look at a picture of a baby girl sitting in a crib. She is wearing a pink Minnie Mouse dress and a head full of barrettes, but, oddly, the camera had caught her in the middle of clapping her hands. Her arms are flaying out to the side, and her tongue is curled up into the awkward beginning of a laugh.

> He saw the baby then left. When he came back to Baltimore he got an honorable discharge, because he was driving over a mine and it blew him all up. He wound up having a plate in his head. But he would start having those nightmares, choking me, and I told my aunt, "I can't handle this no more." We wind up getting a divorce. Later he died of a heart attack, but they said it was from the war. They said it was a lead plate in his head because, at the time, they wasn't using plain steel.
>
> Later I married my second son's father. He was all right except for when he drink. He went crazy, and I said, "I'm not having this no more." I went through this with my father, so I said, "Nope." I said, "You stop drinking." I said, "You don't put another drink in

---

8. Michael Yockel, "Baltimore 100 Years: The 1968 Riots."
9. Kalani Gordon, "From the Vault: Remembering Baltimore's 1968 Riots."

your mouth long as you living here with me." Because see, during the winter he couldn't work for Callahans putting black tar on streets, so he drank instead, but I told him, "No. Uh uh." Then one day I come home sick from work, and he sitting there with a woman. He sitting there, and I say, "Wait a minute what's going on in here?" He said, "No, she's just a friend." I said, "Mm hmm" and went upstairs. When I came back down, both of them was gone because he knew what I was going to do.

"Is this the time when you went and got your pistol?" Harriet had told me a version of this story before.

"Uh huh. Sure was. He left and ain't come back for two weeks. Then he said to me, 'I wasn't thinking,' and I say, 'You sure wasn't. You sure wasn't.' He said, 'Will you accept my apologize? I'll never do it again.' That's what he said."

"Well, did he keep his promise?"

"He didn't do it no more after that, because he knew what I was going to do. He knew I don't play. I don't get mad often, but when I do, just get out of my way."

"Really, Harriet? I've never seen you mad. You seem so easygoing."

"Well, when I'm mad, just don't be over my hand's reach," she says placidly, undermining the credibility of her threat. If Harriet had once been vivacious, then fatigue and the sheer magnitude of her body had taken their toll. "Later, he died. He went down to visit his mother in South Carolina and started drinking corn liquor. Drank corn liquor and went into a diabetic coma. Never came out of it." Harriet gazes above my head and says, "It was about then when my son passed." On the wall, right next to a triptych of the two Kennedys and Martin Luther King, hangs a black and white photograph of a young boy in a suit, his eager eyes looking dutifully into the camera.

"Oh, I didn't know your son passed."

"Yes. Yes, he did. See, Ricardo, my oldest son had a gun and had brought it in the house." Harriet leans forward on her cane closer to me, her billowing frame held up by both hands.

I didn't know he had it, and he was showing it to his brother and it went off. Ricardo come running in the room, "Mama, I shot Caleb! I shot Caleb!" I said, "You what?" "I shot Caleb!" "Oh!" I said, "Bring him here and put him in the tub." And I put pressure on it, on the wound. And when the paramedics came they had to pry my hands off.

They kept saying, "You did good. You did good. Let us finish it. We'll handle it from here." They took him to the ambulance, and I went in the fire truck and followed him. He went to surgery, and the doctors said, "We got the bullet out. He should be doing better." But a week later infection set in, and when they tried to clean him out he started bleeding worse. They had to put a di-nal-sis machine on him to try and stop the bleeding, but that didn't do no good; he bled to death.

After that I turned around, and I blamed his brother for it. I said, "If you hadn't brought that gun in here, Caleb wouldn't be gone from here." I was evil and mean and everything. I wouldn't even let him in the house. Nowhere around me! He went nowhere around me! That's when Sheera said, "Come to church with me." After that, I had my lessons and got baptized and about two weeks later I started feeling different. So, when Ricardo come to the door, and he said, "Ma, you all right? I looked at him and said, "Yeah, I'm all right." He said, "Do you still blame me?" I said, "No, I forgive you." And that brought a whole different thing over me. I felt better and everything. I felt like a new person.

Harriet pauses to rejuvenate herself with a few short breaths. "When I got in the car with Sheera to go to work the next day, she said, 'You all right?' I said, 'Yeah.' She said, 'You look different.' I say, 'Yes, I *am* different.' Then at the daycare, Sarah said I look like I got an uplifting face, like I got a globe on me. I told her, 'Well, I forgave Ricardo,' and Sarah said, 'that's wonderful Harriet.'"

Sheera's Cousin, Sarah

Sarah had also wanted to record her conversion story. We met that Saturday in the Primary room right after Sheera had finished telling me the dream about her sick mother. Sarah had come to help Sheera with the clothing exchange and had spent the morning refolding jeans and straightening out shirts that customers had left crooked on hangers. Sitting across from me now—in one of the undersized chairs—she begins her story, hesitantly at first, with her hands folded in her lap.

"My name is Sarah. I was born in South Carolina. I came up to Baltimore in the early sixties. My mother left me when I was sixteen." Sarah's voice is pinched and gravelly as she tells me fragments of her life. "My cousin, Sheera, she used to have these meetings at her house with the missionary elders and all," she adds.

Sarah is a short, thick-bodied woman with silver hair that curls into a stiff page-boy style around her cheeks. She has kindhearted eyes that reflect decades of hardship but without bitterness, and a permanent smile that is guarded but never scornful. She is a quiet woman who rarely speaks in class and goes out of her way to avoid the limelight, has only missed one day of church—and that was for a funeral—and always sits next to her sister, Rachel, third row from the back in the folding chairs.

"What happened at the meetings?" I ask.

"Well, Sheera would ask us at the daycare to come to her meetings, but she didn't really have to ask me because I loved going over there." Sarah hesitates, and I hope my smile will put her at ease. "You know, being with the missionaries and doing things with them, looking at films and all this kind of stuff, it was real nice." Sarah unfolds her hands and rests them on the table. "That's when I got interested in the Church."

"You moved up to Baltimore when you were young?" I ask, hoping to find out more about the mother Sarah mentioned and her childhood.

"Yes," she replies in a hoarse whisper. "I moved up here to live with Sheera—after my mother died." Sarah pauses and looks up. I see into her eyes, but they are bottomless pools harboring a longing I cannot grasp. Yet somehow, her face shows the opposite. There is no yearning; instead, just fatigue and resignation.

> I loved my mother so much, I follow her everywhere she go. I used to go to the Baptist Church with my mother. She would take me every Sunday with her, and we'd stay there all day. I'd take a break, eat a little something, drink a little something, then after that it'd be right back to church again. But I'd go to sleep most of the time. My mother would say, "Girl, wake up, wake up." I wouldn't wake up. I was sitting there and lay on her lap and lay on her shoulder. I was just so close to my mother, and I wanted to be wherever she was at. And when she passed, I had a nervous breakdown.

Tears fill Sarah's eyes, and she carefully takes a breath. I find myself inhaling along with her as if my breathing would somehow comfort her. I wonder why the years had not softened the ache she had felt for the loss of her mother sixty years ago, and how her feelings of abandonment could still linger with such intensity.

"See, I was fourteen when I got married," Sarah backtracks and gathers composure. "My aunt, my mother's sister, she decide for me to get married, then I had a son. I had some miscarriage, but I had one son." Sarah is speaking more freely now, so I do not interrupt her.

> But when I was sixteen, my mother died in childbirth. I had to take my mother baby, Rachel, and raise her. And my younger brother and sister too. So I brought them up here to Baltimore when I came to live with my cousin, Sheera. She would work all day, and I would take over the kids and send them to school and go pick them up. Do little chores like that. So when Sheera ask me do I want to go to church with her, I said, "Yes." That was Monday. She kept asking every day and I say, "Yes, Sheera." So I got my clothes together and went to church with her that Sunday. And it was—you know I'd been through so much myself, and that Sunday it was just like—I don't know, just like stepping out one place into another one. It was so much love of everybody, you know, they just hugged me like they'd known me for years. And I said, "Oh I never had so much love in my life." So I went that Sunday and you know what? I was getting clothes ready for the *next* Sunday that same day. That's how much I felt so much love. It was just beautiful.

Sarah smiles, and her eyes well up with tears again. "I used to get sick a lot before then. I was always just sick inside, you know, because my mother left me, but when I joined the church I wasn't sick anymore. Everything got better. And right now I'm a happy person," Sarah tells me with tears running down her cheeks. I reach out and Sarah holds my hand for a moment. Her hands are warm and solid, yet how fragile her spirit seems to be. All of us—like Sarah—are tied, heart and soul, to our mothers, intertwined with a bond—an immortal umbilical cord—as we remember through the innocent eyes of a child only the comfort our mothers provided; we forget her imperfections and forgive her transgressions. How we miss mothering when it is gone. In Sarah's story I hear Odetta's soulful words singing the well known Negro Spiritual, "Sometimes I feel like a motherless child, a long way from home."[10]

"A happy person. Yes I am. Now I'm raising my great-granddaughter, and I just hope I'll be living until she grows up, you know, and be there for her. And that just makes me feel strong about the church."

"Well, you raised three generations!"

---

10. Odetta, "Sometimes I Feel Like a Motherless Child."

"Yes. See how many people I done raised? My mother's baby, my own son, my grandson, and now his daughter—my two aunt's sisters and my brother and sister too. I sure did."

Sarah's story was not long. When she was done, she got up from her seat, hugged me, and said, "I'm so glad you're doing this," then left to help Sheera lock up the clothing exchange. Later, I would interview Sarah again, along with her sister Rachel, because they wanted to tell me about their experience in the Washington, DC, Temple.

Sarah and Her Sister, Rachel

Rachel is not at all like Sarah. She is notably thin with a boyish figure and hair smoothed back against her scalp in such a way that it only accentuates her smallness. Her dresses tend to hang a bit too far over her shoulders, and her hips appear to be lost in her skirts; only her child-sized jeans and T-shirts seem to be a good fit. Yet despite her size, Rachel is energetic and decisive. Unlike Sarah, who is tender and emotional, Rachel is unflurried and practical. And while both sisters rarely utter a word at church, it is clear that Rachel is in command at home where two of her grown children and many grandchildren live, each family assigned to a room in Rachel's small apartment.

"See, my mother died after having me, so Sarah raised me," Rachel explains, sitting next to Sarah in a spare classroom after church services. "I joined the Church because of my cousin Sheera, but you know, what *really* caught my eyes was when they said, don't you know that you can baptize for dead people. I done been to many churches, and I ain't never heard anyone say that you can baptize for the dead. That really got my attention!"

Rachel is sitting on top of a table instead of a chair, her legs swinging back and forth while she leans forward, balancing with her hands. "I mean, no Baptist preacher saying you can baptize for the dead. They speak some of the truth but not all of it," Rachel's forehead wrinkles in earnest and her eyes flash as she speaks. "They be so busy trying to collect your money," she concludes, and Sarah nods her head in agreement.

"Yeah, I'm telling you, that's the truth" Rachel continues, "so, in the Mormon Church I say, 'Well dang, I would like to get baptized for my mother.' That's what caught my attention."

"Mm hmm, that's right," Sarah adds even before Rachel is done speaking. "That's right."

"I kept on it and kept on it as I went, and I kept learning more," Rachel explains. "So I say, 'I like this church.' Every Sunday I go, and it's a new thing that I'm learning, something that I can take home." Rachel and Sarah both nod their heads in tandem. "I just enjoy myself. I just feel—how could you say it? I just feel rejoice when I goes to church on Sundays—anytime when I go inside the church I have a good spirit about it."

"That's right," Sarah says again. "So we went down and did baptisms with Sheera and Harriet, you know, at the temple down there, for our mothers."

Harriet had also talked about going to the temple with Sheera. She said, "The temple is like heaven. It's like angels floating over me." She explained how she had stepped down into the baptismal font to perform the baptismal ordinance. "When I went in the water, I could see my mother's face—my aunt and grandmother too. They were telling me, thank you."

"Yes! It was just amazing to us!" Sarah tells me.

"Yeah, that you can do that, "Rachel finishes Sarah's thought "I just felt filled up—it was like my mother was right there!"

"Yeah, that's my mother's baby," Sarah looks at Rachel.

"Coming up out of the water, going back in, coming back—it was really nice."

"And knowing it was her baby that was baptizing for her," Sarah says.

"Yeah, I got filled up."

"I couldn't help but cry. I think about it now and it's—"

"Yeah, it's pretty neat," Rachel says. "I mean, there at first, Sarah was going to do the baptism and—I don't know what made her change her mind."

"Well, I wanted my mama's baby to be baptize for her," Sarah explains to her sister, as well as to me.

"It was amazing, you know; you see these twelve oxen statues around the pool and you're in the midst of it. Then you hear them say all these words, and it's like you're going down in the water in slow motion, then coming up."

As Rachel describes the baptismal ritual of immersion, I see the beauty behind Sarah insisting that Rachel perform the baptism for her mother. Even though Rachel had never known her mother's touch or ached for the loss of her mother in the same way Sarah had, it had been Rachel who had come up out of the amniotic water at her mother's death. So it was Rachel who would offer her mother spiritual birth as she comes up out of the waters of baptism.

"It just seem like I'm moving to heaven, I mean it's so different. You go inside you feel so good," Sarah tells me.

"And you come back out and continue in the world again," Rachel points out.

"Yep, that's right" Sarah says as if she did not hear what Rachel had just said. "People passing each other in the temple halls, and talking, you know, softly . . ."

". . . and it's noisy *out there*," Rachel motions with her head toward the door.

"Yes, mm hmm. Sure is."

7

Having It Out with God

I turn onto Monastery and squeeze by a line of cars parked along both sides of the street. The neighborhood is a maze of two-story row homes, some partitioned off by chain-link fences, others delineated by worn-down walking paths and patches of grass. I inch the truck into a vacant spot in front of Georgia's house and take stock of the activity around me. It is afternoon and the kids are home from school. High-spirited elementary age boys pop wheelies on their bikes imitating Baltimore's infamous Twelve O' Clock Boyz and bounce basketballs uncomfortably close to my windshield.[1] Girls huddle together in semicircles and laugh. Four teenage boys amble by and glance my way with vague curiosity then continue down the street toward the park.

This is the park where someone had tried to shoot two of our missionaries. As they were crossing over the grassy field wearing white shirts and ties, someone fired five shots in their direction. The missionaries immediately hit the ground as bullets whizzed by. Then, when the coast was clear, they ran on to Edmondson Avenue with their lives intact and stories to tell for years to come. Members in our congregation, those who had lived in the city for decades, concluded that the shootings were another gang initiation. Others blamed drugs for running down the neighborhood into outright craziness.

I had texted Georgia earlier that morning to remind her of our interview; she replied, "fine. come on over. i'm not going anywhere"—ending the message with a smiley face. Several weeks earlier, doctors had amputated Georgia's big toe that had turned gangrene, and she was still on crutches from the surgery. As I walk up the steps I notice Keisha standing in the doorway. She greets me with a diffident wave, perhaps wondering why I am there. Keisha is Georgia's twenty-year-old daughter who lives in the house with her two small children. Georgia adores her grandchildren and loves having them underfoot.

---

1. Baltimore's Twelve O'Clock Boyz is a gang whose members pop wheelies on dirt bikes through the city. Police have been banned from chasing the Boyz, creating an illegal underground sport that the city is powerless to stop. See "Twelve O'Clock Boys: Baltimore's Infamous Dirtbike Gang."

"My mom is around the corner talking to a friend," Keisha tells me, assuming the reason for my visit, then turns to her sister who is sitting on the porch ledge. "Roxy, can you go get mom?"

Philomena—Keisha's sister whose given name had somehow been swapped for Roxy—is a tall, quiet girl with large, almond eyes and a sturdy frame. She holds a guitar in her hand. Roxy is entering high school and told me that she hopes to take a music class this year.

"How did your first day of school go?" I ask.

"I didn't go to school," she answers without further explanation. Instead, Keisha fills me in. "Roxy's dad is mourning the death of his mother right now, so Roxy can't go to school for the first week." Then, because of my perplexed face, Keisha adds, "Roxy's dad can't get the money to her right now."

"Money?" I ask, still not getting the connection to school.

"Yes. Money. To. Buy. School. Uniforms," Keisha hyper-pronounces each word slowly, as if talking to a three-year old. This new information only gives way to more puzzlement. Having taught high school, as well as having raised four teenagers, I understood how hard it would be for Roxy to attend a new school away from her neighborhood and to be the only ninth grader without a uniform—that would have been unbearable. But this adolescent ordeal aside, I wondered about the adults in Roxy's life. Shouldn't school take priority? Wasn't education the road to opportunity? In other words, were they letting a navy blue polo shirt and a pair of khaki pants stand in the way of Roxy's future?

I look for further enlightenment on Roxy's and Keisha's faces, but there is not a hint of condemnation or frustration or anger in either countenance—yet neither is there approval or sympathy. They are unreadable.

"So, Roxy, can you go get mom?" Keisha asks again. But Roxy has resisted Keisha's request, shaking her head.

"Please, Roxy, please, please, please, please?" Keisha pleads playfully.

"Yes, please, please, please Roxy" I add, jumping into Keisha's game. Roxy pauses, and I am expecting a smile to creep up at the corners of her mouth, but instead, her eyes brighten and she stands up. Without a word or a even a glance back, Roxy balances her guitar on the porch railing then strides down the steps to go look for her mother.

Not waiting to be invited in, I walk through the opened door where it is cooler. Two large, imitation-leather sofas with matching end tables crowd the entry way, but I manage to squeeze through. The living room is packed as if the family were getting ready to move. Cardboard boxes brimming with plastic toys are stacked against the wall, and garbage bags stuffed with clothes are heaped on top of that. A variety of mismatched items have been deposited here and there, leaving a trail of family artifacts that testify of domestic activity: rolls of masking tape, purple hair ribbons, insect repellent, and two opened bags of potato chips. Thick, fiberglass curtains cover the front window to make the room dark, but it is not so much the density of household goods that pervade the living space as the abrasive odor of cat urine. Georgia and her daughters have soft hearts for abandoned animals and are always taking in strays. For the moment, they are housing Marshmallow, a white, long-haired mother cat, and her four kittens. Little puffs of fur dash in and out among electrical chords and stacks of newspapers strewn on the floor.

Keisha is telling me the events of the day. "Well, Butt Butt never made it to her first day of kindergarten because her father decided not to take her." Butt Butt—an urban term of endearment for children that became another family nickname—is Keisha's five-year-old daughter and the unfortunate beneficiary of a custody dispute. The court had ruled that Keisha would get her daughter every other week, but this was not her week.

"Well, that's too bad," I say. "I guess you will take Butt Butt to school then, when it's your turn?" But I don't catch Keisha's reply because Roxy is coming back up the steps—without Georgia.

"Couldn't find her," she informs us. "She wasn't at the corner."

I wonder where Georgia could have gone, given her surgery. I ask Keisha to help me look for her, which she agrees to do, but only after she changes clothes. She trades her white shorts and tank top—which were barely able to contain her full figure—and returns with a shoulder-length wig, a long, blue T-shirt over tight jeans, and a yellow purse wrapped over her arm. I follow Keisha through the back door out into the alley and around the corner. We walk up the block and across the street where Keisha leans over a fence to talk to a woman. The woman points up the hill then examines me carefully. I smile but feel the heavy August sun beating down on my face with oppressive mugginess. The realization that I am the only White person in the neighborhood puts me on edge. I fight against my inclination to brandish an overly enthusiastic smile as a protective shield, and instead, chat with Keisha as we walk on.

Half way up the hill, Keisha stops to talk to some kids who look like brothers and sisters. They point to their front door. As we step inside, I realize that Black Flight had not entirely gutted Baltimore's neighborhoods of middle-class Black families.² The newly remodeled interior had been painted a stylish mocha brown to match new wood floors. In the kitchen, a smiling woman with an aqua headscarf and numerous bracelets is wiping her marble countertops. Georgia is leaning on the bar-side of the counter, and two men are sitting in the dining room watching ESPN basketball on a flat screen that covers half the wall. They all turn to look at me. I muster a cheery, confident greeting, "How are you? I'm Laura." Georgia immediately remembers our interview appointment. "Oh, I'm sorry! I forgot. I'm so used to not doing anything that I can't remember when I'm supposed to be doing something," she laughs as she gathers up her purse and crutches to get ready to go.

The walk back to Georgia's house is unbearably slow as she fights against the downhill pull on her crutches and the efforts to restrain her body weight. Georgia chats with me cheerfully between gasps for air and wiping sweat from her forehead. "What a hot day!" she points out. I shield my face from the sun and readjust my purse that feels too heavy on my shoulder. Keisha, who began by walking with us, has now disappeared, either running on ahead or out talking to friends.

Once home, Georgia invites me to sit at the dining room table. I've always liked visiting Georgia because her house is quiet—no rap music blaring, no Fox News on full blast, no kids yelling at each other from the bottom of the stairs. Georgia tells me to sit in the middle chair farthest from the wall, "because sometimes the cat box smells," she warns me. And indeed, the litter is so full that the cats have opted to relieve themselves outside the box on the carpet.

Now that we're settled, I ask Georgia to talk about her childhood. She begins her story with a laugh, "So long ago! Well, let me see. I was a quiet child. Stayed to myself, never bothered anyone, played out in front. One of my memories was playing musical chairs for a birthday when I was seven or eight, and the time I got measles. All I remember is the calamine lotion my mother put all over my face. The kids would point and laugh because, you know, you look like a ghost."

Georgia speaks quickly, but her manner is not animated. Instead, she leans into phrases and softens the ends of words creating a swinging cadence, like a soothing lullaby. Her brown eyes radiate as she tells her story,

---

2. Baltimore's population is falling to a 100-year low mainly because of Black Flight to the suburbs. From 1990 to 2015 nearly 40,000 Blacks moved away leaving lower income residents with poverty, crime, and fewer social services. Michael Snidal, "City must fight Black Flight."

"Coming up, my favorite cake was chocolate, and my father'd take me to the bakery and we got a cake. I had birthdays all the way until I was fifteen."

"So you lived with your mother and your father?" I ask, because most of the women I have interviewed had been raised by their mothers.

"Well, my mother left my dad and moved to East Baltimore when I was young, because her and my father were having problems. Then it was just my mother from then on." Georgia bends down to pet Marshmallow who has been busy shedding white fur on her black pants. Static electricity snaps as the cat's fur mats together into an odd array of swirls. "I have three sisters," Georgia continues. "It's four of us girls all together. Three of us had the same father; the oldest one has a different father. My mother did housekeeping for a while until I was about twelve or thirteen, then she started working in Social Service." Georgia keeps talking as she pushes Marshmallow away, probably realizing that the cat is not going to be satisfied with any amount of human affection. "All my sisters dropped out of school except for me. I liked school and I graduated from high school and went to the Community College of Baltimore, or they call it Baltimore Community College—something like that. Then I went and moved on to Coppin State."

Coppin State University, in West Baltimore, was founded in 1900 at what was then called The Colored High School. The school offered a one-year training course for Black elementary school teachers and was attended mostly by female students. In 1926, the facility was renamed in honor of Fanny Jackson Coppin, who was born a slave in Washington, DC, but later gained her freedom and graduated from Oberlin College in Ohio.

> Did a couple of years there, but because of the living situation I wind up dropping out of college. See, I left my mother's house because me and my oldest sister wasn't getting along, and unfortunately my oldest sister was my mother's favorite child. So I went to stay with my father for a while, but he only had a two bedroom house. My father's girlfriend had a younger daughter she wanted to bring into the picture, and the daughter was sleeping on the sofa. The scheme was to get my room for her. So my father said, "Why don't you go over to your mother's house and help her out for a while because she needs you." So I fell for it, and then when I returned, "Oh, you don't have a room anymore." It hurt me really bad, so basically I had nowhere to go. So I slept with this guy for a place to stay. You know, as a child all I ever tried to do was impress my parents and be there for my parents. But all my father cared about was pleasing this woman, and all my mother cared about was her oldest daughter. You know my oldest sister cussed

her out and treated her bad, but that was just her favorite child. And I was the only one trying to do something with myself and go to college. But I had to wind up dropping out, you know to find a way to live. I lost my virginity so I wouldn't be homeless.

Georgia has lost the soft, rhythmic lullaby-way of speaking as her words become more labored. I try to soothe her. "But you got your degree, right?"

"I got my Associate's in the community college," Georgia answers, "but it wasn't like in nothing in particular. I just got credits. Then I was going to Coppin State to become a social worker. Before I dropped out I had a hundred and eight credits."

"Wow, you were almost there!"

"Yeah, almost there, and I had to leave it all behind. Eventually I moved out on my own and met Keisha's father. After I had her I just never got back to college."

"Is it too late for that?" I ask, thinking about my return to the university as a "non-traditional" student.

"Yeah, it's too late. I'm in a career now. I mean, I could take credits here and there, but it wouldn't be the same." Georgia's work as a preschool teacher's assistant began by volunteering when Roxy was young. She would walk Roxy to her class then stay for several hours to help the teacher. Later, the principal hired Georgia as permanent staff.

"You have to talk to children with respect," Georgia explains. "You can't just say, 'Do it! I'm the adult so you do as I say.' You got to respect that; you got to read their faces. Children want to be recognized that they have a problem. So I guess that was one of God's gifts—a blessing to me to know how to deal with children. I can talk in a soft voice, but I can be loud too, and then it's a shock effect."

I've heard Georgia's version of loud. It was on the day I drove her to pay her Baltimore Gas and Electric (BGE) utilities bill, and it was a force to be reckoned with. Georgia was sitting next to me in the front seat, and Roxy, Keisha, and Butt Butt were all crammed into the back of my compact car. Butt Butt's car seat was shoved up against the door as far as it would go, tilting sideward in order to make more sitting space. The family had received a final notice stating that their electricity would be turned off that night unless the bill was paid by 5:00 p.m. If they did not make the deadline, Georgia would have to pay over six hundred dollars in late fees and overdue fines, as well as a security deposit in order to get their power turned back on. But first we had to drive to the Eastside to pick up Georgia's paycheck from school, then find a MECU credit union and cash her check, then drive to the Westside to pay the bill in person at the BGE office. It was already four o'clock, so we were under the gun. As I raced in and out of the afternoon traffic, I was experiencing a pendulum swing of emotions. At one intersection I would feel sympathy and the weight of my responsibility to save the family from living in a dark, cold house; then at the next, I was frustrated and mentally critiquing Georgia for letting the situation get out of hand.

At first, Georgia was calm as she directed me through the city, telling me stories about other hard times in her life. She recalled how one winter, when the girls were still babies, the electricity had been turned off for three months. She had decided to send Keisha and Roxy to live with their cousins while she continued living in the dark house. "I couldn't leave it vacant or someone would break in," Georgia had explained while sitting next to me in the car.

But soon, the minutes began ticking away and we were still backed up in traffic. Tension was mounting and Georgia snapped. She slammed her hand down on the armrest. "Why me?" she yelled. "Why does this always happen to me? I do what I can to provide! I do what I can! But how much am I suppose to bear? Just how much?" Georgia was booming and everyone in the backseat quieted down immediately, keeping wide-opened eyes on her temper. Even Butt Butt seemed to understand the magnitude of the event and just sat in her crooked car seat staring forward.

I assumed Georgia's questions were rhetorical and, instead of answering, rolled down the window a little, as if the outside air would provide a place for the tension to dissipate. But I also made an attempt to accelerate, whizzing through congested lanes, slamming on brakes just in the nick of time, throwing everyone in the back seat to one side. It was three minutes after five when we pulled up to the BGE office. I parked in a no-parking zone while Georgia heaved herself out of the car with surprising speed and boosted herself up the steps. She pushed on the front door right as a BGE worker appeared with keys to lock up. Georgia began talking to the man through the half opened door, her hands making eloquent circles underneath her breath that was condensing in the cool air. Time lapsed into slow motion as we watched the conversation between Georgia and the gatekeeper who held the family's fate in his hands. Then, as if the scene had clicked back to everyday speed, the man opened the door wider and Georgia walked into the building. Everyone in the car exhaled.

That was the day I saw the formidable side of Georgia, and I could understand how, with her temperament and loud voice, the Pre-K students would stop and listen.

"When I was young, I went to church a lot," Georgia continues with her story. Roxy had disappeared upstairs, and Keisha had come back from her jaunt through the neighborhood. She is sitting on the couch looking up at us, and with fixed attention she listens to her mother's storytelling. Even though Keisha has been a single mother herself since her teens, I am touched by the innocence of her twenty-year old face; and even though she has had vicious run-ins with Georgia, right now I see only esteem for her mother.

"See, my mother," Georgia explains, "she always go to church." As Georgia speaks I can hear Roxy strumming guitar chords upstairs: E minor to G, back to E minor. "The Jehovah Witness," Georgia continues, "the Baptist, Seven-Day Adventist—my mother, she tried them all, and I was right there behind her you know, followed whatever church she tried. And then one day about the time I graduated from high school, these two White guys came knocking at the door. I was right there watching my mother studying with them too."

"You mean the missionaries? Those guys?" I smile playfully.

"Yes, the missionaries," Georgia smiles back. "My mother decided to join the Church, and after she got baptized they gave her this big, beautiful bouquet of fresh cut flowers." As Georgia talks, one of the kittens plays with the hem of her pants. She gently pushes it away with her foot. "And I'm like, 'Oh I want me some beautiful flowers.' I'd never had that before."

"And that's why you joined the Church?" I ask, smiling.

Georgia laughs, her eyes reflecting what little bit of light has managed to shine through the opened front door. "Well, I was studying with my mother, and I liked the things they had to say about Joseph Smith and everything." Georgia bends down to pick up the kitten at her feet and holds it in her lap.

> And the other thing I liked was the guys were always respectful, always nice. They always helped if my mom needed something you know. Stuff like, one time she ain't had money for Christmas, and they was just there for her, you know, the Church was there for her. And another thing I like, I never saw a collection plate passed or nothing like that because any monies that was handed over was discreet. It was not about putting somebody on the spot and making her feel like, oh, you should be embarrassed into giving. It was all between you and

God. The Church is your family, your support system. Other churches, they're like, "No we can't help you, sorry." But you go to the Mormon Church, and I don't care if you give them a dollar and you need a hundred, the Mormon Church provides. They take care of their members. This Church does everything a church is supposed to do—poor, rich—everything between you, God, and the Bishop. And that's what made me believe the Mormon Church was true. So right after my mother got baptized, like just a week later, I got baptized and became a member.

"So did you get your bouquet?" I ask, partly in jest.

"Yes! I got my bouquet. I mean, they'd always give the Sunday bouquet to the new members." Georgia had continued the flower-giving tradition in her own way last year when she brought a vase full of pink and yellow fabric lilies and placed them on the podium before worship services, "as a gift to the Church," she had explained.

Georgia's baptism bouquet story also reminded me of a falling out we once had, of how Georgia had lashed out at me, and how I would not yield. Flowers had been part of our reconciliation. The incident happened a few months back when I was the Relief Society president responsible for overseeing the welfare of the women in our congregation. Georgia had sunk into difficult times and had asked me to arrange rides for her to get to work until Mobility could be reinstated.[3] I felt like the request would be too difficult for church sisters who would have to get up at five thirty in the morning to take Georgia through Westside traffic. When I suggested alternative transportation options, Georgia angrily flung texts my way: "nobody cares about nothing no more"; "this is not the church I used to know"; "this is just like the baptist church." And she had told me, "I'm tired of people saying, ride the bus, ride the bus. You don't know how difficult it is for me to walk to the bus stop with this foot!"

Which, of course, was true—I did not know.

We had reconciled at Christmas when my husband and I brought Georgia a potted red Poinsettia and chocolate covered cherries for the family. We had talked and joked together as if there had been no dispute and felt the warmth of the holiday. Happily, I felt like we had cleared the air. Georgia, as always, was forgiving, accepting my flower offering with gratitude.

"Everybody has roadblocks after joining the Church," I continue with our interview, "their own burdens to bear. So is there something that, for you, makes it hard to remain faithful?"

---

3. Mobility is low cost public transportation in Baltimore for people with disabilities.

"Well, the hardest thing," Georgia explains, "is when you try *so* hard, you pray *so* hard, you know you are being faithful—doing things right, living right—and you keep coming up with all this adversity. Once you seem to beat one thing, there's something there to knock you *right, back,* down. It's just hard to get up when you've been beaten so much."

I take a second look at Georgia because I'm wondering if she might be referring to our disagreement. I wonder if she is letting me know, in a round about way, that I was one of those "things" that had knocked her right back down. And still harboring feelings of self-righteousness that I did not know existed, I take my thoughts a step further. Instead of softening, inwardly I resist. I hold my ground, rationalizing that, yes, there is hard luck, but there are also choices that lend themselves to a more difficult life.

But Georgia does not blame me; she blames the Devil. "Lately, the Devil's really been beating me down," she says, and I am thankful that Georgia cannot read my thoughts. "I just talked to the Bishop, and it wasn't a pretty talk, and I know we go through these things to make us stronger. But like I told the Bishop, just how strong am I supposed to be? After two years of fighting, fighting, fighting, how strong am I supposed to be?" Georgia stops talking for a moment and studies the movement of her hands stroking the purring kitten in her lap, then she continues.

> But you never know what's on the road. Only God knows your path and what's over top of that hill; that this little battle right here's going to make you strong enough to fight the next big battle. Or maybe it's not for you. Maybe this little battle right here is so when you get up the road you can help somebody else with their big battle. You know what I'm saying? That your testimony is going to make someone else's testimony stronger. And you just got to keep your head up and not pass out.

Georgia looks at the kitten and smiles, then shifts her weight and leans forward, looking at me with gentle eyes. "But you know my story, Laura. Remember? It started back two years ago."

"Yes. I *do* remember," I tell her, and suddenly I am thankful that Georgia remembers me as part of her life, that I had been with her during some of her most difficult struggles. But I had not heard her story the way Georgia is about to tell it now. I had not understood the magnitude of her hardship, the weight of the burden she had to bear all at once.

> You know when I first found out that I was about to lose my vision. I was going to church one morning, as I told you many times before, and I was happy because I got some money. I could pay tithes today,

and I was just happy, happy, happy! Well, I went down all the steps and missed the last one and ran my head smack into the door. So my head was hurting, but I was all right, said I'm still going to church and pay my tithes. Came home and by that Wednesday my head was hurting really bad; it was over the top of my eye. At the time I didn't know that it was my eye that was the worst of the two when I went to see the doctor for my headache. He referred me right on to my eye doctor. The eye doctor looked in my eyes, and he wouldn't tell me exactly what was wrong, but he sent me to a retina specialist. He said, "You got to go immediately this cannot wait! You got to go immediately." So he set it up for the next day. Well lo and behold God had different plans for me because that very night I had a heart attack.

I was just sitting in the bathroom and had a heart attack, so I went to the hospital, and you know, I was okay. God pulled me through. Then I had another heart attack when I was there. I was talking to the nurse—just talking crazy. She had a jacket on or something, and I was saying, "You're a nurse, you don't need to be wearing no jacket." Just saying all kinds of crazy stuff to her. All I heard them say was, "We're losing her," and I could feel them rushing me out the room on a gurney. They put a stent—what they call a stent—in my groin, not in my heart, but in my groin area that went to my heart. But what else happened, while I was in the hospital, somebody had called CPS[4] on Keisha, so they took little Butt Butt away. I told the CPS workers, I said, "Look, I just had a heart attack and I'm in a hospital room," so they come to the hospital room talking about, you know, the situation and everything.

I remembered vividly that spring morning when Keisha had texted "call us we need u at this time in our life." I had been hesitant to answer back at first, wondering the nature of the crisis. Keisha had called us plenty of times with emergencies and crises, and most of them could be resolved by talking things through. But that day, Keisha had only wanted a ride to Johns Hopkins so she could see her daughter who was under observation for alleged child abuse. Georgia had advised Keisha beforehand not to cry, "because it will upset Butt Butt, and then it will all go worse for her in the long run." After the observation period, the court would decide if Butt Butt would go to foster care, back with Keisha, or a joint custody situation with the birth father who had not seen his child since she was born.

---

4. Child Protective Services.

So when I came home from the hospital on Thursday, it was the week before—now this is crazy—it was a week before spring vacation. The school secretary said, "Well, if you could come in and just sit in the classroom Friday you can get paid for all next week." She said, "If you don't, nobody pay you." So the doctor didn't know it, but I went to school the next day and just sat there. I had to hack a ride,[5] but then all I had to do was sign in and sit there all day, and that got me the whole two weeks of pay that I needed. So you know, God was just looking out. Then that Monday, the first day of spring break, I had to go to court with Keisha for her child.

So you know, God kept my strength because I never thought it at the time, but through the whole incident everybody told me, normally people don't recover that fast to be able to go to work then go to court, back and forth to court, and you know. Normally you had to rest. God kept me through all that. Then when I did go to see the eye doctor they told me if it had been a month later I'd be totally blind. So they was able to save my eyes because both my retinas had detached. It all came from me hitting my head up against the door. The surgeon said that my eyes turned out better than he could even expect it to be. So God saved my eyesight—he saved my life. The process made me strong. I was still able to get around and recover and take care of my family. You have to have faith for God to work in your life like that, and you have to keep going strong, to keep going in the battle for your child and for your grandchildren.

Georgia did not mention that before her heart attack and eye surgery, Keisha, carrying a secret pregnancy, had given premature birth to her second child who weighed only three pounds. As the baby girl lay in an incubator, Keisha considered giving her up for adoption but Georgia was delighted to have another grandchild and convinced Keisha to keep the newborn. My husband and I had visited little Maaka in intensive care; she was small enough to fit into your cupped hands. She had tubes and fluids running into her nose and wrist, and monitors taped all over her delicate

---

5. "Hacking a ride" or "catching a hack" is Baltimore's informal (and illegal) transportation system. People seeking a ride stand on a street corner, extend their arm, and bounce two fingers. Any driver can stop to pick up the potential passenger, then pricing is worked out between the two. See Eman Williams, "How To Catch a Hack in the Hood of Baltimore."

skin. By the time Georgia had her heart attack and Butt Butt had been taken away, Maaka was beginning to thrive under neonatal care.

After that, I did not see Georgia for a while, and summer was almost over by the time she returned to church. It was testimony meeting Sunday, and the Bishop had just announced that the congregation could come up to testify. With the help of a walker, Georgia walked laboriously to the podium with a piece of notebook paper in her hand.

"This is a poem I wrote in my tribulation, " she told us. "I want to read it to y'all 'cause it's my testimony." Then she unfolded the paper and began reading.

The Question

Heavenly Father
I don't understand
why my tears
fall on deaf ears.
I gave people my trust
and they threw it away.
I feel lost and alone
too tired to pray.
Why must change hurt so much?
I don't want to care or reach out or touch.
Why must life be so cruel?
I thought life would be easy if you played by the rules.
So tell me why my life is so hard.
Are you listening?
Where are you God?
You said if I trusted you and believed
there was nothing in life I could not achieve.
You said if I prayed and had faith in you
you'd always be there to see me through.
Why am I going through so much pain?
I feel like I am going insane.
I feel like I want to lay down and die.
I have no more tears left to cry.
Why are wicked people put in our path?
And after they hurt us
they sit back and laugh.
They damage your heart and they really don't care.

Oh God! My burdens are too hard to bear.
I'm sorry God.
This is the end.
I really thought I could depend
on you.
You said if I would take one step
you would take two.
Do you hear me God?
Where are you?

The Reply
I'm right here.
I hear your awesome voice.
My child, I gave you free will
to make your own choice.
I always try to guide you,
which way to go
but you sometimes use your free will to say, no.
The choices we make
affect our life
and decide whether we go through joy or strife.
Wicked people will sometimes come our way.
That's why it's important for you to pray.
Sometimes I have to mold you
which will cause great pain
but you'll never lose
more than you gain.
Broken hearts
I will always mend
but you will be my masterpiece
in the end.
I hear you cry
and see every tear.
I know your heart and pain is sincere.
When you cry,
I cry too.
Because my child,
I love you.
I know sometimes you think life isn't fair

> but I really won't give you more than you can bear.
> From you, my child, I will never hide
> because I will always be right by your side.
> Believe with your heart in what you can't see
> and always remember to have faith in me.
> I'm always here to see you through
> and when you fall down,
> I'll carry you.

Georgia had folded the poem back up into fourths and turned to leave the podium. As I watched her trod slowly toward her seat, making a special effort to keep steady as she clung to her walker, it struck me that it was not Georgia who had almost lost her sight; it was me. I had been blinded looking through the lens of my life experiences, and if I was not mindful I would miss the lessons that Georgia's life story could teach me. I would never know the breadth or the intensity of her hardships—not her anxiety to make ends meet, not the stress of raising children alone, not the racial burdens bequeathed her, and not the ongoing crises she faced every day. Difficulties that would only punctuate my life, such as not having enough money to buy school uniforms, paying a utilities bill on time, or getting a ride to work were the *substance* of Georgia's life. And if she did not prioritize life's demands the same as I, well, who was I to judge?

Later, when I told Georgia how I was inspired by her strength during that difficult time, she had said, "Well, it was definitely adversity, let me tell you. It was no song and dance."

"But, I saw you in the hospital and when you came home; you were so strong."

"Oh no!" she had resisted. "I wasn't. I came home. I cried. I threw my Bible. I said, 'God, why me?'" Then Georgia said something that gave me insight into her strength—it was her humility.

> You know, me and God basically had it out. I had my temper tantrum like children have. And then just like a parent waiting until you're done, God wait until I'm done. I got up and realized I wasn't going to get my way. Then I did what I was supposed to do. God was a loving parent standing there waiting and said, "You done yet? You know 'cause we got stuff we got to do. Because it's not going to be your way. It's going to be the way that it's supposed to be." It's God's will, not your will be done.

Three years after Georgia had read her poem in church, Keisha moved out of the city to the suburbs with her two children, having taken advantage of a Housing First program. My husband and I decided to drive out to see how Keisha was doing and bring Christmas gifts to the girls. We found that Keisha's apartment complex was perfectly situated for a family without a car—close to a grocery store and within walking distance to the mall. The grass was green and plush and there was a playground nearby. We did not see a trace of garbage or a scrap of windblown paper on the sidewalks; the hallways were clean and swept. At the door, the girls greeted us with a hug. Happy and bouncing, they introduced us to their friend who was visiting from next door and showed us their bedrooms, stuffed with a menagerie of pink and purple toys. Butt Butt had lost her nickname, and everyone was calling her by her given name, Keilani. For better or for worse, Keilani's father had lost interest in her and had given up custody rights. According to Keisha, she was now doing well in third grade on ADHD meds and with special attention.

Keisha's premature baby, Maaka, had grown into a first grader. A sensitive, sturdy girl, Maaka sat next to me on the couch—almost on my lap—while she opened our gift. She carefully picked away at the scotch tape until she was able to unfold the nativity scene we had brought. Gently she arranged baby Jesus in the manger encircled about by Mary, Joseph, and the shepherds. Calmness had settled over the household with the fish tank bubbling in the background and the girls asking us questions, touching my feather earrings, and rearranging the nativity scene. When we were about ready to leave, Keisha brought out her new incense burner to show us. After lighting a stick of incense called *Quiet Rain*, the smoke started swirling downwards like a waterfall. Mesmerizing to watch, we ended up staying longer than we had intended.

Things had not gone as well for Roxy, who had dropped out of high school and had sunk into depression. For a while she was seeing a counselor, but she then moved out of her mother's house and was living with two turtles, a kitten, and a boyfriend who was seven years older than she was. From time to time she would come back to see Georgia for a visit. Other times she would come back to take twenty dollars from her mother's purse or drop off pets that she could no longer care for. To this Georgia had said, "There's nothing more I can do. It's time for me to move on with my life, so I leave my children in the hands of God."

8

You Don't Serve God Then Drink with the Devil

I honk my horn at the car stopped in front of me at a green light and glance at the time on the dashboard. I'm going to be late for my interview with Eunice, and she is never late. Once, when I commented on her promptness, she told me that she tries to catch the early bus to church so she will have plenty of time to pick up trash. Impressed by Eunice's faithfulness, my husband and I bought an art print from a Baltimore artist called *Miss Sarah Waiting for Jesus*, a poster that features an African American woman, who looks surprisingly like Eunice, sitting on church steps looking up to heaven.[1] When I showed Eunice the poster she just laughed.

Luckily, I arrive at Eunice's house only two minutes after the hour, and she is waiting for me behind the screen door. "I hope you remembered I was coming," I say, even though it is obvious that she has.

"Of course," she lets me know as she pushes open the door.

When I enter, Eunice's forty-five-year-old son hurries by, but I catch him just before he disappears up the stairs. "Good morning," I yell, assuming an overly cheerful voice. He nods, then continues on up.

"I've learned to hold my tongue," Eunice says, looking toward the stairs. She tells me that her adult children keep coming back to live with her when she could be enjoying the tranquility of an empty nest. But her son had been ill, and she had spent months taking care of him. Now that he had recuperated and was back to work, she was hoping he would move out soon.

Eunice lives in Eastside public housing on a street that intersects New Hope Circle. New Hope, a thoroughfare configured like the rays of the sun, is fortunate enough not to have been christened "The Projects" because the housing units there were built to resemble row homes. The streets at New Hope, while not completely free of trash, are cleaned periodically, and the public dumpsters are hidden from view. Houses are adequately maintained with screen doors repaired and window blinds intact. All the

---

1. Mark Cottman, *Miss Sarah Waiting for Jesus*. According to Cottman, "This painting represents the backbone of Black America because women like her are very wise, even the preachers and reverends of the churches talk to them for advice."

entryways have protective grills that lock and some of the residents have hung wreaths or plastic bouquets on their front doors.

In the living room, I am drawn to the effervescent rhythm of a large fish tank that is the heart of Eunice's household. "I love aquariums!" I tell her, bending down to get a closer look at her orange and black fan-tailed goldfish. "They're so soothing to watch."

"Well, I've had them a long time," Eunice responds, standing behind me with hands on her hips. She is not a tall woman but solid with a sandy-brown complexion and short, straightened ash-colored hair. Her heavy brows accentuate eyes that appear to be sleepy but in reality are taking careful inventory of people around her. After a good, long look, Eunice will don an expressionless face, roll her eyes and turn the other way, or let out a measured, hoarse laugh.

"Maybe your husband can help me move my TV over there so the cable chord will fit into that wall." Eunice asks, but it sounds more like a declaration than a request.

"Of course," I answer then take stock of Eunice's living room. The flat-screen, next to the fish tank, is surrounded by faded photographs of children with outdated, oversized glasses, a large print of the Washington, DC, Temple and a picture of Jesus in the Garden of Gethsemane taped to the wall. Eunice has placed plastic lawn chairs around the room for furniture across from a mauve couch that is covered with a sheet. Her white linoleum floors are spotless, smelling faintly of bleach.

"The TV should be easy to move," I let Eunice know, then follow her into the kitchen and put my recorder on the table. The back window, opened just a few inches, allows a warm April breeze to blow in but also the clatter of traffic. The sound of a siren reverberating from an ambulance on its way to Mercy Hospital disappears into the rumble of Eunice's washing machine behind us as she begins her story.

"I was born up near Hopkins Hospital, and after that my mother moved into public housing—always lived in this vicinity." Eunice appears to be relaxed sitting in her kitchen with her fingers laced together on the table, but her voice has become raspy like she is catching a cold.

"It was neat back then because everybody helped one another, and you didn't have to worry about your door being broken into, stuff like that."

"You mean, you left things unlocked?" This was hard to imagine even back in the forties.

"Right. And like, when my mom got sick, we didn't have to worry because the whole neighborhood would come in and help out. I was a kid and didn't know what to do, so the neighbors got her to the hospital. I didn't have to worry about clothes either, because the neighbors would do the wash and cook the food and if I needed my hair fixed up, it was the oldest girl in the family would do my hair and take me to school.

"So the Eastside was good?" I ask, smiling. "Because Westsiders tell me how bad it is here."

"It's a big battle," Eunice laughs. "Because the Westside says the Eastside is bad, and the Eastside says the Westside is bad. So it's like a war between the two sides."

"I always hear that."

"But things were great on the Eastside for a period of time," Eunice explains, "until, you know, as the years changed and generations changed, then things got *crazy*! 'Specially when the drug scene hit in the eighties."

"Were your kids young then?"

"Yes. And that was that bad part, the drugs. It got to the point you didn't know whether you could go out of your apartment or if you could come back home because things were so bad."

Crack cocaine hit the streets on a large scale by the mid-eighties and proliferated in the poorer communities that were suffering from economic collapse.[2] Blue collar factory jobs, that once had been plentiful, had begun to disappear because of increased technology and the relocation of manufacturing to third world countries. The impact of this industrial shift was felt most strongly among Blacks, because the majority lacked college educations or had previously attended racially segregated and underfunded schools that left them ill equipped to adapt to changes in the economy.[3] As a result, the employment rate for Black men dropped from seventy to twenty-eight percent by 1989.[4] The decline in legitimate employment opportunities increased incentives to sell drugs, and that led to a spike in crime and violence.[5]

In the same decade, Reagan dramatically escalated Nixon's *War on Drugs* campaign even though, by 1979, illicit drug use had been falling[6] and less than two percent of the American public considered drugs to be

---

2. "Illicit Drugs: A Complete History of Crack Cocaine."
3. William Julius Wilson, *When Work Disappears: The World of the New Urban Poor.*
4. John D. Kasarda, "Urban Industrial Transition and the Underclass," 26–47.
5. Michelle Alexander, *The New Jim Crow: Mass Incarceration in the Age of Colorblindness*, 51.
6. National Research Council, "The Underlying Causes of Rising Incarceration: Crime, Politics, and Social Change," 120.

the most important issue facing the nation.[7] In what could arguably be viewed as a deliberate strategy to reach out to White American voters who were motivated by anti-Black sentiment,[8] Reagan framed drug addiction as a moral failing rather than a medical or social issue, and he began a media offensive with a weekly radio address and Nancy Reagan spearheading the *Just Say No* program. Reagan's skillful antidrug rhetoric and anecdotes of undeserving "crack whores" and "crack babies," who would be on government assistance for life, tapped into deeply-held cultural attitudes about illicit behavior among people of color.[9] By 1984, public opinion had shifted along with bipartisan support of his campaign, resulting in an increase of antidrug funding to federal agencies such as the FBI whose budget soared from eight to ninety-five million dollars within a few years. In contrast, funding for agencies responsible for drug treatment, prevention, and education was dramatically reduced.[10] New laws, such as the Anti-Drug Abuse Acts of 1986 and 1988, criminalized even low-level drug offenses and enacted mandatory minimum sentences for drug violations. This legislation resulted in historically unprecedented rates of imprisonment where, by 1997, nearly two-thirds of all federal inmates were drug abuse offenders, and three-quarters of those were African American or Hispanic.[11]

Eunice describes Baltimore city's response to her drug-ridden neighborhood as, "*kind of* a solution but not very much." She says, "We had six high rise buildings over here in Lafayette Courts, and the rest were low. The plan was, first, just to get rid of all the high rises, but then they said, no, if you're going to take 'em down, take 'em all. So they did."

The Lafayette Courts, where Eunice lived for thirty years, were built in 1954 as a solution to the overcrowded "Negro problem" and were considered to be one of Baltimore's largest housing projects. They were comprised of six high rises and fourteen single-story buildings.[12] Residents remember good times when the Courts were "lovely with modern fixtures and clean apartments that were safe enough for neighbors to leave their

---

7. "What do Drugs have to do with Mass Incarceration?"
8. "Race in The Reagan Era."
9. Kenneth B. Nunn, "Race, Crime and the Pool of Surplus Criminality: Or Why the 'War on Drugs' Was a 'War on Blacks,'" 386–91.
10. "What do Drugs have to do with Mass Incarceration?"
11. Christopher Mumola and Jennifer Karberg, "Drug Use and Dependence, State and Federal Prisoners."
12. Alexander von Hoffman, "Enter the Housing Industry, Stage Right: A Working Paper on the History of Housing Policy," 3.

doors unlocked."[13] But three decades later, the high rises had become a "filthy place where people were prisoners in their own homes with broken elevators and trash-strewn grounds patrolled by drug dealers."[14] One tenant recalls, "When I was twelve, I walked into the Rec Center and saw a guy beaten to death with a bat. I will never forget that. Another time a guy got stabbed with an ice pick."[15]

By 1999, the city opted to demolish Lafayette Courts to make way for the row home style housing where Eunice lives now. She remembers standing nearby watching the implosion. "It was a happy event," Eunice tells me. "They were gone in two minutes. And when we first moved into the new apartments, boy! You're talking about happy people! We were some happy people! It was like I got baptized all over again because everything was fresh and brand new and white and smelling good. Over the years it's kind of dwindled a little bit, not too far down, but it's come down some. As they say, good things don't last forever. But we do our best to keep it up so they don't tell us we're going to throw you somewhere else again."

Eunice's voice has become hoarse. She begins to speak in short sentences, probably to give her vocal chords a rest. "But being a single parent—and raising children by yourself—it was rough then."

"Then, do you have more kids besides your son?"

"Four kids."

"And you've always been a single parent?"

"Mmm hmm."

"So you—did you work?"

"Couldn't. Couldn't."

"Couldn't work because of your kids?"

"I tried to, but I always got in trouble."

"In trouble?" I wonder what kind of trouble Eunice means. Trouble with the law? Or does she mean trouble as *in a bind?*

"Yeah, because, somebody would snitch and tell."

"Tell what?"

"What I was doing," Eunice replies almost impatiently. "So I had to either quit or they'd take my kids away. So I quit. I didn't want them to do that! Lots of us did sneaky stuff to try and make it work—to make ends meet."

---

13. JoAnna Daemmrich, "Lafayette Courts Ends in Twenty Seconds of Explosions, Cheers, Tears."

14. Daemmrich.

15. Michael James, "Lafayette Courts: Forty Years from High Hopes to Oblivion."

"Like steal things?" I blurt out the first thing that comes to my mind based on scanty information.

"No! No, no, no—we didn't steal."

"Selling things?" I meant "illegal things" but this time, tread carefully so as not to imply misdeeds.

"No. Working, you know."

"Yes, of course."

But I do *not* know. What kind of work would warrant "them" taking away Eunice's kids other than some kind of illegal activity or neglect? And what about this fear that seemed to loom over Baltimore's mothers that Child Protective Services would take away their children? Had it become an urban legend passed around from household to household?

But Eunice clarifies. "That social security number will kill you! That's the part that kind of got us in trouble. That social security number would tell on you. Because I volunteered at the elementary school first, then they were going to pay me. They started talking about income tax and I'm like, 'what's income tax?' Then I found out with the income tax thing I couldn't get my check."

"You mean they'd take away your welfare check because you were working?"

"Yes. And I even tried going to night school so I could get a better job but that didn't work 'cause somebody told on me for that."

"For going back to school?"

"Oh my gosh, you couldn't do nothing to help yourself—because I didn't want to stay in that situation forever. But whenever you tried to do something it worked against you. So the only thing I could do, and knew I couldn't get into trouble for, was to do childcare. So that's what I did until seven years ago."

"You took kids into your house?"

"Yes, until seven years ago."

"So, you raised other kids for a living."

"*Lots* of other kids!"

Eunice was in a situation where, living hand to mouth on government assistance, she was never able to accumulate a financial safety net. She was caught in a "trap of low assets," an economic catch-22 that perpetuates poverty.[16] The political climate of the time, characterized by Reagan's popular slogan, "government does not solve problems, it subsidizes them," did not

---

16. Mark Schreiner and Michael Sherraden, *Can The Poor Save?: Saving and Asset Building in Individual Development Accounts*.

help the working poor transition out of poverty. Reagan launched his era of New Federalism with the Omnibus Reconciliation Act of 1981,[17] a legislative move that capped welfare expenditures and transferred responsibility for underprivileged and needy families back to the states.[18] But in an ironic twist, the Act also introduced new welfare restrictions by placing maximum allowable assets for welfare eligibility at a meager one thousand dollars per family.[19] A limit that had been previously determined by the state was now in the hands of the Federal Government. In addition to the restrictions of this act, benefits that once aided the working poor such as work incentives, educational programs, and food stamps were now reduced.

"So about the time I moved out of the Courts, that's when I joined the Church," Eunice tells me, "about a year before they tore them down."

"Oh, so you've been a member for quite a while then. Had you been searching for a church?" I ask.

"Well, I went to church a lot when I was in my teens. It was right up there on Gay Street, up there near the train tracks. I liked to go and hear the choir sing. But one Sunday this lady, she was, you know, having this emotional spiritual thing. And the people around her, they was trying to get her glasses off to keep them from getting broke. So I was in front of her, and I turned to help but instead I got it across the face."

"What? She hit you in the face?"

"Yes! She wasn't fighting with me. It was this emotional spiritual thing, but I was upset with her! Then the person who was sitting next to her said, 'Honey, she just feelin' the Spirit. It's all right.'" Eunice mimics the lady, faking a high voice. "So I said, okay."

"Then it was an accident—not on purpose?" I ask.

I think so, but after church was over I was talking to a couple of guys from school. Then I look out the door, and who do I see going to the bar right across the street? It was her—the one who hit me. That really upset me. So when I got home from church my aunt said, "What's the matter? I know something's wrong." I said, "Well, this church lady supposedly had the Spirit, but when I was trying to help take off her glasses she smacked me." My aunt say, "She what?" And I said, "She supposed to be feeling the spirit, but she wasn't feeling the *right* spirit."

---

17. See "Omnibus Budget Reconciliation Act of 1981."
18. Alma Carten, "The Racist Roots of Welfare Reform."
19. Leah Hamilton, "The Forgotten 1980s Rule That's Hurting Poor Families' Savings."

She said, "What'd you mean?" I say, "because after church she went right to the bar across the street." My aunt said, "No. Mm-mmh." She said, "That's not right! You don't serve God and then go on over there and drink with the Devil! Hu-unh!"

Eunice's narration has taken on a certain amount of flair, as if she were telling a story to children. She imitates her aunt, sliding heavily into African American English like a soulful Black preacher calling out the gospel, shaking her finger in my direction.

"So, I didn't go to *that* church any more," Eunice tells me, slipping back into her raspy voice. "I tried this church and that, but it was the same old story. I didn't go to no more churches after that until later when the missionaries found me."

"Then, did you join the Church as a young mother?" I ask.

"Well, I was in my fifties," Eunice laughs.

"Oh, so your kids were all raised."

"Yeah, pretty much—" Eunice answers, her voice trailing off. Then her eyes motion upstairs to where her son is staying. We both burst out laughing, and I enjoy our shared moment when, as long-time mothers and now grandmothers, we embrace each other's maternal wisdom.

"Kids keep coming back, don't they?" I add cheerfully and tell Eunice of a proverb I had learned while living in Spain: *When kids are young they're so sweet you could just eat them. When they get older, you wished you would have.* We laugh again, exchanging insightful nods; then Eunice continues with her conversion story.

See, I had went upstairs for the night and I heard a knock on the door. It was two flights of steps, and I'm tired, so I look out the window, and I'm like, "Why didn't they come before I came upstairs?" So I talk through the window, and they asked me could they talk to me, and I told them could they come back another time. They said, "okay," but they didn't come back. So, one day I was cooking something and I forgot an ingredient, so I had to go upstairs to the bedroom to get the recipe book, but I never went back down because something on TV caught my attention. I sit there watching this good movie, and I'm like, "This is something I've never seen before." Then this lady came on for a commercial talking about the Book of Mormon. I'm like, "Huh? What's that?" Then when she put the phone number up to call she said, "If you like one of the books you call this number, and we'll see that you get one." So I said, "Why not?" A few days later I got another phone call, and they told me the missionaries will bring me the book. And you know what? It was the same two missionaries!

"You're kidding. The same exact ones?"

"Same two. They came over with the book. And I looked at them and said, 'Where you from?' One said Canada, and the other said Utah. I mean, I just knew they were from somewhere else—they didn't look like they were from here, you know?"

"You mean they just didn't have that Baltimore look?" I ask, wondering if Eunice is referring to the curious mix of White suburban naiveté and spiritual confidence that I've seen on our young missionaries' faces as they walk the streets of Baltimore.

"Yeah. They had a different thing. Something different. So I studied with them for a bit, and they left me a pamphlet." Eunice looks down at a wrinkle in her tablecloth and smoothes it out with the adeptness of a mother who has smoothed out things for decades.

> But one of the kids I was taking care of, she took it home because it had a picture of Jesus on it, and she wouldn't give it back, so I couldn't call them no more. I guess they thought I didn't want to be bothered. But one day, I saw them going to my neighbor's house across the street, so I got them back and we started all over again. See, I had a lot of questions that I didn't have answers to even though, you know, I had been going to other churches and hearing stuff on the radio and seeing stuff on the TV, but it still wasn't quite it. Questions like, *What am I going to do after it's done?* you know, because I heard people say when you're dead, that's it. When you're gone, you're gone, but it had to be something else. Because back then when you pass, they didn't discuss it. And when my mother passed—and she passed when I was very young—I asked people questions, but I got no answers. In the Mormon Church I finally found answers. So when I agreed to go, everybody was real nice. Then I got baptized and well, here I am. Never walked away from it. It will be over sixteen years now.

And every Sunday, Eunice sits in the exact same seat: second row on the left side, directly facing the bishopric. If Eunice is not in her spot, people start asking, "Where's that sister who always sits on the second row? You know, the one who always comes early. Is she sick?"

"How about your children?" I venture one last interview question. "Did they say anything about you joining the Church?"

Eunice smiles and her heavy-lidded eyes crinkle up for just a moment. "Well, they told me I was crazy," she laughs, "that the Church was a cult. They said, 'You've been brainwashed.' But I told them, well, I don't *feel* brainwashed! But it does make me feel dizzy! Dizzy to know I have answers to questions I was searching for—those questions I had for so many years."

9

Two Souls

It is a peculiar sensation, this double-consciousness, this sense of always looking at one's self through the eyes of others, of measuring one's soul by the tape of a world that looks on in amused contempt and pity. [We] ever feel [our] twoness—an American, a Negro; two souls, two thoughts, two unreconciled strivings; two warring ideals in one dark body whose dogged strength alone keeps it from being torn asunder.

(W. E. B. Dubois)

"Hi Sister Strickling, this is Tabitha. After our interview today could you help me fill out some church papers?" Tabitha was the new counselor in the women's Relief Society, and the president was out of town that week.

"Sure, I can do that."

"Also, will you be hungry when you come? I was going to prepare some food for you."

"How sweet of you. But it would be best not—with my food allergies—but I appreciate it."

"Okay then, be sure to park on the edge of the street, not in the parking lot, or they'll tow you."

"I will. See you soon."

Tabitha is a hardy woman who moves about with purpose and notable strength in her arms. "Working construction," she had explained, "you get muscles from that." Tabitha's stature, however, is misleading because of the wraps and scarves she wears on her head, and the beads, braids, and dreadlocks that are piled high above that. She has robust facial features with eyes that vacillate from defiant to tender and a mouth that is shaped in a child's pout. Tabitha is opinionated and confident one moment, then shy and thoughtful the next. Her most prominent talents are her spirited determination, her keen sense of responsibility, and her ability to take notes. At church, I don't think I have ever seen her without a ballpoint pen in her hand and a spiral notebook on her lap. One Sunday, when I asked Tabitha what she writes, she told me, "sometimes I write verbatim, but mostly I write my own words and thoughts that come to me when I hear the speakers."

Tabitha lives on the west side of the city in public housing with her elderly husband, Garlin, who converted to the Church after receiving a priesthood blessing that restored his health from a paralyzing stroke. I arrive at the neighborhood and walk through Edison Court, which is nothing more than a bare cement block with dandelions poking out through the cracks and remnants of a basketball hoop off to one side. In front of Tabitha's door is a black, weather-worn grill chained to a metal bar. Tabitha told me that once she had to leave church early because her husband, who was home sick, had called to see if she could chase away the kids who were trying to wreck the grill. At the time, a grill did not seem like an item kids would want to mess with, but now I see how it stands out like a beacon and is the only thing on any porch for as far down as I can see.

I knock hard on the door because there is no doorbell and wait for what seems like too long. I'm about ready to knock again when suddenly the door opens and Tabitha grabs me with a hug and pulls me into the tight space between the opened door and the ascending stairway. Then I follow her up the stairs, the smell of boiled meat getting stronger with each step.

Tabitha's home is only a little bigger than an efficiency apartment and neatly organized. The bathroom is directly in front of the stairs, with the door positioned in such a way that you have to wrap yourself around it in order to fit inside. A newly washed pair of jeans and a button-down shirt are dripping over the tub, hand washed and hung out to dry in the humid air. Immediately to the left of the stairs is a closed door that, Tabitha points out, is the bedroom where her husband is taking a nap. To the right, the living room, dining room, and kitchen are all in one.

"You can sit right here." Tabitha directs me to a table and chairs that are located almost in the middle of the entryway. She continues on into the kitchen, and I watch as she bustles about from stove to sink with spoon and potholder in hand, her purple muslin dress swaying around her ankles. Today her hair is wrapped in a white, twisted turban with dreads spiraling and bouncing out over the top. As I sit down, I notice a large, smiling man standing in the living room.

"This is my brother, Tim," Tabitha introduces us.

"How are you?" I get back up to shake hands. "I'm Laura."

"I was just getting ready to leave," Tim explains, holding his hat in front of him.

"Sister Strickling, is it too hot in here?" Tabitha interrupts us from the sink. "Do you need the air conditioning on?"

Before I can answer, Tim prompts me playfully, "Tell her *yes!*" and smiles as he walks toward the stairs. Even though my clothes are starting to stick to my chest with sweat, I tell Tabitha no, not wanting to be the one to run up her electric bill. Because of my answer, Tim turns to me, teasingly, "I'm mad at you then." Apparently he had been sweating too, but Tabitha reprimands him, "Don't be a baby, Timmy."

After Tim leaves and Tabitha has come back up from locking the front door, she brings me a glass of water and sits down next to me with a sheet of notebook paper, a pencil, and a wadded up paper towel in her hand. She pats her forehead with the paper towel then smoothes it out in front of her.

"When I was a baby," Tabitha begins, "my mom went to New York City where she worked as a maid taking care of other people's children. She sent her earnings back home to my grandparents. I stayed with my grandparents until I was two, then my mom moved to Baltimore and brought me with her. I was raised here on the Westside."

"And did you have brothers and sisters besides Tim?" I ask.

"Yes, it's seven of us, three girls and four boys. It was just my mom and us—because my father and mom was never—" Tabitha pauses, "they weren't married. But later she married my stepfather," Tabitha adds. Tabitha speaks cautiously, and I wonder if she thinks I might look down on her mother for having children out of wedlock.

"We was raised in the Baptist Church, so we had religion in our lives. I remember my mom praying every morning when we get up. All of us get around the cocktail table, and Mama had the Bible, and she read from it. We went to church five days a week."

"Wow! That's a lot of church!" I exclaim. "I didn't know they offered that much in a week."

"Well, Mommy wanted us to behave so we went to different church services. She always disciplined us. I remember an incident when a Social Service lady came to our house—this was before my stepfather came into our life." Tabitha smoothes out the paper towel in her hand as if petting a cat.

"And because my mom was getting some benefits—see, she used to go and clean houses and stuff for other people, because my mother never even went to third grade. But if you spoke with her, you would think that she had a education because she had knowledge—knowledge of people. She was very good with that. And the kids, we took care of everything else as far as what she needed. By the time I got to kindergarten I was already reading and writing, so what I learned I brought home and taught my mom."

"And so what did the Social Service lady do?" I ask as Tabitha takes a drink and wipes the corners of her mouth with her paper towel. I wipe the sweat from my face with the back of my hand.

> So when the Social Service lady came to see her, she said, "I thought you said you had seven kids." My mom said, "I do." The Social Service lady said, "Well, I don't hear them." My mom said, "Because they know better. I have company and they are not supposed to make noise." Well the lady said, "I don't believe you." And I heard the lady talking, and we back there and we're like, "She think Mama ain't got no kids," you know, like that. "We her children back here, talking about she saying, we ain't got no kids." And we heard Mommy say, "Come here let me show you." And we saying, "Watch, mama goin' bring her back here, let her look at us. We goin' look at her *real hard* cause she want to know somethin'." So she come back there, and she peeked in. "Oh, yes you do," the lady said, "They all sitting in the room, sitting on the floor, and on the chair watching television—not making no noise."

"Well, I would have liked to seen that," I laugh, doubting that my four kids, and certainly not my grandchildren, would have been so well behaved.

"Yeah. So see, Mommy really disciplined us, but she was always giving too. I remember one time, see the neighbor kids would come in and we'd be getting ready to eat. She'd say, 'Are you hungry? Do you want something?'" Tabitha makes her voice sweet, imitating her mother.

> But one day I heard that a neighbor boy talk about my mom. He didn't know I was coming around the corner, and they was discussing my mom, "Miss Loretty, she think her kids are White. She always havin' 'em come in the house a certain time, and they always be all clean and stuff." And I'm saying to myself, "We always be clean? I thought we supposed to be clean." That's what I'm saying to myself, and I'm thinking, "You sitting up there talking, coming around all the time, coming 'round dinner time." And my mom fed the whole family *all* the time—it's a whole family! So I told my mother about it, and she said like this, "Don't worry about that. That doesn't hurt me—don't even worry about that. When people talk about you they don't have nothing else to do but talk, so you must be a very important person." She was trying to make me feel better, you know.

The young boy who had ridiculed Tabitha's mother for "acting White" had tapped into a name-calling phenomenon that disparages others for betraying their race either by engaging in behaviors perceived to be characteristic of White society or succumbing to White expectations.[1] While this boy had interpreted attentive mothering as a White attribute, a more common practice has been to scorn academic pursuits.[2] Barack Obama emphasized the negative ramifications of this practice in his Senate campaign speech when he said, "We need to eradicate the slander that says a Black youth with a book is acting White."[3]

There is ample debate as to the origin and implications of the "acting White" slur. Some scholars trace the phenomenon to pre-enslavement times, where education and literacy were the province of White people and when Blacks were denied education. Black folk who were literate were not only perceived as "acting White" but also a threat to the White power structure.[4]

The "acting White" slur has also been explained as the result of an oppositional identity formation in regards to the social, economic, and political subordination that Black Americans have encountered in White society. The pejorative label is viewed as a protective device aimed at promoting Black identity, because it sustains boundaries between Blacks and the dominant White culture.[5]

A similar but more complex explanation is that the "acting White" phenomenon is one phase in a progression of Black racial identity in America. The first is the *pre-encounter stage* that most often takes place during childhood. It represents a Eurocentric view where pro-White attitudes are adopted and the significance of one's blackness is not recognized. The *encounter stage* is a transition where individuals realize they cannot fully be accepted into White society. What follows is the *immersion stage* characterized as a reactionary response to previously held views of self. Here individuals become more interested in their own blackness and awareness of racism increases. Attitudes might become anti-White, and the term "acting White" can become a significant oppositional identity marker. *Internalization* is the final phase where people achieve security

---

1. Roland Fryer, "Acting White: The Social Price Paid by the Best and Brightest Minority Students."
2. Sheryll Cashin, *Place, not Race: A New Vision of Opportunity in America*, 31.
3. Barack Obama, "Transcript: Illinois Senate Candidate Barack Obama."
4. Ron Christie, *Acting White: The Curious History of a Racial Slur*.
5. Signithia Fordham and John U. Ogbu, "Black Students' School Success: Coping With the Burden of 'Acting White,'" 176–206.

with their Black identity and move towards a pluralistic perspective where attitudes are no longer anti-White.[6]

"Were the schools segregated then?" I ask Tabitha, attempting to understand the racial dynamic of her childhood.

"No. Well, not at first. In the beginning, in elementary school, it was integrated. We had um, uh . . . Caucasian students there—and we got along fairly well."

I cannot help but notice Tabitha's grappling with what to call a White person. I respond with a smile but only because I am puzzled at her hesitancy. "That's when I start to realize—" Tabitha continues slowly. "See, me and the kids had fun but when the parents came in and saw who their children was playing with—then I felt hurt because I didn't understand."

"They didn't want their kids playing with you?"

"Right, so—"

"So this was the first time—?"

"My first realization of a separation, because I didn't see it like that. Because my mom always taught us, she said, 'God made all different flowers in the fields and people are the same way inside. There are different people just like the field of flowers.' That's what she said. But then she had to explain to me the segregation part which I couldn't understand. And then because we was getting more of, of . . . of *me* in the area—" Tabitha interrupts her story with a stiff laugh and I add my edgy laugh to hers. She is now attempting to avoid the term Black—or *any* racial label for that matter, using her image as proxy for words. "A lot of other people were taking their kids out of the school because more people, like . . . like, *me*— was moving into the neighborhood and it was getting—" Tabitha pauses.

"—So, White Flight?" I edge in on Tabitha's hesitation because I feel like she is skirting the issue of racism. And I am certain it is because of me, a White woman sitting at her kitchen table. Thinking back, my spur-of-the-moment rationalization was to see if I could make myself less racially threatening by being forthright, because I thought, if so, then maybe Tabitha would speak more freely herself. So I laid, "White Flight" on the table as an offering, as evidence that I am familiar with Black and White racial issues, and that I am willing to be frank about them.

"Yes, right," Tabitha agrees, and I feel like we have taken a step closer toward mutual understanding. "Yeah. So it was getting more populated. I had two very good Caucasian friends. When we was painting and doing

---

6. Vinay Harpalani, "What Does 'Acting White' Really Mean? Racial Identity Formation and Academic Achievement Among Black Youth."

math together we always used to collaborate. So I felt hurt when they left, you know? It's like, what's wrong with me?" Sweating, Tabitha wipes the corners of her mouth. I feel sweat drip all the way down my chest to my legs. I'm starting to regret that I did not accept the air conditioning that Tabitha had offered.

"So mom explained it. She said some people, they feel different about you, but you're not supposed to feel different about other people. Because God made us that way. And she'd talk about the flowers and the field again. She'd say it's okay to talk to other people but not hold them as—" Tabitha searches for the word, "you know the separating or hate thing." Tabitha takes a breath. "Sorry, I'm really sweating," she apologizes as she wipes her head with a paper towel before continuing. "Because my sister, she just—" Tabitha pauses again.

"—hates White people?" In a moment of overzealous confidence, I complete Tabitha's sentence. But then I soften it, "—doesn't like them?"

"Yeah. Yes, that's it."

But just when I decide that Tabitha and I have reached a plateau of conversational comfort, Tabitha suddenly changes the subject. "Let me tell you a story about my name." And she talks about the spelling of her name, how she wanted all A's in her name so she could spell it T-A-B-A-T-H-A, instead of the I.

In retrospect, when I look back at this conversation, I see that Tabitha and I were both struggling—struggling because we were trying to cut our way through a dense social jungle overrun with decades of racially troubled history. Instead of freeing ourselves, we found that we had become entangled, and we did not have the communicative tools to clear the ground and forge a linguistic path where we could both walk. I wondered if, sitting next to Tabitha at the kitchen table, I represented the whole White race and the White people who had abandoned her in her childhood. I wondered if I was emanating "whiteness" in a way that caused distress and, if so, how could I make myself less White? Was I, like W. E. B. Du Bois had explained in *The Souls of Black Folk*, provoking a double consciousness between "two souls, two thoughts, two unreconciled stirrings," one soul of African descent living in a White normative society, and the other, an esteemed American? And because it is impossible to "serve two masters," the African American must continuously trade identities, subduing one while the other dominates, otherwise the "two warring ideals [would be] torn asunder."[7] I wondered if my White presence had brought both souls to the forefront, head to head, deadlocked in a battle for sovereignty.

Or was Tabitha, like Toni Morrison, courageously trying to avoid the "racially informed determined chains" of language that would reinscribe racist thought?[8] Had she sensed that the words available to us were inadequate; that they did not define the essence of who the two of us were?

After that, I decided to move to a safer topic and ask Tabitha to tell me her conversion story. The ease in her voice returns, and the Church becomes our haven. "My mom had met the elders," Tabitha begins. "Mommy was sitting outside on the steps, and they was walking in the area during that time up on McCullah. At the time, I was taking care of my mother who had a stroke, going to school and working part time, and taking care of my son."

"I didn't know you had a son, Tabitha."

"Well, when I got pregnant," Tabitha confides, "I really wasn't ready for it, but I guess had to be ready. I had to grow up because I had made—like they say—choices, so I had to deal with it."

"And was there a father to help?"

"Yeah, there's a father, but he was around only for a while. He was seven years older than me, in the army." Tabitha takes a deep breath and pauses. "My mom never waivered, never fussed at me, never made me feel bad. When I got pregnant she was happy. She showed me no type of scorn or anything. She knew who the father was 'cause I wasn't outgoing like that. I run into somebody, I stick with them. He was actually my first boyfriend, so you know, and he was seven years older than me." Tabitha repeats the age of her son's father, emphasizing her youth.

"I was eighteen when I met him; I got pregnant when I was nineteen; I had my son when I was twenty years old. At that time I was going to the Baptist church, and the people there treated me in a nice way, and it was great. Then after I had the baby and everything, their whole mentality and temperament was totally different. I didn't appreciate that. It's like, they see you at church and give you a hug, then they see you on the street and not speak to you, they just there walking with their head up, and that was hurtful." Tabitha has a pencil in her hand and is scribbling on her notebook paper.

"They were the kind of people that throw stones living in their glass house," she pauses, "I was very, very hurt. But my mother always told me

---

7. W.E.B. Du Bois, *The Souls of Black Folk*, 3.
8. Toni Morrison, *Playing In the Dark: Whiteness and Literary Imagination*, ix.

that God never changes. He remains the same and keeps his promises. So the real thing I got from the Latter-day Saints after I was baptized was, I felt more whole. I felt peace. I felt calmness."

"But tell me from the beginning Tabitha, about your conversion," I urge, wanting to hear the whole story.

"Okay," Tabitha's voice is bright. "So on this particular day I'm coming home and yell, 'Hey Mommy, Mommy,' you know, so she know I'm coming in." Tabitha laughs and puts her pencil down on the table.

> But my mom, she was sitting there quiet with these two boys, and I'm like, "Oh, so sorry," And she's like, "Just come on, come on in here." She said, "These are the elders." And I shake hands with them. Then I'm getting ready to go, but my mom says, she says, "Come on Girl, will you sit down. You sit right here and listen to this. Listen to this for me." So I said, "Yes ma'am." And I just sit right on down. Some of the things I was hearing was sounding right, you know? Sometimes when you hear things, you feel things that are right. Because I have been a Jehovah Witness, I was studying to be an Israelite, a little bit of Islamic faith, and I was born a Baptist. So I had four religions already under my belt. I did a lot of studying on those religions, but drifting from one place to another was telling me that they didn't quite feel right. It wasn't real. So I got baptized a Latter-day Saint a year after my mom. And I must have needed a real good washing, because it took three times to get me baptized. One little plait of hair kept sticking up. But when I came up and opened my eyes, I look and everything was real and bright, really clean you know, and everybody had a glow around them. It was like, the people were just more beautiful. It was so peaceful and good. You get a glee in your heart, and your heart be happy. And when I got confirmed and they put their hands on my head, I could feel myself trying to raise up in the seat. I was raising up from the seat, and it was like they was holding me down.

Tabitha is looking at her rumpled paper towel in her hand and smiling. "After baptism, I was strong—I mean, everybody have challenges—they do things. But I didn't do anything off the wall or out of the ordinary. I mean, I was chastised, me and that man back there." Tabitha points in the direction of the bedroom where Garlin is sleeping.

"What do you mean?" I ask.

"I was chastised for a while as far as, um, taking the sacrament. 'Cause we had started living together. So I was like, 'What? They punishing me like a little kid?' But we did like we was supposed to do and got married. Garlin's been a member for a year now, and we finished temple classes so we're going on to the temple."

"That's wonderful, Tabitha. You will be sealed there then."[9]

Tabitha and Garlin have great affection for each other even though they are a generation apart. Tabitha protectively holds Garlin's hand and guides his arm as he walks feebly into church; Garlin's arm is nestled around Tabitha's shoulder as they listen to the speakers.

"Do you need more water?" Tabitha gets up to refill her glass. I shake my head, and Tabitha comes back to the table with a new paper towel in her hand. "Once, I had an incident with a sister in the congregation," she tells me unexpectedly. "I heard her and some people saying some things about me—about my color—and I didn't appreciate it at all."

"What did they say?" I ask, since Tabitha had brought up the subject of race on her own, but she ignores my question.

"My mom used to say, 'Just because one monkey is acting up doesn't mean all the monkeys are acting up.' She say, 'Don't worry about it, you just worry about yourself. God will show them, and you ask God to show *them* the right way.' So I just prayed on it, and I spoke to the sister about it, but I didn't end up getting close to her." Tabitha pauses, strokes her paper towel, and adds softly, "My heart is a fragile thing."

I look across the table at Tabitha, her mouth pursed into a delicate pout and see a kindhearted woman who wears defiance like a shield to protect her from emotional harm. During those tender years as a little girl growing up in a racialized city, she had been searching for her identity and had trusted with an open heart. Like a butterfly dancing from flower to flower in her mother's field, she had expected fragrance and nectar but had been offered gall instead. Her mother had tried to sweeten the bitterness, but it had been too strong.

As I get ready to go, I gather up not only my recorder and purse but also the weight of my thoughts. Tabitha gives me one last hug, then instructs me, "Now when you get home today call me so I know you are safe—just say, 'Hi Tabitha, I'm home.' That's all."

---

9. Sealing is a temple ordinance typically performed as marriages or as children sealed to parents to bind families together in mortality and after death.

10

The Healing Hands of Sister Clara Haynes

When I first became acquainted with Sister Clara Haynes, she was the Sunday school class president and a soprano in the choir who sang the melody an octave lower than the other women. She had a deep voice that could project across the room when praying, and a slow, heavy laugh that turned into a raspy cough when amused; but I did not think of Clara as a loud woman. Her soft frame moved heavily through the church halls as she nursed an arthritic knee, with her skirt tucked high above her waist to meet her chest. She often wore tennis shoes with white rolled-down socks and a large pair of glasses that engulfed her tired eyes and eclipsed her delicate pearl earrings. Clara's smile was slow and careful with an under bite and not many teeth, and only rarely did she look me in the eye when speaking.

At one time, I had wondered if Clara was bearing the effects of chemotherapy because she was almost bald. But over the months I began to realize that she shaved her head on purpose. This was before "bald and beautiful" and shaved head designs for women came into vogue, so Clara's baldness felt to me like an expression of mourning—except as Sunday school class president when Clara wore her gray felt hat and metamorphosed into an administrator's role. Armed with attendance sheets and the course study guide, she masterfully began the class by introducing and remembering the name of every new visitor, then connecting the reading assignment with the most recent events in Baltimore or the declining condition of the world. With remarkable skill, she summarized the lesson at the end of class explaining what she had learned, then prompted the closing prayer without going a minute overtime. Sister Clara Haynes transitioned us expertly into Sunday school and out again as we made our way to the third-hour meeting.

When I asked Clara if she wanted to record her conversion story she was willing, but did not want me to come to her house for the interview. "I have snoopy neighbors," she had said. "They're always watching, and they'll make a fuss." Then she had explained further, "but God lets me know what they're doing—if they're talking about me, raging about me, this and that. He lets me know when its violence in the neighborhood and when I should stay home, because I'm single and I need his spirit." We decided to meet right after our Sunday meetings.

The cold, grey weather had crept into the church building, so Clara and I sit together in a spare classroom facing each other with coats on. Clara pulls out pictures of her children and grandchildren, and I admire their smiles. "I used to take the kids and drive into the White neighborhoods. It was so uplifting seeing that pretty grass, seeing the yellow flowers. I wanted them out of the city because the city is full of addictions," Clara explains, speaking methodically with heaviness in her voice. "I used to take them out swimming. And horseback riding. Soccer. Sports and things. I just love Catonsville area. I always wanted to move out there after I got my degree. But, I didn't know then the plans God had for me."

Clara takes off her wool hat exposing her bare head and sets it next to the photographs. I notice that she is wearing dainty rhinestone earrings and the fragrance of baby powder. "How about when you were young?" I ask. "Where did you live?"

"I was raised up on the west side of Baltimore."

"Really? I thought the Westside was pretty bad," I ask. Clara's tendency to avoid eye contact leaves me searching for a way to connect, so I jump at the chance to talk about Baltimore.

"The Eastside is more rough—more vicious," Clara tells me. "I remember in elementary school when the word was put out about the gangs that was coming from East Baltimore, coming to the elementary schools beating up the children. It was fearful."

"What would make the East more vicious than the West?" I ask, always interested in how East and Westside residents view each other.

"I don't know. Maybe the culture, the mindset. Maybe the environment of criminal activity," Clara offers, this time looking at me, but I can't see her eyes because her glasses have taken on a reddish tint, reflecting the overhead light.

"Well, tell me more about what it was like growing up on the west side," I nudge her story along.

> Well, I reckon it was a lot of addictions. Addictions to alcoholism in the community. And in the family as well. It was drinking, a lot of drinking. My mom, my brothers, my sister. My grandmother died of alcoholism, abandoned my mom when she was five, so my mom was pawned around to different relatives. There's a lot of—the word they use today—dysfunction, dysfunction in the family. But school was good. I remember winning a lot of spelling bee contests there. I remember a lot

of sad times too because things weren't good at home. I remember that a lot, but school was good. I was an honor roll success student.

Clara pauses again as if rummaging through her memories is an exhausting task. Her eyes becoming cloudy, so I resist the temptation to ask more questions.

"Yes, not all bad, there was good things. My mom was an excellent cook, she was somewhat of a homemaker. She did work—she did, what do you call it? I can't think of the word they used then—cleaning people's houses."

"Domestic?"

"Domestic, yes. She used to clean for one of the Colts—football players. Can't remember which one. When I was born they offered to take her to Florida. But she denied the offer."

"So they liked her work?

"They liked her because she could cook. She was an excellent baker."

In the 1950s when Clara was born, the Colts were based in Baltimore and were named after the region's history of horse breeding and racing. At the time, the Colts had three Black players, and George Taliaferro—the first Black player to be drafted by an NFL team—was among them. One evening after training, Taliaferro walked into the hotel where the Colts were staying to pick up the key to his room but found that he and his Black teammates had been rebooked to a "Coloreds Only" hotel. After the incident, he refused to play at the next exhibition game until Rosenbloom, the owner of the team, offered him a substantial amount of money. Taliaferro's response had been, "discrimination is expensive."

"I don't know how exciting my story is," Clara tells me. Her comment is more like a statement of fact than an indirect request for encouragement. Nevertheless, I smile and hope it is reassuring as I look at Clara's sturdy hands resting on the table and her plaid watchband buckled tightly around her wrist.

> I was always staying inside and reading the Bible. I would tell God when I didn't understand what I'm reading, but I felt compelled that I had to read it. Somehow I felt compelled. I would make myself read the Bible before I went to bed. I felt there was a presence there with me. Now I understand why, because of what I've come through. I've learned that through addictions, that somehow your partner knows what your behavior will be capable of, of feeding into their addictions. They can pick you out. I've been told that. It's like you're wearing neon lights.

"So, you're talking about relationships?"

"Marriage. I'm talking about marriage. Twenty-two years."

"You were married twenty-two years?" I'm not sure why this fact surprised me. Perhaps it was hard for me to imagine Clara in a close relationship because I had always seen her alone. I had never seen her huddled in the hall engaged in a lighthearted chat with Relief Society sisters or playfully gathering children around her like some of the other women in the congregation. She was serious, apologetic, and tearful when speaking in church, and I imagined this to be her demeanor in every aspect of her life.

"I married my ex when I was eighteen. When you're living with addiction it takes a lot from you. He was an alcoholic. Took all the kids' education money and left me for someone younger." Clara's voice has become like a rehearsed script, as if she were playing the part of a character in a play.

Because, that day there was something in my ex's behavior, and I said, "He's going to pick up the drink again." But I had to work that weekend, so I knew I had to make arrangements to get my kids out of harm's way. I tried to take them to that facility—you know where they take you in for domestic violence? But they wouldn't take us because my ex wasn't physically hurting us yet. So, I had to make another plan to get my children out. It was Labor Day weekend when he picked up the drink. I could just feel it. I knew it was coming.

After that, I became obsessed with the crisis, obsessed with—I got to hold onto the bill money, obsessed with him. My world was around him. I was in a place that I didn't know where nothing was coming from. I was taking college classes and the taxes were due, gas and electric bill, telephone bill, food, the children was running amuck you know, because their dad had left—it was all on my shoulders. And I thought, "You've got to get back to who you were." I mean, at that point, I didn't know even what my favorite thing was anymore. So, I remember going to the basement and getting down on my knees to pray. Taking off all my clothes and talking to God. And God told me, "Because of the violence in the city I need you to stop the cycle, Clara. I *need you to stop the cycle*. Let him go. Let him go." So I did. I humbled. I surrendered. I surrendered to God.

Clara catches her breath and her eyes start to water. I too, am holding back tears as I imagine the heart-rending intensity of the scene: Clara in the basement, desperate, bare, and pleading to God. Instead of looking into Clara's eyes, I look at the ruby rhinestone butterfly pin that she has attached to the white embroidered flowers on the pocket of her blouse. I let my mind wander in order to regain composure and offer Clara emotional space. *Butterflies Are Free,* the Seventies movie featuring Goldie Hawn, comes to my mind—a story where a blind man moves into his own apartment to get away from his overprotective mother. And Elton John's "Someone Saved My Life Tonight": "Sweet freedom whispered in my ear. You're a butterfly and butterflies are free to fly."

I can feel the density of Clara's lungs expanding and contracting, but she manages to breathe through it and continue. "You can be permanently scarred from verbal abuse. It's just as worse as being slapped."

"Yes, yes it is," I reply, grateful to be connected with Clara again.

"Apparently he'd been planning to leave anyway, found someone younger, already had home set up." Clara looks down at the photographs of her children.

> Sometimes you live, not by minutes but by seconds. But the healing did begin. The Latter-day Saint Church stepped in for me. And when I had nothing, because the front steps was broken and I needed new doors and the kitchen ceiling had fallen down and sixteen years of taxes due—I just kept going to church and Al-Anon meetings because I was being fed positive things. There is a spirit of positivity here at church. It's a different dimension. People prosper here—not with money but with learning, with education. So I came here, and I learned God in a different way. I lived with no heat for six years and when it was just about to end with bankruptcy and the company was about to take my property, the lawyer said, "We're trying to figure out what we can do." I got the house refinanced and the taxes was paid off and got some things fixed. I've seen the miracle that can come from surrendering and letting go. I've learned that.

I had never been inside Clara's house, because ever since I had known her, she had been taking care of her aging mother and spent most of her time there. "My mother won't let me leave the house much," she had explained. "Sometimes she won't even let me take naps." So, last Christmas we organized a group of Relief Society sisters to go to Clara's house to sing carols for her.

Clara had been waiting for us at the door, and she led us into a living room that was dark and overstuffed with knick-knacks and the unhealthy smell of cigarettes that had been permanently absorbed into the flaking wallpaper. We then made our way, single file, up the narrow stairs, following Clara and stepping over sunken holes in the floor board. We clustered around Clara's bedridden mother with hardly an inch to spare and sang "Oh Come all Ye Faithful" and a two-part version of "Silent Night." Clara was singing with us standing behind her mother next to the wall with tears streaming down her cheeks. "You will never know how much that meant to me," she told us later.

"You know, I always believed in eternal marriage," Clara tells me as we continue with the interview, "but you can't feel like you have to rescue that person or be a doormat for them. So the Church saved me. God blessed me with the Latter-day Saints and Al-Anon."

Then unexpectedly, Clara's voice brightens. "Ever watch that show, *Leave it to Beaver*? The white picket fence? With everything perfect? "

I *had* watched that 1950s show as a child, with Mrs. Cleaver and her string of pearls, and Mr. Cleaver, the breadwinner, with his briefcase and kind, fatherly manner. The show featured the misadventures of an elementary school-age boy, nicknamed "The Beaver," and his responsible older brother, Wally. Every youthful blunder turned out happy in the end thanks to White, suburban family unity and model parenting.

"That's a great blessing to kids—that kind of life," Clara continues, still referring to the TV show. "I've had to learn to let my children feel the consequences of their choices, like in that show—can't be over-enabling or overprotective."

It seemed to me that the parenting Clara had lacked as a child, she had embraced as an adult in *Leave it to Beaver*—which has been called "one of the whitest shows of all time," and not just because it portrayed White characters, but because it represented a neatly-wrapped, naïve worldview where the lives of minorities simply did not exist. I wondered how such a show had been able to cheer Clara. How is it that she had not felt forsaken sitting in her ramshackle living room looking through the shiny, glass screen at an idealized White family? Why had she not felt bitter, sitting on the outside peering in? Just as she had found it uplifting, time and time again, to peer through the car window with her children, looking at White suburban lawns with yellow flowers—a lawn she might never have—she found hope, instead of despair.

The interview that day had not been long. In fact, afterwards, when I was driving home, I wasn't even sure if Clara had told me her conversion story. I could not remember her talking about meeting with the missionaries, or points of doctrine, or the stories of faith that might have inspired her baptism. Instead, she had spoken about her divorced husband as if he were still there, overshadowing her and depleting her life. His betrayal seemed like a permanent wound that would not heal.

I found out later, in an unexpected way, that this observation was not exactly true. If the memory of Clara's ex-husband had been a persistent part of her life, then the burden had strengthened her, not disabled her. It was two months after our interview, on an Easter Sunday, when Clara revealed her spiritual gift to me, and I began to understand.

It started with a chemotherapy treatment my dermatologist ordered, leaving my face red and swollen. My eyes were so puffy that I had turn my contact lenses sideward in order to manipulate them through oversized lids. I had an earache, my head hurt, and I was employing all possible measures—legitimate as well as home remedy—to try and heal my face enough so I could conduct the Easter choir number on Sunday. I had spent the last five days and nights with my face covered in Desitin hoping that the zinc oxide would heal my skin faster.

Miraculously, the swelling subsided Saturday night and I was able to come to our early morning practice. We were singing, "Because He Spoke to Me," one of Clara's favorite songs. In our previous rehearsals it had been difficult to get the sopranos to sing loud enough and the tenors to come in when they should. Some choir members were still not singing the right notes, and we had not yet rehearsed with the flute—so I was anxious about this much-needed practice.

That morning, Clara arrived before the other choir members and approached me at the podium. "Thank you for teaching us this song," she told me. "I *really* feel it. Like I told you before, as a child I always knew there was a higher presence with me. I feel God's presence with this song." I was preoccupied at the time and not able to take in Clara's gratitude, but after a laborious practice, I smiled for the first time when I heard Clara in the women's restroom hum the words we were about to sing, "I have been, forever changed, because He spoke to me."

As it turned out, we performed our Easter number without a flaw; the flute came in at the right time and people were on pitch. The choir members seemed happy with their performance, and I certainly was. Now I could sit back and just let my head spin like it wanted to. But as I went to sit down Clara appeared out of nowhere. "Could we meet together for ten minutes some time?"

Thinking that this must be a question about the choir, I answered, "How about now?" and followed her out the chapel door into the hall.

But when she kept on walking, I realized that she must have wanted to meet more privately. Clara led me into a classroom and closed the door.

"Can we have a prayer?" She was asking me. In the split second that I automatically said yes, I was also wondering which one of us would be praying and for what purpose. But I was not left to ponder long because Clara immediately grabbed my hands, facing me. She pulled me close and started praying out loud in a strong voice. But she had crossed her arms in front of her chest so that she was holding onto my hands, right to right and left to left. I did not hear what Clara was saying at first, because I was trying to figure out the meaning of this hand position.

She was praying for me. "Heavenly Father, thank you for Sister Strickling. She was inspired to come today. Help heal her with the treatment she is going through. Thank her Heavenly Father. **Heal** her. **Heal** her Heavenly Father."

I was taken by surprise, wondering how Clara knew about my chemo treatment and tears started to well up in my eyes. I was engulfed in a headache and Clara's words, but also cognizant that I was simultaneously resisting the intimacy of this encounter. Clara, perhaps sensing my hesitancy, pulled my head toward hers, causing us to bump together with the staccato of her prayer. Her hands would shake like she was playing the maracas as she held on to mine, so I was pulled into the rhythm of her voice, my hands shaking too.

"Thank you for *inspiring* me to come this *morn-ing*. Thank you for the *mu-sic*. I saw Sister Strickling, and I could *see* her humbleness. I could *see* her humbleness. I could *see* her humbleness. Her *hu-mil-i-*ty." There was even rhythm in her pauses. She was getting louder, more confident. "Let Sister Strickling know that *you will* be with her. I've been praying for her, but I *need* to pray for her *now*."

Like grains of sand slipping through an hourglass, I could feel myself letting go, falling into her soulful melody. Clara was accelerating now. "I am **thankful** and grateful, **thankful** and grateful, **thankful** and grateful that Sister Strickling came **here** to be with us—that she **came-here**-to-be-with-us!"

Came here to be with us? What did that mean? The phrase lingered in my mind. Perhaps it was because I was new to Baltimore, to this city. Or was it because I was a White sister, an outsider to the Black community? But Clara was not rejecting me, she was pulling me in, pulling me into her life with the ebb and surge of her impromptu refrain. I could feel Clara's spiritual energy, her warm, billowy body, and her wholeness. This time I surrendered and let go completely.

Then it was over. Clara said, "Amen," pulled me closer and hugged me. For a finale, she patted my back. "Thank you Sister Haynes." That was the best I could do. Besides I wasn't even sure how to transition out of a cross-handed prayer. But I did not need to worry because Clara was on her way.

"There's somebody else I need to go to today," she said as she picked up her oversized purse and stepped out into the hall. I turned the opposite way toward the bathroom, still reeling from her rhythms. I needed a moment alone in the women's stalls to take in what had just happened. Standing next to the toilet, I took a deep breath and pondered Sister Clara Haynes.

I believe I had not understood the gift of healing until that day—at least not how the gift is shaped and expressed by the one who owns it. It had not been a physician or an experienced church leader who had succored me, but rather a woman with a wounded soul. It had been a woman who had been rejected and had felt the brokenhearted anguish of betrayal, who opened her heart to mine with unquestionable trust. It was from a woman who had been born into the bondage of addiction who called upon God, with her breath of faith, to offer me emotional freedom.

Now, when I think of healers, I see Sister Clara Haynes. Eclipsed in a congregation whirling about with busy members, Clara is quietly going about her work among the sick and injured. And among the distressed, again, I see her. Clara, who is carrying much more in her hands than her organized church books and her heavy bag.

11

Pray For These Three Things

It is a hot summer afternoon and my husband and I are trying to find Sunnydale Assisted Living so we can visit Helen, but the GPS on Google Maps has led us to a subdivision west of the city limits. I double check the address and decide to try our luck at the house in front of us. Quickly, I walk across the damp, uncut grass to the front porch while my husband waits in the car for me to signal him in. At the entrance I see that the door is open, and through the screen there are regulations tacked on the wall: "Report abuse," "Thank you for not smoking," and another document with small print and a signature at the bottom. I wave to my husband as a young Black man comes to the entrance hall. He has a teenage face, purple gloved hands, and *Jasmine* tattooed up the side of his wrist. It is impossible to overlook his bright yellow golf shirt, yellow baseball cap, and friendly smile—not always the response one encounters at care facilities in Baltimore. As he opens the screen door for us to come in, I notice that his nametag says "Tiger (Ti) Johnson."

"Is Helen Sawyer here?" I ask.

"Yes, back there," he answers, pointing inside.

"I wasn't sure if this was a care facility—it looks like a house," I explain, but instead of responding, the young man turns toward the hall. I glance around, expecting the facility manager to appear, then realize that Tiger—or Ti—is in charge, so we turn to follow him through the living room.

The care facility is a ranch-style house, haphazardly furnished with no particular design in mind: beige carpets, motel-type pictures on the walls, and the un-homey smell of too many people using the bathroom without ventilation. I hear the rumble of a washing machine behind us and *The Price is Right* booming from someone's bedroom. As we round the corner, I see a wisp of a woman sitting in a straight-backed chair, peering out from a dark room. Immediately, Helen recognizes us and her face brightens. She holds out her arms as I bend down to hug her. Ti turns on the light.

The woman before me is such a painful contrast to the church sister I have known for years. Every Sunday Helen would walk through the chapel doors, sometimes late, but always in high heels or knee-high boots, hats of all colors—and different ones every week—finger nail polish the exact color of her dress, bust lifted high, and her wig styled short with reddish highlights. She wore rings on every finger except her thumbs, gold and semi-precious stones, diamonds catching the light, and her neck adorned with scarves in contrasting colors, purple with red, leopard print, and gold held together with colorful pins.

In front of me Helen sits crooked in her chair too weak to straighten herself out. Her hands, folded in her lap, bear the weight of her heavy gold rings. She wears a green headband over short, naturally-twisted hair; oxygen tubes hang from her nose. She has lost weight, and her polyester pants cling to thin legs; her sagging chest is lost among the folds of her everyday shirt. Helen's eyes droop with fatigue, but for her declining state of health I am drawn to her shining face; her ebony skin is still firm and lustrous. Apparently her skin treatment had paid off. I recall how she had pulled me aside after Sunday School just a few months ago, shooing away my husband, saying, "I need to talk to your wife, so run along. Now, I hope you don't think I'm too bold, but I was noticing your neck."

"Oh great," I had thought. I knew my neck was remarkably more wrinkled than my face. "You need to do exercises like this." Helen tensed her lower jaw: tighten, release, tighten, release. My jaw was following hers as she demonstrated the technique. "And take some olive oil and rub it on your neck at night."

"Okay. Thank you Sister Sawyer." I had decided that instead of taking offense, I would take her advice. After all, she was eighty-six years old and strikingly well-preserved. So I started rubbing olive oil on my neck at night, but never did manage to do the jaw exercises.

Helen whispers something to me, but I find it hard to understand her against the noisy oxygen machine—and because she is not wearing her upper denture. During her last hospital stay the staff had lost her teeth. She repeats more slowly, "What's happening at church?" Helen had not been to Sacrament meeting or choir practice for months.

At church, Helen did not hesitate to express her opinions and did so frequently. Newer members of the congregation—Johns Hopkins students or visitors from the West who were just passing through—might become impatient and chime in before she was done. But Helen would not let people interrupt her and ignored patronizing smiles, saying, "Let me finish please, I'm talking now." She would talk about the unfortunate side of Baltimore as if everyone understood what she meant. Not everyone did. You could bypass the homeless and street hustlers with a little foresight, avoid the boarded up row homes and mothers with bags in arm hacking rides. One could go from the Water Front Marriott, to valet parking, to the Jones Falls Expressway, and manage to exit the city unscathed from the most neglected and hopeless neighborhoods.

One Sunday, in our women's Relief Society class, Helen's comment brought to light the racialized, socioeconomic difference that existed among the church sisters. The teacher had asked for examples of how the institution of the family had been attacked in recent years and women in the room had raised their hands: "Couples are living together before marriage," "There's been a re-defining of the family" (code for same-sex couple households), "Mothers are not at home anymore." But Helen's response had reflected the reality of the city, "Mothers can't get government assistance if the father is living in the house. He has to leave in order for the mother to get food stamps and things like that, you know what I'm saying? *This*, is an attack on the family."

The teacher had wavered at what was, apparently, an unexpected response and, taking her cue, the class chatter had begun to taper off. Government welfare was an ideologically-charged topic for some, but a fact of life for others. And whether Helen's claim was accurate or not,[1] it was premised, without apology, from the position that government welfare is an acceptable economic mainstay.

The Church's stance on welfare appears to oppose this perspective. Articulated by President Heber J. Grant in his 1936 conference address and reproduced today in Church handbooks, Church welfare aims to establish "a system under which the curse of idleness would be done away with." Work, the president said, would "be re-enthroned as the ruling principle of the lives of our Church members" and would facilitate financial independence, promote thrift, and restore self-respect.[2]

President Grant issued his statement at the height of the Depression when one-sixth of the Mormons living in the Intermountain West were

---

1. "While recent fatherhood initiatives have sought to offer benefits for fathers and debunk what they claim to be a decades-old myth, welfare reform continues to marginalize fathers." Cynthia Gordy, "Welfare, Fathers and Those Persistent Myths." "Most programs in the U. S. have such low eligibility thresholds that only the poorest single mothers with children qualify. Cohabitating with a boyfriend who is not biologically related to any of the household's children is the most advantageous setup in most states. The children get the benefit of government help, but still have a second adult in the house to bring in cash." Elizabeth Stuart, "How Anti-Poverty Programs Marginalize Fathers," 3.

2. Heber J. Grant, October 2, 1836, *Report of the SemiAnnual Conference of the Church of Jesus Christ of Latterday Saints*, 3.

receiving government assistance. The increasing lack of necessities among members became a significant concern for Church leaders. They not only estimated that 15,000 would be in dire need of assistance by the coming winter, but also feared that members would become comfortable with "the dole."[3] The Church responded to this dilemma by organizing a security program based on membership tithes and fast offerings, as well as voluntary gifts of money, food, clothing, and fuel. These donations were managed by a Bishop's storehouse and were made available to every "needy and worthy Church family unable to furnish for itself."[4] But members were also admonished, if not required, to "labor with energy." Local congregations helped facilitate this mandate by organizing a work force where welfare recipients and others could help with food preservation projects, the planting of gardens, and harvesting fruit.

But Blacks living in the Eastern Seaboard were not so fortunate. At the time when President Grant was reassuring the Saints in the Salt Lake Tabernacle, Black folk looking for work were met with White protest: "No Jobs for Niggers until Every White Man Has a Job" and "Niggers, Back to the Cotton Fields—City Jobs are for White Folks."[5] In an attempt to escape destitution and increased racial violence in the South, four hundred thousand Blacks—the majority of whom were laborers or sharecroppers who had lost their livelihood to White landowners—journeyed north to cities seeking employment. However, the scarcity of jobs and discrimination left well over 50 percent unemployed.[6] Blacks became disproportionately represented in breadlines and relief centers, perpetuating White stereotyping of Blacks as inherently lazy.[7] In desperation, urban Black women would congregate at street corner "slave marts" where they would bid their housekeeping and other services to middle, and even lower class Whites, working for as little as fifteen cents an hour—or sometimes less if their employer decided to change the wage at the end of the day. These conditions produced a hopelessness that James Baldwin describes as *a labyrinth of fear*, where "[Negroes] would never defeat [their] circumstances by working and saving pennies; [they] would never, by working, acquire that many pennies, and . . . the social treatment accorded even the most successful Negroes

---

3. Grant, 2–3.

4. Grant, 3.

5. Joe W. Trotter, "African Americans, Impact of the Great Depression on," 8–17.

6. William Sundstrom, "Last Hired, First Fired? Unemployment and Urban Black Workers During the Great Depression," 415–29.

7. "Issues of Race in the 1930s."

proved that one needed, in order to be free, something more than a bank account."⁸ Poverty for the Western Saints existed temporarily within a sociality based on tenets of Christianity and equal access to work. But Black poverty in the East proceeded from decades of institutional racism.

Helen's remark in Relief Society class about fatherless homes and eligibility for government assistance spoke to Baltimore's racialized socioeconomic legacy and its vestiges that have continued today, with a Black unemployment rate that is three times higher than unemployment for Whites.⁹ The issue of who is to blame for Black poverty has been a politicized debate for decades. The "pull-yourself-up-by-your-boot-strap" camp claims that civil rights acts have eradicated institutional racism and that the roots of Black America's problems lie in the self-defeating attitudes and dysfunctional behavior of Blacks themselves.¹⁰ Social justice advocates contend that our nation has not yet eradicated racial discrimination because there is a distinct difference between the kind of government policy that is, in and of itself, racist, and policies that seek to remedy or prevent the effects of prior racism.¹¹ From this standpoint, Black people will not be able to thrive without exposing the deep-seated institutional racism that still exists, such as the decades of housing segregation that directly correlates with educational disadvantage,¹² the role of public policy in the

---

8. Baldwin describes the conditions of urban Blacks in the 1930s: "For the wages of sin were visible everywhere [in the Negro ghetto], in every wine-stained and urine-splashed hallway, in every clanging ambulance bell, in every scar on the faces of the pimps and their whores, in every helpless, newborn baby being brought into this danger, in every knife and pistol fight on the Avenue, and in every disastrous bulletin: a cousin, mother of six, suddenly gone mad, the children parcelled out here and there . . . someone's bright son blown into eternity by his own hand; another turned robber and carried off to jail. One would never defeat one's circumstances by working and saving one's pennies; one would never, by working, acquire that many pennies, and . . . the social treatment accorded even the most successful Negroes proved that one needed, in order to be free, something more than a bank account." James Baldwin, "Letter from a region in my mind."

9. Carrie Wells, "Report Highlights Economic Disparities between Races in Baltimore."

10. Tommie Shelby, *We Who Are Dark*, 5.

11. See Justice Thurgood Marshall's dissent in City of Richmond v. J. A. Croson Co., 488 U. S. 469 (1989).

12. Research from Census 2000 reveals little change in neighborhood segregation since 1980. The average Black household with an income over $60,000 lived in a neighborhood with a higher poverty rate than did the average White household

widening gap of racial wealth,[13] and U. S. prison demographics where 70 percent of those interned are African Americans and Hispanic males.[14]

Yet the relevancy of this debate is likely to be lost in Utah, because the state has been successful in relieving poverty; Salt Lake City has the highest rate of upward mobility in the nation.[15] This achievement has been attributed not only to the Church's welfare system staffed by volunteers, but also to its racial homogeneity with less than two percent of the population identifying as Black.[16] This lack of racial diversity is manifested in state meetings on economic inequality, where the topics of race and racism are nearly non-existent. "When the poor are, by and large, the same race as the richer ones, a different discussion takes place." The conversation is not so much about *victim/oppressor* or *us/them*, but instead, "one that recognizes that poor people often make choices that keep them in poverty, but also, that the constraints of poverty, including the social environment of poor neighborhoods, make it very difficult to make another choice."[17]

"Do you have any gum?" Helen asks us through her oxygen tubes. "I drink water all day, but my mouth is still dry."

My husband, who always has gum, pulls a pack from his pocket. "Here, you can have the whole thing" he says, and hands it to Helen. But even though her finger nails are long, she can not break the seal behind the Chiclets-style tablets. She fumbles with the aluminum foil. As I watch

---

earning the same. And similarly, while the average White elementary student attended a school where about 35% of classmates were eligible for the reduced-price meals program (an indicator of poverty) the average Black student attended a school where 65% of classmates were eligible. Analysis of 2010 Census shows that there has been only a slow decrease in these neighborhood statistics. See John Logan and Brian Stults, "Separate and Unequal in Suburbia."

13. The Brandeis study followed 1700 families from 1984 to 2009 and shows that the wealth gap between White and African American households has tripled and that the disparity is largely due to public policies and institutional practices. The researchers were able to statistically validate five fundamental factors that together account for two-thirds of the proportional increase in the racial wealth gap. See Thomas Shapiro, Tatjana Meschede, and Sam Osoro, "The Roots of the Widening Racial Wealth Gap: Explaining the Black-White Economic Divide."

14. "Quick Facts: Career Offender."

15. Raj Chetty, et al., "Where is the Land of Opportunity? The Geography of Intergenerational Mobility in the United States."

16. "Population Demographics for Salt Lake City, Utah in 2017, 2018."

17. Megan McArdle, "How Utah Keeps the American Dream Alive."

her fingers, I wonder if she can even chew gum without her top teeth. "We can open them all for you now so you'll have them for later," my husband says. He breaks the seal behind each piece and hands them back to her. Helen slowly, slowly, with shaking hands, lifts a piece of gum to her lips and manages to slip it into her mouth.

"I came fast into the world and I've been fast ever since," Helen had told me at the start of our interview a few months back. Sitting at the kitchen table I was taking note of Helen's faded lime-green paisley wallpaper—a pattern that had recently made its way back into popularity. The room had the feel of a second-hand store stacked with vintage novelties and everyday house wares that were significant only because, for decades, their owner had held them in her hands. Cardboard boxes of documents and photograph albums were piled high next to a jar of peanut butter, bottles of spray starch, and Windex. An unplugged microwave, toaster oven, and iron rested on top of a washing machine under lacy curtained windows, and a big, outdated TV sat on a wood utility table next to that. With so little space left, Helen had planted her exercise bike right in front of the door next to a plastic garbage pail. But what really dominated the space was a giant seventies-style, mustard-colored refrigerator peppered with fruit magnets, school pictures of great-grandchildren, and a pyramid nutrition chart. A picture of Jesus held up by a hook magnet drooped to one side.

Helen continued her story. "See, back before I was born my mother was working for a rich lady. They loved her work, but they used to get angry with her for having so many children and told her if she had another baby they were going to fire her. So she kept me close, and they didn't know she was pregnant. When she got home that night she had me. My mother had seven children in all."

It was clear that Helen had told this story before, and perhaps it had become one of those treasured narratives passed down from mother to daughter to granddaughter—and now to a church sister, a narrative that linked the maternal generations through the years. And this was a story worth retelling. In the face of inequality, Black motherhood had flouted the ultimatum of a wealthy White employer and bequeathed the newborn baby girl with her mother's defiance. Helen's mother might not have been able to change her social position, but she owned the right to be a parent.

Now, my father, he worked in a restaurant, and even though he was a waiter we ate good. On Third Street and St. Paul, Miss Polly had a restaurant, and my father would bring home all the food from there:

roast beef, Chicken-a-la-King, and all this stuff left over. My father fed the neighborhood children because things were a mess back then. Every morning they'd knock on the door, and my daddy would say, "You had your breakfast?" "No Mr. Ja—ckson," they'd reply. Then I'd say, "But daddy, that girl ran me home from school yesterday." He said, "Did she catch ya?" And I said "No," so he'd feed them anyway. And they would do the same thing the next day—run me home. They'd chase me because you see, my mother was a beautician and would do my hair up in Shirley Temple curls. And she was a seamstress too. That rich lady she worked for, she would give my mother clothes, and she'd cut them down for us. My mother always had us dressed up and starched up so the kids, they used to call me prissy. They'd run me home from school every day.

We had both laughed. "Yes, I was always running," she admitted. Helen had a tendency to speak rapidly, blurring together words and phrases into a mumble, so sometimes it was hard to understand what she was saying. Yet, it was her confidence and commanding presence that governed her storytelling. At one time, I had been afraid of her brassy confidence. I had taken Helen's frankness for aggression and her fiery spirit for anger, but that day, she seemed almost vulnerable sitting across from me with her doo-rag and kitchen apron, laughing about her childhood. I did not know then how vulnerable Helen would become.

In the care facility, Helen's room is too hot. We are sitting on the edge of her unmade bed, facing her with my feet planted firmly on the ground to keep from slipping off. My face is beading up with sweat. Ti, the caregiver, is rustling about in the hall helping a resident to the bathroom, so I make an effort not to look. He leaves the bathroom door ajar and comes into our room. "Here, let me turn on the fan," he offers. Then, with a certain amount of effort he also opens the window and a little breeze creeps in. Helen is sucking on her piece of gum.

"Remember when I was interviewing you in your kitchen?" I ask. "You were talking about how you were always in trouble as a kid."

"Yes," Helen replies without energy, and I do not detect any light of remembrance in her eyes.

"You were telling me about how in school the principal always used to have a chair for you out in the hall—a permanent chair just for you," I laugh, hoping that it will jog Helen's memory. She makes an effort to sit up straighter. "You said you had to be first in line all the time and would never be last. The kids were always moving over for you, because they knew you'd fight them if you were last." The corners of Helen's mouth lift into a vague smile. She grips her hands together tighter on her lap but then shrinks back down to a crooked position in her chair.

In our kitchen interview that day, Helen had continued talking about school. "I was in trouble a lot back then, but I graduated from high school in 1938."

"Oh, so during the Depression" I replied, thinking of my father's stories about rough times in the 1930s. "How did that time go for you then?"

Helen's laugh was almost a rebuke. "I didn't know nothing about no Depression! It's all the same for us Blacks." She dismissed the thought with a wave of her hand, reminding me how easily racial disparity can go unnoticed. "To tell the truth, I didn't know I was Black until I was fourteen. I had a job in a restaurant on Lexington Street, and when I got my first paycheck I tried to go shopping. But I found out I couldn't go into *this* store, or try on clothes in *that* store because I was Black. See, before that, my mother, she'd take us to Richmond. We'd have to sit at the back of the bus, but we could try on clothes in Richmond."

Helen's mother had taken her children to Richmond, Virginia's thriving Jackson Ward—also known as Black Wall Street, Black Mecca, and the Black Harlem of the South. Originally a German-American neighborhood, Jackson Ward became home to freed Black shop owners in the late 1700s. After the Civil War, the Black population in the district grew as segregation laws separated the races and the city's boundaries expanded. By the late 1800s, the neighborhood became a hotbed of Black entrepreneurship and a national center for Black economic and cultural activity. The community continued to flourish until the 1950s when the Ward was split to build Interstate 95.

"Now my husband, he was a macho-man." Our kitchen interview had progressed to Helen's adult life. "But he was a good husband, and I ain't never had no trouble with other women. He always worked hard, and he said many times that he didn't want to get up and go to work, but then he said, 'I know I got children to feed.' He worked hard and brought home the money, and I was extravagant and selfish at the time." Helen was twisting one of the rings on her finger as she spoke. "But now I know," she had said, "I know if I'm sick, what good is money going to do me? It don't mean nothing. Let me get well, then I can think about spending some more money." Helen had laughed at that, but then her face softened, "I hope God forgives me for my extravagance."

Helen had always been the first one up to the pulpit during Sunday testimony meetings. She would stand up, straighten her narrow skirt and start walking to the front of the chapel before the Bishop was even done announcing to the congregation that it was testimony time. Helen had her own particular style of testimony bearing. She never eased into her speech like most testifiers starting with an introduction, producing evidence, then wrapping up with a statement of belief. Instead, Helen carried on a conversation with God while the congregation was her witness.

> Heavenly Father, bless the children, because there are so many in Baltimore who are hungry and they've done nothing wrong. I just hate to see them suffer. I send money every month to sponsor a child in Africa. I know it's a small thing. Bless the prophet and the elders of the church, Elder Spencer and Ford sitting behind me today. And I hope you don't think I'm frivolous because I like to look nice. I pray Heavenly Father will forgive me. In the name of Jesus Christ, amen.

"We've had our ups and downs, me and my husband, but he always suffered me." Helen was still talking about her marriage. "My husband, he always said he's going to leave me, but he never left. My father told him when he married me, 'Now, if Helen give you some trouble you bring her back home.' After my third child my husband said, 'Mr. Jackson, can you take Helen back now?' My father said, 'No, not now—she got children!'" This time Helen's laugh ended in what sounded like a smoker's cough that left her in a sweat. She wiped her forehead with her hand. "After that, we moved to Cherry Hill. We were one of the first families to move there in the fifties."

"Cherry Hill? It seems like such a rough place now with drugs and gangs. What was it like back then?" I asked.

"Oh it was nice. We had a brand new house. I had all my children there," Helen told me, "five boys and one girl."

Cherry Hill is located at the southern tip of Baltimore and began as a housing project in 1945 for the Black World War II veterans who, like the southern Whites, had come north seeking work in shipyards and defense plants. The influx of workers during that decade had spawned a severe housing shortage that especially affected Blacks who had been confined to the densely populated and segregated city center dubbed the "Black Belt." Baltimore's City Commission declared the situation a crisis and proposed several sites for Black housing construction, but they were consistently met with White opposition: "It's all right for colored people to fight for democracy abroad, but this is not the time to try to break down [racial] barriers at home."[18] Instead of expanding land areas for Black occupancy, the city developed an urban renewal plan aimed at razing Black slums and replacing them with higher density public housing that would contain the "slum dwellers." However, this plan resulted in destroying more housing than was rebuilt, with half of the new units reserved for Whites. As a result, almost twenty-three thousand Blacks were displaced. In addition, the city ratified the passing of racially restrictive housing covenants that maintained certain neighborhoods as "Colored" and others as "White." These discriminatory housing practices prompted Civil Rights activist Clarence Mitchell Jr. and the NAACP to ask the federal urban renewal agency to withdraw federal funds from Baltimore because its "slum clearance and redevelopment program . . . places the Federal Government behind a policy of rigid segregation in the city."[19]

By 1950, the isolated Cherry Hill peninsula was proposed as a site for the construction of permanent public housing for Black people and was met with little White opposition. However, the NAACP and Urban League asserted that the site was unsuitable because it was surrounded by polluted water and would be an environmental hazard next to the city's incinerator. Under such circumstances they feared that the housing area would become a slum and that Blacks would be blamed for the outcome.

Today, Cherry Hill remains isolated and economically distressed with the highest rate of single mothers in the U. S.[20] Forty-five percent of its households are struggling with an income below the national poverty level, and the neighborhood has a crime rate that is more than twice the national average.[21]

"By the time I moved away from Cherry Hill in the Seventies," Helen continued, "all my children were grown. I moved here, to the Westside, and started to go to the AME Community Church[22] on Lafayette. I en-

---

18. "Negro Housing Foes Boo and Cheer Mayor."
19. Barbara Samuels, "Segregation and Public Housing Development in Cherry Hill and Westport: Historical Background."
20. "Cherry Hill, Baltimore."
21. "Cherry Hill: Crime Rates and Statistics."
22. The AME, or African Methodist Episcopal Church, is the oldest independent Black Protestant church in the United States, established in Philadelphia in 1787 after White church officials pulled Black worshippers off their knees while praying. Richard Allen, a former Delaware slave, gathered Black followers and successfully sued the courts in 1807 for the right to exist as an independent institution.

joyed the church service there. They did a lot of preachin' and there was a lot of nice people."

"So you were a regular church-goer?"

"Yes. My mother was a member, and I went there for years too. The thing is, after I came out of church, you know, you get on fire with the Spirit, but then, most of us would wind up at the bar across the street. And the one that halleluiah-ed the most would be at the bar first!"

Helen's boisterous laugh made me suspect that she had been one of the halleluiah-bar-goers herself. Yet, now in church, her testifying was subdued—even soft spoken.

"But then I flew to Las Vegas," she continues, speaking faster with her hands in the air.

> I flew there with some of the AME members, and enjoyed myself—had a good time drinking and gambling. But on the way back the flight captain came over the loudspeaker and said that we had to fasten our seat belts and close the bar because we had to prepare for a crash. At that moment I had a Bloody Mary in my hand, but I put the drink down. Then they gave us lessons on how to protect ourselves when we crashed. They said it was the hydraulics that was out—I had no idea what a hydraulics was. Two couples had children, and they had to take them and put them on the floor—put their feet on them to give them balance. That's when I prayed, "Oh dear God, I don't want to die. Please save me and please save the children because they are the quietest children I've ever seen. They didn't cause no one trouble." But when we got to Chicago instead of crashing, the plane went down like this, tunk, tunk, tunk—three times softly—then it stopped. And everybody ran to the terminal right to the bar. But I just sat there. God had heard my voice and took the taste of liquor from me; I had no desire to drink anymore.
>
> Then a couple of days later, I got a phone call, and these two missionaries said they were the Mormons from the Church of Jesus Christ of Latter-day Saints. They asked if I believed in Jesus Christ, and I said, "Yes, I do." They said, "Well, can we come and see you?" and I said, "Of course." When they came to my house, I asked them how they had found me and they said, "in the phone book." They just opened the book, and there was my name. I believed what they were saying, so I was baptized. That was back in 1976, and I've been at this church ever since.

"In 1976?" I asked. "So you became a member of the Church before Blacks were allowed to have the priesthood?" I perked up at this unexpected discovery. Helen was the only Black sister I had interviewed who had converted to Mormonism before the priesthood ban was lifted in 1978.

Helen was quick to answer. "Yes. We weren't allowed. The Blacks didn't have their priesthood then—not until President Kimball. He was my prophet! Yes, I loved President Kimball!"

"Then, there weren't many Blacks in the congregation I suppose?" I wondered how Helen fared in a predominately White congregation.

"I had one Black Mormon friend. We used to go downtown on Charles Street and help the homeless—feed them you know—and talk to them, but they had odors you wouldn't believe!" Helen laughed.

> But we said to each other, we are Christians, and sometimes people are in situations where they don't put themselves in it, but they get into it. And then, some be putting themselves in because they're lazy and don't want to work. So different situations you have to look at, and if you don't know, you don't judge. You do what you got to do.

But Helen's explanation had only partly answered the question on my mind. I wondered how she had reconciled joining a Church that, in the Seventies, could only offer complete salvational ordinances to White people. And how had she navigated issues of race at a time when the Church had not yet come forth to declare its conflicted racialized past?

"Helen," I asked, "What are your thoughts on why the Blacks weren't able to hold the priesthood?" I was hoping she would not gloss over the issue because I was White.

"You know," she said, "I've read books on Black Mormons, and I've thought a lot about that—because the Blacks *did* hold the priesthood for a while—until, it was the second prophet."

"Brigham Young."

"Yes, and the Blacks held the priesthood then too. Then by the third prophet they were told they couldn't hold it anymore."

"Why do you think?"

> Because I believe there was a racist thing there. Because some of those Mormons came from the South and had slaves as they moved to Utah. The White Mormons would have the slaves prepare a place for *them*, and make sure that *they* had plenty of wood to keep warm, but the Whites never worried about the slaves—where they would live. And the slaves would freeze to death sometimes because of the way they

were treated. So I believe the Mormons then mostly believed in the prophet more than Christ. If you believe in Christ then you're all one. You're all one, and you all serve together.

"So you're saying a little racism slipped in?" I had asked, but it was not so much a question as a prompt.

"Of course!" Helen had replied, as if the answer were obvious. "Because the Whites were so tied up with what was happening at the time, you know? And even though the Blacks helped build the temple—put their heart and backs into bringing rocks up—they weren't able to go in. See what I'm saying?" Helen had become animated, waving her hands with a flourish while her rings reflected the afternoon sunlight. "But what I don't understand is how the White Mormons back then would make the Blacks cook for them and whistle out loud—you know how they did—to indicate that they weren't messing with the food. You know what I'm saying? Mormons were supposed to be people who had the truth."

To this, I could only nod, looking to Helen for more insight.

"It happens today too," she continued, "but in subtle ways. Lots of people, even here, at our Baltimore church, don't like Blacks. But that's the way life is. You have to go along with the program, try your best, and ask forgiveness. We're not going to see peace until Jesus Christ comes." Helen tossed her hands in the air. "Well, all churches have their problems of people not believing in their teachings."

This was a merciful explanation from one who had experienced racism in the Church. It was also a dialectical conversation. On the one hand, racism was personal and had been a vivid part of Helen's life, yet on the other, she did not harbor resentment or seek retribution. Helen was troubled by the unchristian, racist behavior of Mormons who had espoused spiritual truth, yet she acknowledged, "That's the way life is." She had reconciled racism in the Church and the priesthood ban by conceptualizing doctrine as a separate entity existing within a larger Church organization. The doctrine of Christ was absolute, immovable, and available to all, both Black and White, but the Church organization—one that consisted of prophets, leaders, members, revelations and practices—evolved with the tide of social change, like a living organism. In the end, Helen had resolved, "You do what you got to do—as Christians. If you don't know, you don't judge."

The kitchen interview was ending. Helen smoothed out her apron then laid her hands on the table in front of me. I had not noticed her long, shapely fingers before, because I was always looking at her rings. They were the adept, expressive hands of a mature woman who had worked for decades, yet surprisingly smooth and youthful. "Well, I'm eighty-six years now, and God has been with me ever since my birth," Helen had concluded. "I was running around doing things I shouldn't be doing, and if it wasn't for the grace of God I should have been dead a long time ago." She was laughing again then added softly, "I'm just so thankful he cleansed me and gave me something to live for. You just feel the weight lift off. I want to be a good Christian so when Jesus Christ comes he will say, 'Well done my good and faithful servant.'"

I look at Helen facing me now at the Sunnydale facility and see only the remnants of a woman who was once burning with spiritual zeal and undeviating devotion. I wipe sweat from my forehead again and push myself up to keep from sliding off Helen's bed. "Close that window, I'm cold. And turn off the fan, would you?" Helen asks us loudly. I can see Ti in the hall passing by. He glances our way, and I smile back to signal that everything is fine.

"I get so cold at night. I'm always cold now." I pull the chain to stop the fan, and my husband rattles the window closed.

Helen's weak state of health reminds me of the last thing she had said in our kitchen interview. "Before I pass from this world I want to play a song for this church, play a song on the piano and sing. That's what I want to do." Helen had not yet accomplished her dream, but she had sung in the choir for as long as I could remember. She had a deep contralto voice like so many of the other older sisters in the group. She did not ornament or embellish notes but sang a plain and simple melody with a strong vibrato. At one choir practice, I was struggling to get the singers to memorize their parts to a rousing arrangement in E-minor: "Come let us go up to the mountain of the Lord." I wanted them to memorize the words and master the four-part harmony of the refrain. But the choir persisted in looking down at their music. I began to stomp my feet to the rhythm, I slapped the piano so they would look up. I bellowed out the more difficult phrases so the words would burn into their memory. I was exhausted by the end of that practice when I asked who would like to say a prayer to close the practice session. Helen had jumped up immediately without asking and started praying out loud, "Dear God, help us to learn these words. Help us to memorize the tune. Help us to *feel* it. We have to *feel* it Lord. Sister Strickling is *so into it* Lord, she is *so-o* into it. Help us to please her and please you. Amen."

It was at that moment, when Helen had said "Amen," that I began to see her in a new light. I had been intimidated by her boldness. I had judged her as too abrasive and unfeeling. I had attributed her confrontational manner to *playing-the-dozens-in-yo-face*-Black speech and left it at that.[23] I had been out of touch with her—I wasn't *feeling* her.

But I could feel Helen now at Sunnydale. I could feel her head-on approach to life, her husky voice that did not blend in a crowd, the softness of her testifying, the direct way she spoke to God, and her refusal to soft-pedal issues of race at church. But the persistent image in my mind was Helen bringing a tuna casserole to a sister who had just had her third baby. This new mother was the wife of an Oriole baseball player and Helen had brought a simple casserole to a church family who was probably wealthy enough to hire not just a cook but also a nanny for each child. "We all need the same things," she had said. "Doesn't matter who you are."

Helen leans over to me and pulls me close to her with surprising deliberation. "I'm a peeing woman," she whispers between puffs of oxygen. I look into Helen's face, not sure what she means. "I drink water all day long because of my medication, but my mouth is still dry. So I pee a lot. I wet the bed at night. I hate it."

I have to lean over more to catch what she is saying. "Pray for me," she says in my ear. "Pray for me to be able to get to the bathroom by myself. Pray for me to use my walker. Pray for me to bathe myself."

At first I am troubled by the rawness of Helen's condition, that the elegance and dignity of her life had been stripped away so abruptly here at Sunnydale. But then, almost at the same time, I am touched by the intimacy of her request, that at the most vulnerable moment of her life, she sees me as a sister and trusts my faith.

"Okay, Sister Sawyer. I will," I whisper.

"Pray for these three things."

"I will."

---

23. "Playing the dozens" is a form of ritual insulting in African American vernacular that is traditional and widespread. The linguistic sparring is also called "snaps," "talking trash," "dissing," and "busting caps."

EPILOGUE

God Reclaims with Dandelions

Before Helen died, she had written her own eulogy and had made a list of funeral plans. "So my kids won't fight," she had laughed, "because I know them." Among the plans, she had asked that I go to the mortuary and help dress her body in her burial clothes.¹ This unexpected request left me feeling painfully inadequate, yet, at the same time, loved—and in a remarkable sort of way. Helen had remembered me at a time when the substance of this life was losing significance and afflictions of the heart had begun to find rest in the next; at a time when one's heritage becomes more important than the lost cause of good health, so we cling to the hope that our life was well spent and our efforts were fruitful in our endeavors to impart wisdom to our unsettled children and grandchildren—some wandering aimlessly, others with promise, yet ignorant of the struggle that lies ahead. During the travail of her crossing this hallowed juncture, Helen had thought of me, a White sister in the gospel, to carry out one last favor. And because of this request, I could feel her even in death, that she was with me; but it was more than that—I felt that Helen was instructing me; I felt that she was teaching me the meaning of love. And I was listening because I believed the words of Lorraine Hansberry when she said, if you want to know the meaning of love and life, talk to Black people.

> [Do you want to know about] despair? Listen to . . . those who have known little else if you wish to know the resiliency of this thing . . . Of life? Ask those who have tasted of it in pieces rationed out by enemies. Love? Ask . . . those who have loved when all reason pointed to the uselessness and fool-hardiness of love. Out of the depths of pain we have thought to be our sole heritage in this world—oh, we know about love! Perhaps we shall be the teachers when it is done.²

---

1. It is common practice for Mormons who have participated in temple ordinances to be buried in their special clothing reserved for temple worship.

2. Lorraine Hansberry, *To Be Young, Gifted and Black: A Portrait of Lorraine Hansberry in Her Own Words*, 104. Hansberry (1930–1965) was author of *A Raisin in the Sun* (1959) and the first Black playwright to have a play performed on Broadway.

In Helen, and the Black Mormon women I had come to know as sisters, I saw the words of author bell hooks calling for a return of the love ethic because love "is our hope and salvation,"[3] and the fulfilling of Martin Luther King Jr.'s "double victory." Referring to the capacity of Black people to endure suffering and turn the other cheek, King said that Black folk would not only win freedom for themselves but also for White people, saying, "we will so appeal to your heart and your conscience, that we will win you in the process. And our victory will be a double victory."[4] Helen had turned the other cheek on my whiteness, on all the racialized, brutal history that my skin bore, on the privilege that it stood for—and had asked me to clothe her body, her mortal black skin, with the robes of her faith.

I thought of Helen again, after the 2015 riots had raged through the streets of Baltimore, and when our congregation had gathered for our monthly testimony meeting. I missed her because she was not there to be the first to thank God for the city's children, for our church leaders in Salt Lake City, and for safety walking the streets; but instead of Helen, Pearl's sister stood up and filled me with her prayerful declaration of faith.

> I was walking through my neighborhood where it's been collecting debris and trash, and was looking at these places that had been neglected. They were filled with dandelions and it was breathtaking! Heavenly Father reclaims his own with dandelions, and I feel that he is reclaiming me now. I have been neglected, but he has moved challenges out of my way, he is showing me love. He wants to reclaim me—just like these derelict buildings in Baltimore that he reclaims with dandelions; he reclaims me.

Growing in neglected places, despised by land and lawn owners, their seed throughout history tossed to and fro with the current of the wind until they could find a scrap of nourishing dirt, a foothold—the dandelions then strike a taproot ten inches long, strong, and practically immovable. But in this neglected place, the value of the flowers, like the disparaged of any society, grows undetected, worthless to the superstructures and institutions that are attractive but derelict of spirit and to the social architecture that casts an oppressive shadow. Nevertheless, the dandelions

---

3. bell hooks. *Salvation, Black People and Love*, xxiv. Born Gloria Jean Watkins, bell hooks has chosen the lower case pen name based on the names of her mother and grandmother to emphasize the importance of the substance of her writing as opposed to who she is.

4. Martin Luther King Jr., "Transcript of Dr. Martin Luther King's Speech at Southern Methodist University on March 17, 1966."

not only survive among the trash and debris but blossom with vigor until, with faith born of tribulation, they begin to reclaim the derelict. And like the spiritual beauty I witnessed in the lives of these Black sisters, for those who have eyes to see, it is breathtaking.

Bibliography

"2017 Baltimore City Homicides: List and Map." Baltimore City Blog. Accessed January 10, 2018, http://chamspage.blogspot.com/2017/01/2017-baltimore-city-homicides-list-and.html.

Alexander, Michelle. *The New Jim Crow: Mass Incarceration in the Age of Colorblindness.* New York: The New Press, 2012.

Allen, James B. "Would-Be Saints: West Africa Before the 1978 Priesthood Revelation." *Journal of Mormon History* 17 (1991):207–47.

Anzaldúa, Gloria. *Borderlands/La Frontera: The New Mestiza.* San Francisco: Aunt Lute Books, 1999.

Associated Press. "Fans at Orioles-Red Sox Asked to Stay in Camden Yards After Violent Protest." *USA Today*, April 25, 2015. Accessed August 17, 2018, https://www.usatoday.com/story/sports/mlb/orioles/2015/04/25/baltimore-orioles-boston-red-sox-camden-yards-freddie-gray-protest/26390977/.

Baldwin, James. "Letter From a Region in My Mind." *The New Yorker*, November 17, 1962, http://www.newyorker.com/magazine/1962/11/17/letter-from-a-region-in-my-mind.

"Baltimore Homicides." *The Baltimore Sun.* Accessed January 16, 2018, http://data.baltimoresun.com/news/police/homicides/index.php.

"Baltimore, Maryland Ordinance No. 654." *The Ordinances of the Mayor and City Council of Baltimore.* Baltimore: Meyer Thalheimer Public Printer, 1911.

"Baltimore, Maryland. Ordinance No. 692." *The Ordinances of the Mayor and City Council of Baltimore.* Baltimore: Meyer Thalheimer Public Printer, 1911.

Berkman, Elliot. "Poor People Don't Have Less Self-Control. Poverty Forces Them to Think Short-Term." *New Republic,* September 22, 2015, https://newrepublic.com/article/122887/poor-people-dont-have-less-self-control.

Berkowitz, Edward. "Baltimore's Public Schools in a Time of Transition." *Maryland Historical Magazine* 92, no. 4 (Winter 1997): 413–32.

Berlin, Ira. *Many Thousands Gone: The First Two Centuries of Slavery in North America.* Cambridge: The Belknap Press of Harvard University Press, 1998.

Bernheim, Douglas, Debraj Ray, and Sevin Yeltekin. "Poverty and Self-control." *Econometrica,* 83, no 5. (September 2015): 1877–1911.

Black, Susan. "Name of the Church." In *Encyclopedia of Mormonism,* 4 vols., edited by Daniel H. Luldlow, 3:979. New York: Macmillan Publishing Company, 1991.

Bouie, Jamelle. "The Deep, Troubling Roots of Baltimore's Decline." *Slate,* April 29, 2015, http://www.slate.com/articles/news_and_politics/politics/2015/04/baltimore_s_failure_is_rooted_in_its_segregationist_past_the_city_s_black.html.

Byrne, Bridget. "Troubling Race. Using Judith Butler's Work to Think about Racialised Bodies and Selves." Paper for Queering Development, IDS Seminar Series, 2000, https://www.ids.ac.uk/files/dmfile/byrne.pdf.

Campbell, Colin. "Demonstrators Interrupt Baltimore Monument Lighting Event." *Baltimore Sun,* December 5, 2014, http://www.baltimoresun.com/news/maryland/baltimore-city/bs-md-ci-morgan-protest-20141204-story.html.

Carten, Alma. "The Racist Roots of Welfare Reform." *The New Republic,* August 22, 2016. Accessed January 23, 2018, https://newrepublic.com/article/136200/racist-roots-welfare-reform.

Carter, Aaron. "Taliaferro, One of Colts' First Black Players Recounts Times in Baltimore." CNS Sports, April 12, 2012, http://cnsmaryland.org/2012/04/13/taliaferro-one-of-colts-first-black-players-recounts-times-in-baltimore/.

Cashin, Sheryll. *Place not Race.* Boston: Beacon Press, 2014.

"Cherry Hill: Crime Rates and Statistics." Point2Homes. Accessed January 24, 2018, https://www.point2homes.com/US/Neighborhood/MD/Baltimore-City/Cherry-Hill-Demographics.html.

Chetty, Raj, Nathaniel Hendren, Patrick Kline, and Emmanuel Saez. "Where is the Land of Opportunity? The Geography of Intergenerational Mobility in the United States." National Bureau of Economic Research, revised June 2014, http://www.nber.org/papers/w19843.

Christie, Ron. *Acting White: The Curious History of a Racial Slur.* New York: Thomas Dunne Books, 2010.

City of Richmond v. J. A. Croson Co., 488 U. S., 1989. *Justia: US Supreme Court,* 469. Accessed January 24, 2018, https://supreme.justia.com/cases/federal/us/488/469/case.html.

Cottman, Mark. *Miss Sarah Waiting for Jesus.* March 2013. Painting. Baltimore, https://www.facebook.com/events/226316227513203/.

"Crime and Despair in Baltimore." *The Economist,* June 29, 2017. https://www.economist.com/news/united-states/21724399-america-gets-safer-marylands-biggest-city-does-not-crime-and-despair-baltimore.

Crummell, Alexander. *Destiny and Race: Selected Writings, 1840–1898.* Edited by Wilson Jeremiah Moses. Amherst: University of Massachusetts Press, 1992.

Daemmrich, JoAnna. "Lafayette Courts Ends in Twenty Seconds of Explosions, Cheers, Tears." *The Baltimore Sun,* August 20, 1995, http://articles.baltimoresun.com/1995-08-20/news/1995232004_1_lafayette-rise-murphy-homes.

Delgado, Richard, and Jean Stefancic. *Critical Race Theory.* New York: New York University Press, 2012.

DeShields, Inte'a. "Baldamor, Curry, and Dug': Language Variation, Culture, and Identity among African American Baltimoreans." Language in Baltimore. Accessed August 17, 2018, https://baltimorelanguage.com/baldamor-curry-and-dug-podcast/.

Dickinson, J., and T. Jefferson. "A Declaration by the Representatives of the United Colonies of North-America, Now Met in Congress at Philadelphia, Setting Forth the Causes and Necessity of Their Taking Up Arms." Yale Law School: Documents in Law, History and Diplomacy. Accessed August 17, 2018, http://avalon.law.yale.edu/18th_century/arms.asp.

Du Bois, W. E. B. "Criteria of Negro Art." *The Crisis* 32 (1926).

———. *The Philadelphia Negro: A Social Study*. Philadelphia: University of Philadelphia, 1899.

———. *The Souls of Black Folk*. New York: Bantam Books, 1989.

Durham, Erin. "Mapping Inequality: Historical Context of Baltimore's Neighborhoods." Mapping Inequality: Baltimore, March 30, 2016, http://dcicblog.umd.edu/redliningbaltimore/baltimores-history/.

Ehlers, Nadine. "'Black Is' and 'Black Ain't': Perfromative Revisions of Racial 'Crisis.'" *Culture, Theory & Critique* 47, no. 2 (2006): 149–63.

———. *Racial Imperatives: Discipline, Performativity, and Struggles against Subjection."* Bloomington: Indiana University Press, 2012.

Embry, Jessie. *Black Saints in a White Church: Contemporary African American Mormons*. Salt Lake City: Signature Books, 1994.

Ericson, Edward. "Mapping Baltimore: A Layered Look at our City—Neighborhood by Neighborhood." City Paper, June 2016, http://www.citypaper.com/bcpnews-mapping-baltimore-a-layered-look-at-our-city-neighborhood-by-neighborhood-20160628-storygallery.html.

Fleming, Thomas. "Reflections on Black History: The Great Experiment." *Sun-Reporter: San Francisco's African American Weekly*, 1998. Accessed August 17, 2018, http://www.sfmuseum.org/sunreporter/fleming19.html.

Fordham, Signithia, and John U. Ogbu. "Black Students' School Success: Coping With the Burden of 'Acting White.'" *The Urban Review* 18, no. 3 (1986): 176–206.

Fryer, Roland. "'Acting White': The Social Price Paid by the Best and Brightest Minority Students." *Education Next* 6, no. 1 (Winter 2006).

Fullwiley, Duana. "Race in a Genetic World." *Harvard Magazine* (May/June 2008), http://harvardmagazine.com/2008/05/race- in-a-genetic-world-html.

Gordon, Kalani. "From the Vault: Remembering Baltimore's 1968 Riots." *Baltimore Sun*, April 28, 2015, http://darkroom.baltimoresun.com/2015/04/from-the-vault-remembering-baltimores-1968-riots/.

Gordy, Cynthia. "Welfare, Fathers and Those Persistent Myths." *The Root*, June 17, 2011, http://www.theroot.com/welfare-fathers-and-those-persistent-myths-1790864434.

Report of the Semi-Annual Conference of the Church of Jesus Christ of Latter-day Saints. Salt Lake City: Church of Jesus Christ of Latter-day Saints, semi-annual.

Griffin, Gabriele. "The Compromised Researcher: Issues in Feminist Research Methodologies." *Sociologisk Forskning* 49, no. 4 (2012): 333–47.

Gross, Ariela J. "Litigating Whiteness: Trials of Racial Determination in the Nineteenth-Century South." *Yale Law Journal* 108, no. 1 (1998): 111–85.

Hamilton, Leah. "The Forgotten 1980s Rule That's Hurting Poor Families' Savings." *The Atlantic*, March 11, 2015, https://www.theatlantic.com/business/archive/2015/03/the-forgotten-1980s-rule-thats-hurting-poor-families-savings /387373/.

Hansberry, Lorraine. *To Be Young, Gifted and Black: A Portrait of Lorraine Hansberry in Her Own Words*. New York: Samuel French, 1971.

Harpalani, Vinay. "What Does 'Acting White' Really Mean? Racial Identity Formation and Academic Achievement Among Black Youth." *Perspectives on Urban Education* 1, no. 1 (Spring 2002), https://papers.ssrn.com/sol3/papers.cfm?abstract_id=3153173.

Healy, Allie. "Baltimore is Burning: Witnesses Share Photos, Video of City in Chaos as Riots Rage On." *Syracuse.com,* April 27, 2015, https://www.syracuse.com/us-news/index.ssf/2015/04/baltimore_is_burning_witnesses_share_photos_of_city_in_choas_as_riots_rage_on.html.

hooks, bell. *Salvation: Black People and Love.* New York: Harper Perennial, 2001.

Hughs, Camille, and Laura Strickling. "Camille." *Exponent II* 30, no. 3 (Winter 2010): 27–28.

"Illicit Drugs: A Complete History of Crack Cocaine." Rehabs.com, February 23, 2013, http://www.rehabs.com/a-complete-history-of-crack-cocaine/.

"Issues of Race in the 1930s." *The New Yorker,* March 19, 1938, http://archives.newyorker.com/?i=1938-03-19#folio=CV1.

J. Correspondent. "Interrupters: Linguist Says It's the Jewish Way." *The Jewish News of Northern California,* May 12, 2000, https://www.jweekly.com/2000/05/12/interrupters-linguist-says-it-s-jewish-way/.

Jackson, Michael. *Dancing the Dream.* New York: Doubleday, 1992.

James, Michael. "Lafayette Court: Forty Years from High Hopes to Oblivion." *The Baltimore Sun,* August 16, 1995, http://articles.baltimoresun.com/1995-08-16/news/1995228005_1_demolition-lafayette-rise.

Kasarda, John D. "Urban Industrial Transition and the Underclass." *The Annals of the American Academy of Political and Social Science* 501, no. 11 (January 1, 1989): 26–47.

Katzman, David M. *Seven Days a Week: Women and Domestic Service in Industrializing America.* Chicago: University of Illinois Press, 1981.

Kimble, Julian. "The 25 Whitest Shows of all Time." *Complex,* March 4, 2013, January 22, 2018, http://www.complex.com/pop-culture/2013/03/the-25-whitest-tv-shows-of-all-time/.

King Jr., Martin Luther. "Transcript of Dr. Martin Luther King's Speech at Southern Methodist University on March 17, 1966." Accessed January 23, 2018, https://www.smu.edu/News/2014/mlk-at-smu-transcript-17march1966.

———. "MLK: A Riot is the Language of the Unheard." *60 Minutes Overtime,* August 25, 2013. A reprint of an interview with Mike Wallace September 27, 1966, https://www.cbsnews.com/news/mlk-a-riot-is-the-language-of-the-unheard/.

———.. "Statement on Poverty, Black Power, and Political Power, October 14, 1966." Southern Christian Leadership Conference. Accessed January 12, 2018, http://www. crmvet.org/docs/6610_mlk_power-poverty.pdf.

Lean, Spence. "Oldtown Mall: Youtube Worthy." Baltimore City's Past Present and Future, September 30, 2007, http://baltimorefuture.blogspot.com/2007/03/oldtown-mall-you-tube-worthy.html .

LeBaron, Dale. "African Converts Without Baptism." BYU Speeches, November 3, 1998. Accessed January 13, 2018, https://speeches.byu.edu/talks/e-dale-lebaron _african-converts-without-baptism/.

Lericos, Vasilis. "Forbes: The Baltimore Ravens Franchise is Worth $1.93 billion." Baltimore Beatdown, July 14, 2016, https://www.baltimorebeatdown.com/2016/7/14/12187160/forbes-the-baltimore-ravens-franchise-is-worth-1-93 -billion.

Logan, John, and Brian Stults. "Separate and Unequal." American Communities Project, October 2011, https://s4.ad.brown.edu/Projects/Diversity/Data/Report/report12012014.pdf.

López, Ian Hanley. *White by Law: The Legal Construction of Race.* New York: New York University Press, 2006.

Malcom X. *By Any Means Necessary (Malcolm X Speeches and Writings).* New York: Pathfinder, 1992.

McArdle, Megan. "How Utah Keeps the American Dream Alive." *Bloomberg*, March 28, 2017, https://www.bloomberg.com/view/articles/2017-03-28/how-utah-keeps-the-american-dream-alive.

Morrison, Toni. *Playing in the Dark: Whiteness and Literary Imagination.* New York: Random House, 1994.

Mumola, Christopher, and Jennifer Karberg. "Drug Use and Dependence, State and Federal Prisoners." *Bureau of Justice Statistics Special Report.* NCJ 213530 U. S., October 2006.

National Research Council. "The Underlying Causes of Rising Incarceration: Crime, Politics, and Social Change." In *The Growth of Incarceration in the United States: Exploring Causes and Consequences.* Washington, DC: National Academies Press, 2014.

"Negro Housing Foes Boo and Cheer Mayor." *Baltimore Sun*, July 14, 1943.

Nunn, Kenneth B. "Race, Crime and the Pool of Surplus Criminality: Or Why the 'War on Drugs' Was a 'War on Blacks,'" *Journal of Gender, Race and Justice* 6 (2002): 381–445.

Obama, Barack. "Transcript: Illinois Senate Candidate Barack Obama." *Washington Post*, July 27, 2004, http://www.washingtonpost.com/wp-dyn/articles/A19751-2004Jul27.html.

Obinna, Anthony Uzodimma. "Story of a Nigerian Member: Obinna's letters." *The Liahona*, June 1981, https://www.lds.org/liahona/1981/06/story-of-a-nigerian-member.

Odetta. "Sometimes I Feel Like a Motherless Child." *Odetta at Carnegie Hall.* Vanguard, 1960, vinyl record.

Omi, Michael, and Howard Winant. *Racial Formation in the United States: From the 1960s to the 1990s.* New York: Routledge, 1994.

"Omnibus Budget Reconciliation Act of 1981." Congress.gov. Accessed January 23, 2018, https://www.congress.gov/bill/97th-congress/house-bill/3982.

Pitts, Jonathan. "Rebranding of Sparrows Point Bittersweet." *Baltimore Sun*, January 13, 2016, http://www.baltimoresun.com/news/maryland/bs-md-sparrows-point-name-change-20160113-story.html.

"Population Demographics for Salt Lake City, Utah in 2017, 2018." Suburban Stats. Accessed August 21, 2018, https://suburbanstats.org/population/utah/how-many-people-live-in-salt-lake-city.

Power, Garrett. "Apartheid Baltimore Style: The Residential Segregation Ordinances of 1910–1913." *Maryland Law Review* 42, no. 2, Article 4 (October 9, 2012): 289–328.

"Quick Facts on Career Offenders." *United States Sentencing Commission*, 2015.

Accessed January 24, 2018, https://www.ussc.gov/sites/default/files/pdf/research-and-publications/quick-facts/Quick_Facts_Career_Offender_FY14.pdf.

"Race and Ethnicity in Baltimore, Maryland." Statistical Atlas. Accessed January 12, 2018, https://statisticalatlas.com/place/Maryland/Baltimore/Race-and-Ethnicity.

"Race in the Reagan Era." Shmoop. Accessed August 14, 2017, https://www.shmoop.com/reagan-era/race.html.

Rappaport, Mike. "The Peculiarity of the Three-fifths Rule." *Library of Law and Liberty*, October 13, 2013, http://www.libertylawsite.org/2013/10/13/the-peculiarity-of-the-three-fifths-rule/.

Rector, Kevin. "Baltimore Reaches Highest Per Capita Murder Rate on Record in 2017." *Baltimore Sun*, December 29, 2017, https://www.policeone.com/patrol-issues/articles/468304006-Baltimore-reaches-highest-per-capita-murder-rate-on-record-in-2017/.

Resnick, Brian. "Zooming into Baltimore, a Segregated City." *The Atlantic*, April 28, 2015. Accessed January 18, 2018, https://www.theatlantic.com/politics/archive/2015/04/zooming-into-baltimore-a-segregated-city/453606/.

Reuter, Edward Byron. *Race Mixture: Studies in Intermarriage and Miscegenation*. New York: Whittlesey Press, 1931.

Rickford, John. R., and Russell. J. Rickford. *Spoken Soul: The Story of Black English*. New York: John Wiley & Sons, 2000.

Ross, Thomas. *Just Stories: How the Law Embodies Racism and Bias*. Boston: Beacon Press, 2001.

Samuels, Barbara. "Segregation and Public Housing Development in Cherry Hill and Westport: Historical Background." *American Civil Liberties Union of Maryland*, 2008. Accessed January 24, 2018, http://docplayer.net/24529690-Segregation-and-public-housing-development-in-cherry-hill-and-westport-historical-background.html.

Sandler, Gilbert. "How the City's Nickname Came to Be." *Baltimore Sun*, July 18, 1995. Accessed August 20, 2018, http://articles.baltimoresun.com/1995-07-18/news/1995199190_1_charm-city-bill-evans-loden.

Schreiner, Mark, and Michael Sherraden. *Can The Poor Save? Saving and Asset Building in Individual Development Accounts*. New Jersey: Transaction Publishers, 2007.

Schultz, Mark. *The Rural Face of White Supremacy: Beyond Jim Crow*. Chicago: University of Illinois Press, 2007.

Shapiro, Thomas, Tatjana Meschede, and Sam Osoro. "The Roots of the Widening Racial Wealth Gap: Explaining the Black-White Economic Divide. *Institute on Assets and Social Policy: Policy Brief*, 2013. Accessed January 24, 2018, http://iasp.brandeis.edu/pdfs/Author/shapiro-thomas-m/racialwealthgapbrief.pdf.

Shelby, Tommie. *We Who Are Dark*. Cambridge: Belknap Press of Harvard University Press, 2005.

Singewald, James. "Photographing Old Town, East Baltimore." *Baltimore Sun*, September 25, 2012, http://darkroom.baltimoresun.com/2012/09/

photographing-old-town-east-baltimore.
Smith, Joseph. *General Smith's Views of the Powers and Policy of the Government of the United States*. Nauvoo, IL: John Taylor, 1884.
Smith, Joseph F. Letter to Alfred M. Nelson, January 31, 1907. Microfilm of original typescript, MS 14591, LDS Church History Archives, Salt Lake City, UT.
Smith, Phillip. "Check out the States with the Most Dry Countries—As If Prohibition Never Ended." *Alternet*, January 27, 2016. Accessed January 22, 2018, https://www.salon.com/2016/01/27/which_state_has_the_most_dry_counties_partner/
Smith, Mother Mary Carter. "Mary Carter Smith." Maryland Women's Hall of Fame. Accessed January 30, 2018, http://msa.maryland.gov/msa/educ/exhibits/womenshall/html/smith.html.
Smitherman, Geneva. *Talkin and Testifyin*. Detroit: Wayne State University Press, 2000.
Snidal, Michael. "City Must Fight Black Flight." *Baltimore Sun,* March 3, 2017, http://www.balti0moresun.com/news/opinion/readersrespond/bs-ed-shrinking-letter-20170330-story.html.
Sollors, Werner, ed. *Interracialism: Black-White Intermarriage in American History, Literature, and Law.* Edited by Werner Sollors. New York: Oxford University Press, 2000.
"Spirit of Baltimore Dinner Cruises." Spirit Cruises. Accessed August 13, 2018, https://www.spiritcruises.com/baltimore/cruises/dinner-cruises.
Stevenson, Russell W. *For the Cause of Righteousness: A Global History of Blacks and Mormonism, 1830–2013*. Salt Lake City: Greg Kofford Books, 2014.
Stuart, Elizabeth. "How Anti-Poverty Programs Marginalize Fathers." *The Atlantic,* February 25, 2014, https://www.theatlantic.com/politics/archive/2014/02/how-anti-poverty-programs-marginalize-fathers/283984/.
Sundstrom, William. "Last Hired, First Fired? Unemployment and Urban Black Workers During the Great Depression." *The Journal of Economic History* 52, no. 22 (1992): 41–429.
Swingle, Anne Bennett, and Neil Grauer. "A Dream of a Deal." *Dome: A Publication for All the Members of the Johns Hopkins Medicine Family* 55, no. 3 (April 2004).
"The State of Maryland: Not Much Work for Colored People on the Eastern Shore." *The Baltimore Afro-American*, January 23, 1904, 1.
"The Westside Baltimore: A Vision for the Westside Neighborhood." *Urban Land Institute*, Washington, DC 20007-5201, 2010, 9. Accessed January 18, 2018, http://uli.org/wp-content/uploads/ULI-Documents/BaltimoreReport.pdf.
Toward Equality: Baltimore's Progress Report. Baltimore, MD: The Sydney Hollander Foundation, 1960.
Joe W. Trotter. "African Americans, Impact of the Great Depression on." In *Encyclopedia of the Great Depression*, edited by Robert S. McElvaine, 1:8–17. Vol. 1. New York: Macmillan Reference USA, 2004.
"Twelve O'Clock Boys: Baltimore's Infamous Dirtbike Gang." Youtube, December 2, 2013, https://www.youtube.com/watch?v=SmNUEAE1xY4.
von Hoffman, Alexander. "Enter the Housing Industry, Stage Right: A Working Paper on the History of Housing Policy." *Joint Center for Housing Studies*

Harvard University, February 2008, 3.

Weishampel, John F. *The Stranger in Baltimore: A New Handbook Containing Sketches of the Early History and Present Condition of Baltimore.* New York: Harvard College, 1866.

Wells, Carrie. "Report Highlights Economic Disparities between Races in Baltimore." *Baltimore Sun*, January 30, 2017, http://www.baltimoresun.com/news/maryland/ baltimore-city/bs-md-racial-wealth-divide-20170130-story.html.

Wells, Megan."The FBI's Ten Most Dangerous Cities." EfficientGov, February 2, 2017, https://efficientgov.com/blog/2017/02/02/fbi-10-dangerous-cities/.

"What Do Drugs Have to Do With Mass Incarceration?" Harm Reduction and Drug Law Reform Caucus. Accessed January 24, 2018, http://harmreductionma.org/history-of-drug-reform/what-does-drugs-have-to-do-with-anything/.

Williams, Eman. "How To Catch a Hack in the Hood of Baltimore." Youtube, July 18, 2015, https://www.youtube.com/watch?v=feA6x5HYIhw.

Wilson, William Julius. *When Work Disappears: The World of the New Urban Poor.* New York: Vintage, 1997.

Wood, Julia T. "Feminist Standpoint Theory." In *Encyclopedia of Communication Theory*, edited by Stephen W. Littlejohn and Karen A. Foss, 397–99. Thousand Oaks, CA: SAGE, 2009.

Yglesias, Matthew. "How Baltimore Invented Neighborhood Segregation." Vox, May 10, 2015, https://www.vox.com/2015/5/10/8578077/baltimore-segregation-pietila.

Yockel, Michael. "100 Years: The 1968 Riots." *Baltimore,* May 2007, http://www.baltimoremagazine.com/2007/5/1/100-years-the-riots-of-1968.

Zelinsky, Wilbur. *The Enigma of Ethnicity: Another American Dilemma.* Iowa City: University of Iowa Press, 2001.

Index

A–B

acting White, 128–29
African American English, xx–xxi, 122
African Methodist Episcopal Church, 156
Agnew, Spiro, 90
American Zion, 9
Anderson, Harry, 1
Anti-Drug Abuse Acts, 118
Asante, Molefi Kete, xi
Baldwin, James, xi, 148
Baltimore Colts, 137
Baltimore Community College, 103
Baltimore Gas and Electric, 104
Baltimore language, xxi
Baltimore Ravens, xv
Baltimore
   black belt, 154
   crime, 13
   discriminatory housing, xvi, 23, 155
   Inner Harbor, xv
   segregated neighborhoods, 22
baptism, 11, 15, 23, 51, 106–7, 123, 133, 156
   proxy, 79, 95–96
Baptists, 39, 50, 63–64, 71, 86–87, 93, 107, 132–33
Bay View, 58
biracial, 2
Black agricultural laborers, 40
Black child labor, 43
Black Diaspora, xi
Black flight, 101
Black movements, 5
Black preachers, xviii
Black slang, 24
Black unemployment, 148
Black vernacular, xviii
Black/White binary, 6
blackness, 3, 42
Bolton Hill, 38
Book of Mormon, 9, 14, 65, 70, 85, 87, 122
bootlegging, 81
Brown v. Board of Education, 19

C–D

Cain, 9
Camden Yards, xv, xvi
Catonsville, 136
Charlottesville, Virginia, 6
Charm City, xvi
Cherry Hill, 154
Chesapeake Bay, xv
Child Protective Services, 32, 109, 120
Chitlin' Circuit, 49
Church welfare, 147, 150
Civil Rights Acts, 1964, 1968, 6
Civil War Amendments, 4
Colored High School, The, 103
consonant cluster reduction, xxi
constitutional compromise of 1787, 3
Coppin State, 103
Coppin, Fanny Jackson, 103
cotton, 82
crack cocaine, 117
Critical Race Theory, xi, 6
Crummell, Alexander, 12
curse of Cain, 9
D'Alesandro, Tommy, 89
discriminatory housing, xvi, 23, 155
Druid Hill Park, 90
Du Bois, W. E. B., xx, 12, 125, 131

E–F

East Baltimore City Hospital, 58
Eastside/Westside, 136
Edmondson Avenue, 99
Eighteenth Amendment, 81
essentialist ideology, 3, 5
ethnicity, 5
Eurocentricism, 5
existential *it*, xxi
Feminist Standpoint Theory, xix
Feminist Theory, xix
food stamps, xvii, 25, 121, 147
Fort Meade, 56
Fourteenth Amendment, 6

G–J

Garner, Eric, 69
Garvey, Marcus, xi
government assistance, 147
Grant, Heber J., 147
Gray, Freddie, xv
  riots, xv, xvii, 162
Hansberry, Lorraine, 161
Hawn, Goldie, 139
Holy Week Uprising, 89
hooks, bell, 161–62
Housing First Program, 114
indentured servitude, 3
insider/outsider role, xx
Jackson Ward, 153
Jackson, Michael, 18, 29
Jamestown, 3
Jim Crow, 6, 42
John, Elton, 139
Johns Hopkins, 146
Jones Falls Expressway, 147
Just Say No, 118

K–M

Karenga, Maulana, xi
kickin' up dust, 80
Kimball, Spencer, 11, 157
Kimbrough Army Hospital, 57
King, Martin Luther, Jr., xvii, 6, 162
  riots, xv, 69, 88
Lafayette Courts, 118
Latter-day Saint, xi
Leave it to Beaver, 140
Legg Mason, xv
M & T Stadium, xv
Madison Avenue Apartments, 65
Malcolm X, 6
Marriott, xv
Mar-Va Theatre, 41
McCullah Street, 132
Mercy Hospital, 116
"Miss Sarah Waiting for Jesus," 115
missionaries, 15, 21–24, 50–51, 63–64, 71, 74, 85, 92–93, 99, 106, 122–23, 133, 156
Mitchell Jr., Clarence, 155
Monastery Road, 99
Monument East Apartments, 86
Morrison, Toni, 7, 132
Murder City, xvi

N–P

NAACP, 155
Naturalization Act of 1790, 4
neo-imperialism, xix
New Federalism, 121
New Hope Circle, 115
non-linear storytelling, 61
Obama, Barack, 129
Obinna, Anthony, 10
Odetta, 94
Old Town Mall, 89
Omnibus Reconciliation Act of 1981, 121
Orioles, xv, xvi
Pan Africa, xi, 6
playing the dozens, 160
Pokomoke City, Maryland, 40
poverty, 33, 117, 119, 146, 149, 155
premortality, 10
priesthood, 9
  ban, 11–12, 157–58
Projects, The, xvi, 17, 115

Q–S

Quorum of the Twelve Apostles, 11
"Race and the Priesthood," 11
race, 2–4
racial binary, 5
racism, xix, 60, 73, 158
  implicit, 7
  institutional, 148–49
rape, 25, 44
Reagan, Nancy, 118
Reagan, Ronald, 117, 120
Richmond, Virginia, 153
riots, xv, xvii. *See also* Freddie Gray, Martin Luther King Jr.
Rosenbloom, 137
Royal Theatre, 49
Second Great Awakening, 8
segregation, 41, 130
Sinai Hospital, 88
slave marts, 148
Smith, Joseph, 8
Smith, Joseph Fielding, 10
smoking, 75–76, 83–86
Social Services, 25, 128
Sparrow's Point, 13

T–V

Taliaferro, George, 137
temple, 11, 73, 79, 96, 134, 158, 161
tobacco, 82. *See also* smoking.
Tradepoint Atlantic, 14
Twelve O'Clock Boyz, 99
Tyson Alley, 68
Under Armor, xv
Unite the Right, 6
University Hospital, 72
upward mobility, 150
Urban Land Institute, 17
Urban League, 155
visions, 15, 20, 77, 79, 96
visiting teaching, 38

W–Y

War on Drugs, 117
Washington, DC, Temple, 18, 95, 116
Washington Monument, 69
West African Christians, 10
West Baltimore/East Baltimore, 13
Westside/Eastside, 117
White church, 12, 22, 24, 65, 157
White flight, 20, 130
White supremacy, 6
whiteness, 4, 37, 101, 131, 140
Young, Brigham, 9, 157

Also available from
GREG KOFFORD BOOKS

For the Cause of Righteousness: A Global History of Blacks and Mormonism, 1830-2013

Russell W. Stevenson

Paperback, ISBN: 978-1-58958-529-4

**2015 Best Book Award,
Mormon History Association**

"In Russell Stevenson's *For the Cause of Righteousness: A Global History of Blacks and Mormonism*, he extends the story of Mormonism's long-standing priesthood ban to the broader history of the Church's interaction with blacks. In so doing he introduces both relevant atmospherics and important new context. These should inform all future discussions of this surprisingly enduring subject."
— Lester E. Bush, author of "Mormonism's Negro Doctrine: An Historical Overview"

"Russell Stevenson has produced a terrific compilation. Invaluable as a historical resource, and as a troubling morality tale. The array of documents compellingly reveals the tragedy and inconsistency of racial attitudes, policies, and doctrines in the LDS tradition, and the need for eternal vigilance in negotiating a faith that must never be unmoored from humaneness."
— Terryl L. Givens, author of *Parley P. Pratt: The Apostle Paul of Mormonism* and *By the Hand of Mormon: The American Scripture that Launched a New World Religion*

"You might wonder what a White man could possibly say to two Black women about Black Mormon history. Surprisingly a whole lot! As people who consider ourselves well informed in African-American Mormon History, we found a wealth of new information in *For the Cause of Righteousness*. Russell Stevenson's well-researched exploration of Blacks and Mormonism is an informative read, not just for those interested in Black history, but American history as well."
— Tamu Smith and Zandra Vranes (a.k.a. Sistas in Zion), authors, *Diary of Two Mad Black Mormons*

Saints, Slaves, and Blacks: The Changing Place of Black People Within Mormonism, 2nd ed.

Newell G. Bringhurst

Paperback, ISBN: 978-1-58958-649-9

Originally published shortly after the LDS Church lifted its priesthood and temple restriction on black Latter-day Saints, Newell G. Bringhurst's landmark work remains ever-relevant as both the first comprehensive study on race within the Mormon religion and the basis by which contemporary discussions on race and Mormonism have since been framed. Approaching the topic from a social history perspective, with a keen understanding of antebellum and post-bellum religious shifts, *Saints, Slaves, and Blacks* examines both early Mormonism in the context of early American attitudes towards slavery and race, and the inherited racial traditions it maintained for over a century. While Mormons may have drawn from a distinct theology to support and defend racial views, their attitudes towards blacks were deeply-embedded in the national contestation over slavery and anticipation of the last days.

This second edition of *Saints, Slaves, and Blacks* offers an updated edit, as well as an additional foreword and postscripts by Edward J. Blum, W. Paul Reeve, and Darron T. Smith. Bringhurst further adds a new preface and appendix detailing his experience publishing *Saints, Slaves, and Blacks* at a time when many Mormons felt the rescinded ban was best left ignored, and reflecting on the wealth of research done on this topic since its publication.

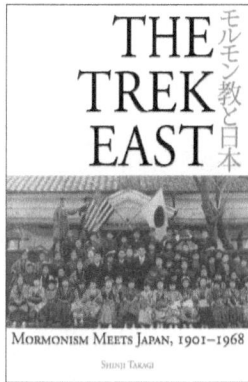

The Trek East: Mormonism Meets Japan, 1901–1968

Shinji Takagi

Paperback, ISBN: 978-1-58958-560-7
Hardcover, ISBN: 978-1-58958-561-4

**2017 Best International Book Award,
Mormon History Association**

Praise for *The Trek East*:

"In *The Trek East*, Dr. Shinji Takagi has produced a masterful treatment of Mormonism's foundation in Japan. Takagi takes an approach that informs us of Mormonism in Japan in a manner that focuses on inputs and results, environmental conditions in Japan and cultural biases of a Mormonism informed by western assumptions."
— Meg Stout, *The Millennial Star*

"This is a wonderful book, full of historical knowledge on a lesser-known subject in LDS history. The author, who is Japanese, LDS and lives in Virginia, is deeply invested in the subject and carefully includes all sides of the history."
— Mike Whitmer, *Deseret News*

"A monumental work of scholarship. . . . I can't imagine that any future study of this period could hope to provide a more thorough and engrossing analytical study of the origins and growth of the Church in Japan. This remarkable contribution is unlikely ever to be supplanted."
— Van C. Gessel, *Journal of Mormon History*

Mormon and Maori

Marjorie Newton

Paperback, ISBN: 978-1-58958-639-0

**2015 Best International Book Award,
Mormon History Association**

Praise for *The Liberal Soul*:

"*Mormon and Maori* is the result of a labor of love that reflects not years but decades of diligent research. Indeed, in combination with Newton's earlier Tiki and Temple, it constitutes the most detailed discussion in print of the fascinating 160-year saga of accommodation and adjustment between Maori culture and Mormonism. Unflinchingly honest yet unfailingly compassionate, *Mormon and Maori* is a must-read for anyone interested in the extraordinary history of the LDS experience in New Zealand."
— Grant Underwood, Professor of History, Brigham Young University

"*Mormon and Maori* offers a substantial historical account that structures and organizes *te iwi* Māori's (The Māori people's) often complex relationship and attachment to an American religion. In this respect Newton's work should be considered groundbreaking."
— Gina Colvin, *Journal of Mormon History*

Mormon Women Have Their Say: Essays from the Claremont Oral History Collection

Edited by Claudia L. Bushman and Caroline Kline

Paperback, ISBN: 978-1-58958-494-5

The Claremont Women's Oral History Project has collected hundreds of interviews with Mormon women of various ages, experiences, and levels of activity. These interviews record the experiences of these women in their homes and family life, their church life, and their work life, in their roles as homemakers, students, missionaries, career women, single women, converts, and disaffected members. Their stories feed into and illuminate the broader narrative of LDS history and belief, filling in a large gap in Mormon history that has often neglected the lived experiences of women. This project preserves and perpetuates their voices and memories, allowing them to say share what has too often been left unspoken. The silent majority speaks in these records.

This volume is the first to explore the riches of the collection in print. A group of young scholars and others have used the interviews to better understand what Mormonism means to these women and what women mean for Mormonism. They explore those interviews through the lenses of history, doctrine, mythology, feminist theory, personal experience, and current events to help us understand what these women have to say about their own faith and lives.

Praise for *Mormon Women Have Their Say*:

"Using a variety of analytical techniques and their own savvy, the authors connect ordinary lives with enduring themes in Latter-day Saint faith and history." --Laurel Thatcher Ulrich, author of *Well-Behaved Women Seldom Make History*

"Essential.... In these pages, Mormon women will find *ourselves*." --Joanna Brooks, author of *The Book of Mormon Girl: A Memoir of an American Faith*

"The varieties of women's responses to the major issues in their lives will provide many surprises for the reader, who will be struck by how many different ways there are to be a thoughtful and faithful Latter-day Saint woman." --Armand Mauss, author of *All Abraham's Children: Changing Mormon Conceptions of Race and Lineage*

Voices for Equality: Ordain Women and Resurgent Mormon Feminism

Edited by Gordon Shepherd, Lavina Fielding Anderson, and Gary Shepherd

Paperback, ISBN: 978-1-58958-758-8

Praise for *Voices for Equality*:

"Timely, incisive, important—this book teaches us that our sometimes very personal struggles with gender and equality in Mormonism have profound and far-reaching significance. In these pages, some of Mormonism's finest researchers and thinkers bring a richness of historical and scholarly perspective and a powerful new survey of tens of thousands of Mormon people to bear on headline-making issues like women's ordination, sister missionaries, church discipline, the internet and faith, and change in the LDS church. They offer us a rare and precious opportunity to grasp the full significance of this moment. This book is a much needed mirror for our time."

— Joanna Brooks, co-editor of *Mormon Feminism: Essential Writings* and author of *The Book of Mormon Girl: A Memoir of an American Faith*

"*Voices for Equality: Ordain Women and Resurgent Mormon Feminism* is a very important contribution to the discussion of Mormon feminism and the struggle for the ordination of women to the priesthood in the LDS Church. Anyone interested in this subject, any library concerned to be up-to-date on these issues, needs to have this book."

— Rosemary Radford Ruether, world-renowned feminist scholar and Catholic theologian, author of *Sexism and God-Talk: Toward a Feminist Theology* and *Women-Church: Theology* and *Practice of Feminist Liturgical Communities*

Women at Church: Magnifying LDS Women's Local Impact

Neylan McBaine

Paperback, ISBN: 978-1-58958-688-8

Women at Church is a practical and faithful guide to improving the way men and women work together at church. Looking at current administrative and cultural practices, the author explains why some women struggle with the gendered divisions of labor. She then examines ample real-life examples that are currently happening in local settings around the country that expand and reimagine gendered practices. Readers will understand how to evaluate possible pain points in current practices and propose solutions that continue to uphold all mandated church policies. Readers will be equipped with the tools they need to have respectful, empathetic and productive conversations about gendered practices in Church administration and culture.

Praise for *Women at Church*:

"Such a timely, faithful, and practical book! I suggest ordering this book in bulk to give to your bishopric, stake presidency, and all your local leadership to start a conversation on changing Church culture for women by letting our doctrine suggest creative local adaptations—Neylan McBaine shows the way!" — Valerie Hudson Cassler, author of *Women in Eternity, Women of Zion*

"A pivotal work replete with wisdom and insight. Neylan McBaine deftly outlines a workable programme for facilitating movement in the direction of the 'privileges and powers' promised the nascent Female Relief Society of Nauvoo." — Fiona Givens, co-author of *The God Who Weeps: How Mormonism Makes Sense of Life*

"In her timely and brilliant findings, Neylan McBaine issues a gracious invitation to rethink our assumptions about women's public Church service. Well researched, authentic, and respectful of the current Church administrative structure, McBaine shares exciting and practical ideas that address diverse needs and involve all members in the meaningful work of the Church." — Camille Fronk Olson, author of *Women of the Old Testament* and *Women of the New Testament*

Common Ground—Different Opinions: Latter-day Saints and Contemporary Issues

Edited by Justin F. White and James E. Faulconer

Paperback, ISBN: 978-1-58958-573-7

There are many hotly debated issues about which many people disagree, and where common ground is hard to find. From evolution to environmentalism, war and peace to political partisanship, stem cell research to same-sex marriage, how we think about controversial issues affects how we interact as Latter-day Saints.

In this volume various Latter-day Saint authors address these and other issues from differing points of view. Though they differ on these tough questions, they have all found common ground in the gospel of Jesus Christ and the latter-day restoration. Their insights offer diverse points of view while demonstrating we can still love those with whom we disagree.

Praise for *Common Ground—Different Opinions*:

"[This book] provide models of faithful and diverse Latter-day Saints who remain united in the body of Christ. This collection clearly demonstrates that a variety of perspectives on a number of sensitive issues do in fact exist in the Church. ... [T]he collection is successful in any case where it manages to give readers pause with regard to an issue they've been fond of debating, or convinces them to approach such conversations with greater charity and much more patience. It served as just such a reminder and encouragement to me, and for that reason above all, I recommend this book." — Blair Hodges, Maxwell Institute

Mormonism at the Crossroads of Philosophy and Theology: Essays in Honor of David L. Paulsen

Edited by Jacob T. Baker

Paperback, ISBN: 978-1-58958-192-0

"There is no better measure of the growing importance of Mormon thought in contemporary religious debate than this volume of essays for David Paulsen. In a large part thanks to him, scholars from all over the map are discussing the questions Mormonism raises about the nature of God and the purpose of life. These essays let us in on a discussion in progress." —RICHARD LYMAN BUSHMAN, author of *Joseph Smith: Rough Stone Rolling*.

"This book makes it clear that there can be no real ecumenism without the riches of the Mormon mind. Professor Paulsen's impact on LDS thought is well known.... These original and insightful essays chart a new course for Christian intellectual life." —PETER A. HUFF, and author of *Vatican II* and *The Voice of Vatican II*

"This volume of smart, incisive essays advances the case for taking Mormonism seriously within the philosophy of religion–an accomplishment that all generations of Mormon thinkers should be proud of." —PATRICK Q. MASON, Howard W. Hunter Chair of Mormon Studies, Claremont Graduate University

"These essays accomplish a rare thing—bringing light rather than heat to an on-going conversation. And the array of substantial contributions from outstanding scholars and theologians within and outside Mormonism is itself a fitting tribute to a figure who has been at the forefront of bringing Mormonism into dialogue with larger traditions." —TERRYL L. GIVENS, author of *People of Paradox: A History of Mormon Culture*

"The emergence of a vibrant Mormon scholarship is nowhere more in evidence than in the excellent philosophical contributions of David Paulsen." —RICHARD J. MOUW, President, Fuller Theological Seminary, author of *Talking with Mormons: An Invitation to Evangelicals*

The End of the World, Plan B: A Guide for the Future

Charles Shirō Inouye

Paperback, ISBN: 978-1-58958-755-7

Praise for *End of the World, Plan B*:

"Mormonism needs Inouye's voice. We need, in general, voices that are a bit less Ayn Rand and a bit more Siddhartha Gautama. Inouye reminds us that justice is not enough and that obedience is not the currency of salvation. He urges us to recognize the limits of the law, to see that, severed from a willingness to compassionately suffer with the world's imperfection and evanescence, our righteous hunger for balancing life's books will destroy us all."
— Adam S. Miller, author of *Rube Goldberg Machines: Essays in Mormon Theology* and *Letters to a Young Mormon*

"Drawing on Christian, Buddhist, Daoist, and other modes of thought, Charles Inouye shows how an attitude of hope can arise from a narrative of doom. The End of the World, Plan B is not simply a rethinking of the end of our world, but is a meditation on the possibility of compassionate self-transformation. In a world that looks to the just punishment of the wicked, Inouye shows how sorrow, which comes from the demands of justice, can create peace, forgiveness, and love."
— Michael D.K. Ing, Assistant Professor, Department of Religious Studies, Indiana University

"For years I've hoped to see a book that related Mormonism to the great spiritual traditions beyond Christianity and Judaism. Charles Inouye has done this in one of the best Mormon devotional books I've ever read. His Mormon reading of the fourfold path of the Bodhisattva offers a beautiful eschatology of the end/purpose of the world as the revelation of compassion. I hope the book is read widely."
— James M. McLachlan, co-editor of *Discourses in Mormon Theology: Philosophical and Theological Possibilities*

From Above and Below: The Mormon Embrace of Revolution, 1840–1940

Craig Livingston

Paperback, ISBN: 978-1-58958-621-5

**2014 Best International Book Award,
Mormon History Association**

Praise for *From Above and Below*:

"In this engaging study, Craig Livingston examines Mormon responses to political revolutions across the globe from the 1840s to the 1930s. Latter-day Saints saw utopian possibilities in revolutions from the European tumults of 1848 to the Mexican Revolution. Highlighting the often radical anti-capitalist and anti-imperialist rhetoric of Mormon leaders, Livingston demonstrates how Latter-day Saints interpreted revolutions through their unique theology and millennialism."
--Matthew J. Grow, author of *Liberty to the Downtrodden: Thomas L. Kane, Romantic Reformer*

"Craig Livingston's landmark book demonstrates how 21st-century Mormonism's arch-conservatism was preceded by its pro-revolutionary worldview that was dominant from the 1830s to the 1930s. Shown by current opinion-polling to be the most politically conservative religious group in the United States, contemporary Mormons are unaware that leaders of the LDS Church once praised radical liberalism and violent revolutionaries. By this pre-1936 Mormon view, 'The people would reduce privilege and exploitation in the crucible of revolution, then reforge society in a spiritual union of peace' before the Coming of Christ and His Millennium. With profound research in Mormon sources and in academic studies about various social revolutions and political upheavals, Livingston provides a nuanced examination of this little-known dimension of LDS thought which tenuously balanced pro-revolutionary enthusiasms with anti-mob sentiments."
--D. Michael Quinn, author of *Elder Statesman: A Biography of J. Reuben Clark*

Future Mormon: Essays in Mormon Theology

Adam S. Miller

Paperback, ISBN: 978-1-58958-509-6

From the Introduction:

I have three children, a girl and two boys. Our worlds overlap but, already, these worlds are not the same. Their worlds, the worlds that they will grow to fill, are already taking leave of mine. Their futures are already wedged into our present. This is both heartening and frightening. So much of our world deserves to be left. So much of it deserves to be scrapped and recycled. But, too, this scares me. I worry that a lot of what has mattered most to me in this world—Mormonism in particular—may be largely unintelligible to them in theirs. This problem isn't new, but it is perpetually urgent. Every generation must start again. Every generation must work out their own salvation. Every generation must live its own lives and think its own thoughts and receive its own revelations. And, if Mormonism continues to matter, it will be because they, rather than leaving, were willing to be Mormon all over again. Like our grandparents, like our parents, and like us, they will have to rethink the whole tradition, from top to bottom, right from the beginning, and make it their own in order to embody Christ anew in this passing world. To the degree that we can help, our job is to model that work in love and then offer them the tools, the raw materials, and the room to do it themselves.

These essays are a modest contribution in this vein, a future tense apologetics meant for future Mormons. They model, I hope, a thoughtful and creative engagement with Mormon ideas while sketching, without obligation, possible directions for future thinking.

www.ingramcontent.com/pod-product-compliance
Lightning Source LLC
Chambersburg PA
CBHW022101160426
43198CB00008B/303